Emerging Metaverse XR and Video Multimedia Technologies

Modern Streaming and Multimedia Systems and Applications

Jong-Moon Chung

Apress®

Emerging Metaverse XR and Video Multimedia Technologies: Modern Streaming and Multimedia Systems and Applications

Jong-Moon Chung
Seoul, Korea (Republic of)

ISBN-13 (pbk): 978-1-4842-8927-3   ISBN-13 (electronic): 978-1-4842-8928-0
https://doi.org/10.1007/978-1-4842-8928-0

Managing Director, Apress Media LLC: Welmoed Spahr
Acquisitions Editor: Susan McDermott
Development Editor: James Markham
Coordinating Editor: Jessica Vakili

Distributed to the book trade worldwide by Springer Science+Business Media New York, 233 Spring Street, 6th Floor, New York, NY 10013. Phone 1-800-SPRINGER, fax (201) 348-4505, e-mail orders-ny@springer-sbm.com, or visit www.springeronline.com. Apress Media, LLC is a California LLC and the sole member (owner) is Springer Science + Business Media Finance Inc (SSBM Finance Inc). SSBM Finance Inc is a **Delaware** corporation.

For information on translations, please e-mail booktranslations@springernature.com; for reprint, paperback, or audio rights, please e-mail bookpermissions@springernature.com.

Apress titles may be purchased in bulk for academic, corporate, or promotional use. eBook versions and licenses are also available for most titles. For more information, reference our Print and eBook Bulk Sales web page at http://www.apress.com/bulk-sales.

Any source code or other supplementary material referenced by the author in this book is available to readers on the Github repository: https://github.com/Apress/Emerging-Metaverse-XR-and-Video-Multimedia-Technologies. For more detailed information, please visit http://www.apress.com/source-code.

Printed on acid-free paper

To my father and mother for their love and devotion, to my wife Seung-Won and daughters Yonhee and Yonju for their love and care, and to God for all these blessings and love.

Table of Contents

About the Author

Jong-Moon Chung received B.S. and M.S. degrees in electronic engineering from Yonsei University (Seoul, South Korea), and at the Pennsylvania State University he received his Ph.D. in electrical engineering and served as assistant professor. From 2000 to 2005, he served at the Oklahoma State University as a tenured associate professor in the School of Electrical & Computer Engineering and director of the Oklahoma laboratory for communications, networking, and bioengineering. Since 2005, he has been with Yonsei University where he serves as a tenured professor in electrical and electronic engineering, associate dean of the College of Engineering, and professor (joint appointment) of emergency medicine in the College of Medicine. Since 2021, he has been serving as the Principal Investigator (PI) of South Korea's largest metaverse eXtended Reality (XR) flagship project to build XR digital twin emergency training systems for the Ministry of Science and ICT, Ministry of Interior and Safety, National Fire Agency, Korea Fire Safety Institute, National IT Industry Promotion Agency, and the Korea Evaluation Institute of Industrial Technology. Before this, as PI he developed South Korea's government augmented reality (AR) composite disaster training system. Due to these contributions, he received prestigious government awards in 2019 and 2021. He has developed XR training and smart factory control systems for industry, autonomous driving technologies and ADAS/CAN/DSRC/C-V2X as well as BEV/

FCEV technologies for Hyundai Motors, 5G/LTE/Wi-Fi and smartphone technologies for Samsung, LG, and Google, and AI optimized electronic circuit designs for LG Display. His courses in Coursera on deep learning, big data, AR/XR, multimedia streaming, MPEG-DASH, cloud/edge computing, smartphones/smartwatches, 4G, 5G, Wi-Fi, Bluetooth, TCP/IP, Internet, security, and IoT technologies have been accessed by over 1.8 million users and were listed among the top 33 industry recommended courses. He is currently the Vice President of the IEEE Consumer Technology Society (CTSoc), IEEE Product Safety Engineering Society (PSES), and Korean Society for Internet Information (KSII) and serves as Senior Editor of the IEEE Transactions on Consumer Electronics, Section Editor of the Wiley ETRI Journal, EiC of the KSII Transactions on Internet and Information Systems and served as Editor of the IEEE Transactions on Vehicular Technology from 2011 to 2021. He is also a member of the Eta Kappa Nu (HKN) honor society and Fellow member of the IEEE.

About the Technical Reviewer

Massimo Nardone has more than 22 years of experience in security, web/mobile development, cloud, and IT architecture. His true IT passions are security and Android.

He has been programming and teaching how to program with Android, Perl, PHP, Java, VB, Python, C/C++, and MySQL for more than 20 years.

He holds a Master of Science degree in Computing Science from the University of Salerno, Italy.

He has worked as a project manager, software engineer, research engineer, chief security architect, information security manager, PCI/SCADA auditor, and senior lead IT security/cloud/SCADA architect for many years.

Acknowledgments

I sincerely thank the Springer Nature and Apress executive editor Susan McDermott, senior editor Aaron Black, and editors James Markham, Jessica Vakili, Nirmal Selvaraj, and Dulcy Nirmala for their excellent work and for inviting me to write this book. I also appreciate the hard work of the technical reviewer Massimo Nardone. I am also grateful to Yonsei University, the Oklahoma State University, and the Pennsylvania State University and to all my former/current graduate students. I thank the research assistants who worked on my government metaverse XR flagship project and AR disaster response project and the teaching assistants of my Coursera courses, which include Yong-Suk Park, Jong-Hong Park, Taeyoung Ha, Hyoungjun Cho, Jinbae Lee, Junsung Kim, Changsung Lee, Sooeun Song, Jusik Yun, Younghwan Shin, Seungwoo Seo, Wonsuk Yoo, Sihun Heo, Wonsik Yang, Minsu Choi, Yunyeong Goh, Jaewook Jung, Sangdo Kim, Minsoo Joo, Dongjun Jung, Jeongyoon Shin, Byounghoon Son, Jungmin Seo, Giyoung Hwang, Sunghyun Kim, and Youngwook Kim. In addition, I thank Daniel Park for reviewing the contract. Especially, I deeply thank my father Chin O. Chung and mother Young C. Chung, wife Seung-Won H. Chung, and daughters Yonhee Chung and Yonju Chung, and cordially thank God for all the blessings.

Introduction

The metaverse world has become a reality. Metaverse and eXtended Reality (XR) technologies will rapidly spread widely and will soon influence a vast range of products and services that we use. In addition, the way we view shows and movies and the way we have meetings have also radically changed. Television programs were first broadcasted using wireless signals, and were later delivered through cables, and now multimedia content is streamed through the Internet on-demand using over-the-top (OTT) technology. As multimedia real-time support technologies and networking services have significantly evolved (and due to the COVID-19 pandemic), online meetings are more frequently held. In this book, the core technologies that enable metaverse XR services and advanced multimedia streaming services are introduced. The XR technologies covered in this book include mixed reality (MR), augmented reality (AR), virtual reality (VR), haptic and 3D-motion user interfaces (UIs), as well as head mounted displays (HMDs) like Microsoft HoloLens 2 and Meta Quest 2. The core technologies that are used in advanced multimedia services like Netflix, Disney+, YouTube, and Skype are described. An overview of H.264 Advanced Video Coding (AVC), H.265 High Efficiency Video Coding (HEVC), H.266 Versatile Video Coding (VVC), and Moving Picture Experts Group – Dynamic Adaptive Streaming over HTTP (MPEG-DASH)-based adaptable video streaming technology, as well as Content Delivery Networks (CDNs), cloud computing, and edge cloud technologies (e.g., Amazon Web Services (AWS) and Microsoft Azure) is provided. This book ends with an overview of emerging technologies with some predictions on how these technologies may evolve and recommendations for future endeavors.

Who This Book Is For

This book is for anyone interested in metaverse and multimedia technologies. You do not need to be a student in this field or an engineer or computer scientist to understand the material in this book. Only your interest is needed. This book is for businesspeople and marketing experts that realize the market potential and may have plans to apply XR, metaverse, and multimedia technologies in their organization and need to work with engineers, programmers, and scientists. This book is also for government, academia, and public administrators that plan to use XR, metaverse, and multimedia technologies to enhance education, job preparation, re-education, and field training. This book is also for entertainment artists, musicians, scriptwriters, and designers that see the potential in new trends of XR, metaverse, and multimedia technology which can be used to significantly grow their creative potential and content. Especially, this book is for students that are seeking knowledge in state-of-the-art technologies that have longevity and are extremely exciting, fun, admirable, and full of creativity. Indeed, the metaverse and multimedia technology field has great value and is worthy of investment. Not all chapters of this book may be needed for now, so selective reading of chapters is welcome. The contents of the chapters are interconnected and can provide a synergistic effect in understanding the technical details. However, the chapters are written in a way such that selected chapters can be read without needing to read all chapters. The chapters initially skipped may become useful later when more technical details are needed. The following chapter description may help you in selecting the chapters that you may want to read first. Thank you for choosing this book and I hope you enjoy it and that it helps you in your studies and work.

Chapter Overview

This book starts with an introduction of metaverse, eXtended Reality (XR), and multimedia streaming services by first focusing on the technology evolution and business aspects in Chapter 1. A brief history of these technologies is provided with an overview of the market's past and future expectations. In addition, the reason why these technologies are important and how much potential they have are explained. Chapter 2 introduces the core XR components starting with a description of XR, Mixed Reality (MR), Augmented Reality (AR), and Virtual Reality (VR) technologies. Then the XR system components and workflow are described followed by an introduction of the hardware and software engines as well as the system platforms. Various XR haptic devices and three-dimensional (3D) motion treadmills are also introduced. Chapter 3 covers the technologies used in XR head mounted displays (HMDs) as well as the XR operation process, and feature extraction/detection technologies. Because metaverses, XR, and multimedia streaming systems use a lot of Artificial Intelligence (AI), Chapter 4 focuses on how AI and deep learning can be used to provide accurate decision making and control services. A description of how deep learning is used in computer vision, speech recognition, sensor signal tracking, and future predictions is provided. Chapter 5 focuses on the video encoding and decoding technologies, which include the H.264 Advanced Video Coding (AVC), H.265 High Efficiency Video Coding (HEVC), H.266 Versatile Video Coding (VVC) standards, and holography technology. Descriptions of how these video codecs are used in Meta Quest 2, Microsoft HoloLens 2, Netflix, Disney+, Skype, and YouTube are provided. In addition to the video codecs, the progressive download and adaptive streaming techniques used over networks are introduced in Chapter 6. The specifications of the Moving Picture Experts Group – Dynamic Adaptive Streaming over HTTP (MPEG-DASH) are described along with details on how the Multimedia Presentation Description (MPD) and Group of Pictures (GOP) are used. Chapter 7 focuses on the benefits and operations of Content Delivery Networks (CDNs), which are used in all global OTT video streaming and metaverse services. A description of how Netflix, Disney+, and Facebook use CDNs is provided along with details of CDN hierarchical content delivery, caching services, and content updating operations. Chapter 8 provides details of cloud computing and edge cloud technologies and how they are used by companies like Netflix and Disney+. In addition, details on Amazon Web Service (AWS) edge cloud services and the Microsoft Azure edge cloud services are introduced. This book concludes with Chapter 9, which presents some emerging technology predictions on the future evolution of media streaming, XR, and metaverse services, in hope to serve as a guidance to the reader.

CHAPTER 1

Introduction to Metaverse and Video Streaming Technology and Services

This book was written to serve as a guidance to assist the evolution of media streaming, eXtended Reality (XR), and metaverse services (`www.coursera.org/learn/ar-technologies-video-streaming`). Media streaming and metaverse services share many core technologies in which each can provide a synergistic effect to the others' future evolution and growth.

Future technical advancements in XR devices will significantly help metaverse services and massively multiplayer online games (MMOGs) to improve. At the same time, advanced XR devices will also enable multimedia streaming services to reach new levels in 3D and holographic immersive presence media content.

© Jong-Moon Chung 2023
J.-M. Chung, *Emerging Metaverse XR and Video Multimedia Technologies*,
https://doi.org/10.1007/978-1-4842-8928-0_1

It is expected that standalone XR devices will become lighter, sleek in design (fashion XR glasses), and more powerful in functionality, such that they will become much more popular in the market. At the same time, wireless networks (based on future 6G, Wi-Fi 7, etc.) and edge computing will become faster such that the wireless tethered (non-standalone) XR devices will also become very popular.

My personal desire is to help technology evolution toward a very light and cool XR smart device in eyeglasses form that is standalone, which switches to wireless tethered mode only when needed, and supports real-time metaverses, MMOGs, and multimedia streaming services with charge intervals exceeding 72 hours even under heavy usage.

The chapters of this book show that the core technologies applied to metaverse XR and multimedia systems are mostly the same and the networks and cloud computing requirements are very similar. In addition, considering that metaverse XR services are in search of new creative socializing themes, and multimedia streaming services are in need of new and unique content for their platforms, the merge of metaverse XR services and multimedia streaming services seems like a win-win make, which is one of the purposes of combining these two massive topics into one book.

This chapter focuses on the characteristics of metaverse, XR, and video streaming services, including technology and business aspects. The importance of these technologies and future potential are described. The chapter provides a brief history of the technologies as well as an overview of the market's past and future expectations. This chapter consists of the following four sections:

- Metaverse XR Technology Introduction

- Metaverse XR Products and Business

- Video Streaming Technology Introduction

- Video Streaming Services and Business

Note   All dollar "$" figures are based on the US dollar (USD).

Metaverse XR Technology Introduction

The term "metaverse" was coined from the Greek word *meta* (which means "beyond") and "verse" (which comes from the word "universe") by the American novelist Neal Stephenson in 1992 based on the science fiction novel titled *Snow Crash* (www.randomhousebooks.com/books/172832/). The term "metaverse" was used to describe what a virtual reality (VR) society could provide. The metaverse would be a digitally created virtual world that people could use avatars to work, play, and socialize. Metaverse was described as a future successor of the Internet, which could serve as an escape from the dystopian reality. The metaverse virtual society could be used to avoid suffering or injustice in the real-world society and enable a fresh new start in socializing through avatars. The realization of metaverses has already started, where it is used for new types of socialization, exploring, traveling, work, entertainment, games, and education. Although there may not be a dystopian reality that everyone wants to avoid, metaverses can serve as an escape from the dysfunctional or unsatisfying aspects of one's society by entering a virtually created environment that could be customized to satisfy personal desires and be less stressful. One benefit of a metaverse is that it is a virtual world based on digital VR designs. So, a metaverse can be erased, modified, or rebuilt when needed, mostly requiring computer designing and programming efforts as well as one's creativity and investment. Social value of a metaverse is added when multiple participants start to join and interact, forming a virtual society. When such a virtual society is formed, then the metaverse value increases, and from then, changes must be made more carefully such that the metaverse social ecosystem and values are

3

maintained. When social values of a metaverse are not maintained, users
will leave, thereby decreasing the size of the society and its total value.
In some cases, inappropriate users may be forced to leave the metaverse
to maintain a sufficient level of social values (`https://youtu.be/
ydWYJSpsCLE`).

Metaverse and VR were first mentioned at a time when the Internet
was still in its early stages. The origin of the Internet began in 1966 based
on a project operated by the Advanced Research Projects Agency (ARPA)
of the US Department of Defense (DoD). This project was focused on
creating a military network called ARPANET, which grew extensively in
functionality, size, and coverage. Extending from the military ARPANET,
the modern Internet was formed in the early 1990s, which is when various
enterprises and academia were connected through commercial networks,
which triggered an exponential growth on the Internet in terms of content
and services (`https://en.wikipedia.org/wiki/Metaverse`).

Recently, advancements in computing hardware, video display
technology, content delivery technology, artificial intelligence (AI), VR
and augmented reality (AR) software programming, head mounted display
(HMD) devices (e.g., VR and AR goggles, headsets, or glasses), digital twin
technology, edge computing, wireless and wired networks, development
of Web3, smart devices, 5G and 6G mobile communication, and Wi-Fi and
Bluetooth networking, as well as the COVID-19 pandemic, are all reasons
why metaverse services and XR technology continuously grew.

As metaverse users are rapidly increasing and wider age groups start
to use metaverse services in forms of massively multiplayer online games
(MMOGs) or social network media, it is significantly important to properly
deal with user safety and information privacy. In addition, user addiction
issues related to mental and physical health as well as time waste need to
be considered.

Currently, most metaverse services are based on VR user
environments. This is mainly because many types of MMOG applications
have been using VR technology to enable player avatars to compete in

virtual game environments, which may include multiple domains, worlds, and universes. MMOGs are online video games that enable many players to simultaneously participate individually or collaborate in teams while competing in the same game environment. MMOG users rely on the Internet for worldwide connectivity, and they depend on the game server to provide a fun experience and fair competition and protect the user while providing privacy. All these features are expected from a metaverse as more personal activities are to be conducted in the metaverse while socializing. MMOGs require high-quality networks, game servers, high-performance player computer terminals, as well as virtually created multiple game domains, worlds, universes, and dimensions. Thus, MMOGs can be considered as one of the original purposes to create and use a metaverse.

However, it is predicted that XR will be used in creating future metaverse services, as XR technology can enable users to experience both real and virtual environments by interpolating mixed reality (MR) (which combines AR with VR) with various haptic user interfaces to make the user's environment more interactive, realistic, broader, diverse, and immersive. New XR application programming interfaces (APIs) can enable various types of human-to-human, human-to-animal, human-to-machine, and machine-to-machine interaction.

Future metaverse services will need advanced XR equipment as well as high-performance wired and wireless networks to support the required data rate, time delay, and reliability requirements. Advanced metaverse services require high levels of Quality of Service (QoS) and Quality of Experience (QoE) to enable the XR system to provide a satisfying level of virtual immersive presence.

Based on this focus, new standards on XR equipment and networking services are being prepared by global organizations, like the 3rd Generation Partnership Project (3GPP) and the Institute of Electrical and Electronics Engineers (IEEE). Standards provide a way for new products and services to interoperate, safely be used, while satisfying the basic commonly required functionalities.

Just like MMOGs, metaverse systems can be supported by many types of networking platforms and be played using a personal computer (PC), video game console, smartphone, HMD, as well as various Internet of Things (IoT) wireless devices. Therefore, metaverse applications must be designed considering users in diverse environments using various interactive XR interfaces. The social connection aspect of the metaverse is what makes it different from most 3D virtual world-based video games like MMOGs. Some noticeable metaverse services are described in the following.

Sandbox Games

Sandbox games are video games that enable a player to freely explore options and the environment, select options, and create virtual features with or without any predetermined goal related to a game (www.merriam-webster.com/dictionary/sandbox). In addition, multiple player interaction and collaboration can be conducted in the sandbox. This unburdening personal exploration and socializing platform provided by sandbox games mimics a sandbox that children play in and socialize, which is where the name came from. From this aspect, the "sandbox" of sandbox games can be considered as an original form of the metaverse. Some of the early sandbox games are introduced in the following, which include Elite, The Sim, Habbo, Second Life, Minecraft, and more (https://en.wikipedia.org/wiki/Nonlinear_gameplay).

Elite

In September of 1984, Elite was released as one of the earliest sandbox-type games (www.frontierstore.net/games/elite-dangerous-cat/elite1984.html). It was focused on space trading and combat scenario competition. Based on a player's performance, one's combat rating could be increased, where reaching the exalted level of "Elite" could be achieved, which is where the name of the game originated from. Elite originated as a three-dimensional (3D) arcade game, so it originally did not have an online interface, nor did it have multiplayer trading features. Elite was originally programmed using assembly language, which is a machine coding software, which took 2 years of research and development. Elite was originally made for BBC Micro and Acorn Electron computers and was officially published by Acornsoft, which has its headquarters located in Cambridge, England. Elite contributed to initializing both the sandbox game era as well as advanced 3D graphics technology, as it was the first to enable wire-frame 3D graphics with hidden-line removal technology on home computer games. The Elite series of games are among the most successful and oldest ongoing video game franchises in history, which has significantly influenced many game models (`https://en.wikipedia.org/wiki/Elite_(video_game)`).

SimCity

In 1989, SimCity was released, which is a simulation-based city-building video game created by Maxis (`www.ea.com/games/simcity`). Maxis was founded in 1987 in Redwood Shores, California, USA. Due to the company's great success in simulation games like SimCity, The Sims, and Spore, the company was acquired by Electronic Arts (EA) in 1997. SimCity started as a black-and-white two-dimensional (2D) graphics video game focused on building a new city as its mayor. The game's objective is to build a city with the highest population based on a limited budget, which is based on taxes collected. A higher standard of living of the residents triggered the virtual city's population to grow. As the city grew, it became more challenging to balance improvements considering each region's environmental standards and issues while needing to continuously develop higher-quality residential and industrial areas. Based on this high level of strategic planning involved in playing the game, SimCity contributed to breaking the barrier of thought that video games were only for the young and were not challenging enough for adults. SimCity was extremely popular and successful and won many accolades. However, due to the lack of multiple user avatar based social networking aspect of SimCity, some do not consider it as a true metaverse game. However, it is the origin of the urban simulation video game genre that is based on virtual environment strategic planning and designing, which is a metaverse feature. In addition, its spinoff "The Sims" has many aspects that significantly contributed to metaverse designs and technology, which is described in the following (`https://en.wikipedia.org/wiki/SimCity`).

The Sims

In February of 2000, "The Sims" was released which began the popular Sim game series, which are life simulation and social simulation-based sandbox-type video games (`www.ea.com/games/the-sims`). The Sims and its series were developed by Maxis and published by EA. Players would create their avatar (which are called "Sims") and place them in existing homes, or players can create new homes. The original video games did not define any goals for the avatars to accomplish, thus socializing was the main purpose. However later expansion pack versions of the game included a gameplay-style factor to provoke more interaction among players. Worldwide, The Sims game series sold approximately 200 million copies and is one of the all-time best-selling video game series (`https://en.wikipedia.org/wiki/The_Sims`).

Habbo

In August of 2000, Habbo was launched by Sulake located in Finland, where it was formerly known as "Habbo Hotel" (`www.habbo.com/`). The service platform name and Internet domain name were changed from "Habbo Hotel" to "Habbo" in May of 2006. Habbo is a popular social

world-building game that enables users to create their avatar and talk
with other players. Habbo's social network community was focused more
on teens and young adults. On the social activity side, Habbo enabled
users to provide caregiving for virtual pets and design and build rooms.
On the gaming side, Habbo enables players to create new games and play
games, which include completing team quests. By October of 2020, Habbo
had accumulated 316 million avatars. In January 2021, it was reported
that Habbo had over 800,000 monthly active users from more than 150
countries. Habbo has been classified as a metaverse platform, and due to
the game activities included, some classify it as a massively multiplayer
online role-playing game (MMORPG) (https://en.wikipedia.org/
wiki/Habbo).

Grand Theft Auto III

In October of 2001, Grand Theft Auto III was released
(www.rockstargames.com/games/grandtheftauto3). It was published
by Rockstar Games (located in New York City, USA) and developed by
DMA Design as a series following Grand Theft Auto II, which was released
in 1999. Grand Theft Auto III is played by controlling the avatar Claude
in Liberty City, which is a 3D virtual space that somewhat resembles
New York City. The game received many praises and awards based on its
3D design, concept, and gameplay. In addition, it also received criticism
due to its content related to violence, sex, and crime (e.g., grand theft
auto). Grand Theft Auto III sold over 14.5 million copies and was the
2001 best-selling video game. Due to its 3D landmark designs and open
world concept, it can be considered as an innovative sandbox game and
contributor to metaverse technologies (https://en.wikipedia.org/wiki/
Grand_Theft_Auto_III).

Second Life

In 2003, Second Life was launched by Linden Lab located in San Francisco, California, USA (`https://secondlife.com/destination/metaverse-city`). Second Life enables users to create their avatar that would live in an online virtual world, thereby enabling users to live a virtual "second life" by connecting to the application's Internet platform. The popularity of Second Life grew, where it reached approximately one million users in 2013. The most recent upgraded stable release was provided in February of 2021. Second Life is different from a massively multiplayer online role-playing game (MMORPG) as it focuses on providing an online virtual social environment for user avatars but does not impose any required set of objectives for the users, nor does it create any manufactured conflict as games do. Due to these reasons, many consider Second Life as the first metaverse service realized (`https://en.wikipedia.org/wiki/Second_Life`).

Roblox

In September of 2006, the online game platform Roblox was released by the Roblox Corporation (located in San Mateo, California, USA) for use on computers based on Microsoft Windows (`www.roblox.com/`). Roblox enables its users to create new video games by programming. As new games are made, users can participate in games created by other users. This characteristic of Roblox served as a major contribution to the metaverse self-building features. The Roblox platform is based on the programming language Lua and hosts a library of multiple genres of online video games that are user-created. Although Roblox provides free games, in-game purchases can be made using the ROBUX cryptocurrency, which is a unique token used in Roblox. The popularity of Roblox significantly grew in the mid to late 2010s and especially during the COVID-19 pandemic. By August of 2020, the number of monthly active users of

Roblox reached 164 million, which amazingly included more than half of all American children under 16. Roblox has received many positive reviews and accolades (https://en.wikipedia.org/wiki/Roblox).

Minecraft

In 2009, Minecraft was first made public in 2011 with its first full release. Minecraft was developed by Mojang Studios (in Stockholm, Sweden) as a sandbox video game (www.minecraft.net). Minecraft is considered as one of the best-selling video games of all time based on its 2021 status of having sold over 238 million copies and having nearly 140 million monthly active users through its publishers Mojang Studios, Xbox Game Studios, and Sony Interactive Entertainment. One characteristic of Minecraft is the virtual 3D world designed with blocky and procedurally generated terrain, which needs to be explored and in which new structures and earthworks need to be established. In Minecraft, players can modify their avatar, design new gameplay mechanics, as well as add new items and assets. Minecraft has several game modes. In the survival game mode, players use their avatars to obtain resources and build a virtual world, in which maintaining one's avatar health while accomplishing multiple goals is the objective. In another game mode, players can use their avatar to join team-based or competition-based fighting games against computer-controlled mobs. Due to these aspects, Minecraft received many awards and is considered as one of the greatest video games of all time. The intellectual property rights of Minecraft and the company Mojang were acquired by Microsoft in 2014 for $2.5 billion, and since spin-off games of Minecraft have been released (https://en.wikipedia.org/wiki/Minecraft).

VRChat

In January of 2014, VRChat was released by VRChat, Inc. for the Oculus Rift DK1 prototype that was supported by Windows operating system (OS) computers (https://hello.vrchat.com). VRChat is based on a Unity

engine and enables users to socialize using 3D avatars and worlds created
by the users. The world and avatar creation capability of VRChat is similar to
Second Life and Habbo Hotel. The VRChat platform has a versatile interface
that allows various VR HMDs like the Oculus Quest and Rift series, Windows
Mixed Reality (MR), and SteamVR headsets like the HTC Vive but also allows
user access through a personal computer (PC) when using the "desktop
mode" in which the mouse, keyboard, and/or gamepad are used for control.
In VRChat, users are divided into "trust levels" and corresponding colors
based on their experience of programming and creation on the platform.
The beginner rank is the "Visitor" represented by gray. The next higher rank
is the "New User" represented by blue. A "New User" can upload the content
they have created using the VRChat software development kit (SDK).
This Unity programming SDK was released to help creation and stable/
secure importing of avatars as well as virtual spaces and infrastructure onto
the VRChat platform. The higher ranks are "User" represented by green,
"Known User" represented by orange, "Trusted User" represented by purple,
and "Friends" represented by yellow. In addition, VRChat Plus was released
in November of 2020, which enables up to 100 avatars to be saved in a user's
favorites (the earlier limit was 25), supports nameplates with custom images
and invite requests with in-game photo attachment, and grants trust rating
increases (https://en.wikipedia.org/wiki/VRChat).

Fortnite

In 2017, "Fortnite: Save the World" and "Fortnite Battle Royale" were
released by Epic Games located in Cary, North Carolina, USA
(www.epicgames.com/fortnite/en-US/home). Fortnite is an online video
game that uses a common gameplay and game engine to support the
three very popular game modes: "Fortnite Battle Royale," "Fortnite: Save
the World," and "Fortnite Creative." The "Fortnite Battle Royale" early
access title released in 2017 became a great success by accumulating
approximately 125 million players within a year. "Fortnite Battle Royale"

is playable on various platforms such as Microsoft Windows, macOS, iOS, PlayStation 4, PlayStation 5, Xbox One, Xbox Series X/S, Nintendo Switch, and Android. In "Fortnite Battle Royale," up to 100 players can participate in a last person standing free-to-play battle. "Fortnite: Save the World" is playable on various platforms such as Microsoft Windows, macOS, PlayStation 4, and Xbox One. In "Fortnite: Save the World," up to four players can participate in a survival game using cooperative hybrid tower defense-shooters, traps, and fortifications to defend objects from zombie-like creatures. "Fortnite Creative" was released in December of 2018 as a sandbox game playable on various platforms such as Microsoft Windows, macOS, PlayStation 4, Xbox One, iOS, Nintendo Switch, and Android. In "Fortnite Creative," players have full freedom to create new worlds and battle arenas. A significant part of the success of Fortnite games is based on the Unreal Engine developed by Epic Games. The Unreal Engine is a very powerful video game engine that is commercially available. The performance of the Unreal Engine earned official world-record recognition as the "most successful video game engine" from the Guinness World Records in 2014. The great success of Fortnite games resulted in a gross revenue of $9 billion by December of 2019. More details on the Unreal Engine will be provided in Chapter 2 (https://en.wikipedia.org/wiki/Fortnite).

Meta

Facebook rebranded its name to Meta in October of 2021, in which the company has invested a lot into metaverse technology and service development (https://about.facebook.com/). In December of 2021, Quest users in the United States and Canada were able to access Horizon Worlds. As of February of 2022, it was reported that 10,000 metaverse worlds have been created and there are 300,000 users. In addition, Meta's creator groups consist of more than 20,000 members. This is a significant accomplishment within a very short period, which shows the interest in metaverse technology and services. Meta's Horizon metaverses require a

Quest headset for proper access. Considering that the Quest 2 VR HMD
costs $299 or more, an investment from the user is required to actively
participate. By the fourth quarter of 2021, Meta's Quest 2 occupied 80%
of the global VR, AR, MR, and XR headset shipment market share, which
shows Meta's dominant success. For virtual ware sales made on the Meta
Quest store, a creator fee will be charged which includes Meta's platform
fee and a fee for using Horizon Worlds. This fee will apply to all metaverse
products, apps, and games of Meta (`https://en.wikipedia.org/wiki/
Meta_Platforms`).

Microsoft

Microsoft's metaverse is focused more on enterprise-centric work, design,
research, development, and education rather than social networking,
entertainment, or games (`www.microsoft.com/en-us/mesh`). Microsoft's
Mesh MR collaboration platform will work with Microsoft's Teams, in
which both will be supported by Azure edge cloud technology (`https://
docs.microsoft.com/en-us/mesh/overview`). Microsoft's Mesh will
provide virtual holographic MR systems that will be combined with
Team's virtual meetings, chats, and shared documents tools such that
collaborative work and virtual presence sharing is possible (`https://
docs.microsoft.com/en-us/mesh/mesh-app/`). Microsoft has
accumulated experience from earlier projects that combined MR with
Office tools, such as the "SharePoint Spaces" that was introduced in 2018.
SharePoint enables users to create 3D virtual spaces to visualize and
collaborate on product models and conduct data analysis (`www.zdnet.
com/article/microsoft-to-extend-its-enterprise-metaverse-
strategy-with-mesh-for-teams/`).

There are many more companies that have been providing metaverse
services, where unfortunately not all can be described in this book. In
the following, an overview of XR-, MR-, AR-, and VR-based metaverse
technologies are provided, where more details will be provided in Chapter 2.

XR-, MR-, AR-, and VR-Based Metaverse Technologies

Virtual reality (VR) is the best technology to implement a metaverse as it can provide an immersive presence into totally new virtual domains where interaction in the metaverse is possible through an avatar (or parts of an avatar, like the user's hands) and the metaverse design range is unlimited or limited to only the designer's programming/design skills and creative capacity.

Compared to VR, AR requires additional projected augmented images and information that have to be accurately positioned to blend in with the user's view of reality, which is a more difficult process. AR technology is based on the actual environment that the user is in, where augmented objects and/or information are added to provide information or conduct application-based functions. However, the actual environment view of the user is only partially augmented with objects and/or information. In order to be synchronized with the user's actual view (which can quickly change), the augmented process has to be conducted very fast and has to comfortably match the environment of the user.

Mixed reality (MR) combines AR and VR services with seamless crossover capability such that the MR user's actual AR service environment can transition into a virtual domain that is serviced by VR technology and seamlessly return from the VR domain to the AR environment as well.

XR adds various haptic interfaces to MR technology such that a more realistic experience can be obtained by the user. Various XR haptic interfaces are currently able to influence vision, hearing, and touch, which are three of the five human senses. In the future, the level of these three senses will be enhanced in many ways, and the missing two senses "taste" and "smell" may be added to XR haptic interfaces.

XR Implementation History

Head-up display (HUD) is commonly used on transparent displays/
windows to allow the user to see the surrounding viewpoints/
environment without requiring any additional head movement
(https://en.wikipedia.org/wiki/Comparison_of_virtual_reality_
headsets#Tethered_VR). On April 30th of 1958, the first HUD prototype
was used in the Blackburn Buccaneer attack aircraft of the British Royal
Navy. More HUD systems were developed for many other aircrafts in the
1950s and 1960s where flight instrument data and directional lines were
projected on screens or cockpit windows so the pilot(s) could keep their
"head up" while controlling the aircraft and not look down to read the
flight control instruments. This is where the name "head-up display" came
from. HUD is an original and practical form of AR technology.

In 1992, the Virtual Fixtures technology developed at the US Air
Force's Armstrong Laboratory is known to be the first MR system. In
addition, projection mapping technology uses projectors to display
graphical information or images onto physical objects. Projection
mapping technology has been used for many purposes which include
education, science, engineering, and military, and it is especially useful in
architecture and art.

Ever since the first smartphone (the "iPhone") was introduced by
Apple in 2007, smartphones have been the most convenient platform to
implement XR technology. This is because smartphones are a complete
form of a portable computer that has numerous sensors, multiple wireless
network interfaces, touch screen display, sufficient memory, high-
performance computing processors (CPU, GPU, and SoC), high-resolution
camera(s), and haptic devices. One of the earliest and most successful
XR models implemented on a smartphone is "Pokémon Go" that was
released by Niantic in collaboration with Nintendo and The Pokémon
Company in 2016. Pokémon Go is an AR game for iOS- and Android-based

16

smartphones. The GPS on smartphones were used to locate Pokémon virtual creatures which could be captured, trained, and put to battle the other Pokémon creatures. Pokémon Go was free to use as its business model was based on local advertisement and in-app purchases of various in-game items. XR technology combined with modern smartphones can implement simultaneous localization and mapping (SLAM)-based images and map creation. SLAM is a technology used to build a map using information or images collected from one agent roaming around or using a wireless network to collect information or images from multiple agents. SLAM uses the agent's location and the sensor's data or image of that location and combines all data to create an overview of the larger territory. The SLAM map can consist of sensor data and statistics and/ or can be a combination of partial images to form a larger image map (picture connecting technology is needed). SLAM maps may have parts where data or images are missing. There are a variety of SLAM methods that are used in AR applications, such as parallel tracking and mapping (PTAM) technology (`https://en.wikipedia.org/wiki/Simultaneous_ localization_and_mapping`).

XR headsets, HMDs, and eyeglasses are the most common types of XR devices, in which a list of various devices based on release date order is provided in the following section. XR devices (including all VR, AR, and MR systems) can be divided into "tethered" or "standalone." Tethered XR devices require a computer (including laptops and tablets) or video game console to process the application where the user video information is sent to the XR headset wirelessly (commonly using Wi-Fi or Bluetooth) or through a wire connected to the computer or video game console. Wired XR headsets receive power through the wired line, so they do not need an internal battery. Standalone XR devices conduct all processing of the application in its system and therefore do not need a supporting external computer or video game console to support it. This is why tethered devices are commonly lighter than standalone devices and can be used longer. However, tethered devices that need a wired connection have a limited range of usage that is based on the length of the wire, and wireless tethered devices also require the user to be in the reliable range of the networked computer or the video game console. Due to this reason, standalone devices are expected to become more popular in the future. Some XR devices have been released as both tethered and standalone products. In the following is a list of XR devices ordered based on date of release.

Tethered XR Devices

The following list introduces the chronological order of tethered XR device releases.

- In 2015, Razer OSVR HDK 1.4 was released.

- In 2016, Oculus Rift, HTC Vive, Razer OSVR HDK 2, StarBreeze StarVR, and PlayStation VR were released.

- In 2017, Fove 0, Pimax 4K, VRgineers VRHero 5K, Deepoon VR E3, Dell Visor, Acer AH101, HP WMR headset, Lenovo Explorer, Samsung Odyssey, and VRgineers VRHero 5K Plus were released.

- In 2018, Asus HC102, HTC Vive Pro, VRgineers XTAL, StarVR One, Samsung Odyssey+, and Pimax 5K Plus were released.

- In 2019, Varjo VR-1, Varjo Aero, Pimax 8K, Valve Index, HP Reverb, Oculus Rift S, HTC Vive Cosmos, Varjo VR-2, and Oculus Quest were released.

- In 2020, Oculus Quest 2, HP Reverb G2, HTC Vive Pro 2, and Varjo VR-3 were released.

Standalone XR Devices

The following list introduces the chronological order of standalone XR device releases:

- In 2015, Samsung Gear VR was released.

- In 2016, Avegant Glyph, Pico VR Goblin, Qualcomm Snapdragon VR820, Alcatel Vision, Microsoft Hololens, and Helmet Vision were released.

- In 2017, Pico Neo CV, Qualcomm Snapdragon 835 VRDK, and Woxter Neo VR100 were released.

- In 2018, HTC Vive Focus, Oculus Go, Lenovo Mirage Solo, GFL Developer Kit, and Google Daydream View were released.

- In 2019, Pico G2 4K and Oculus Quest were released.

- In 2020, Oculus Quest 2 was released.

- In 2021, HTC Vive Focus 3 and Pico Neo 3 Pro were released.

- In 2022, HTC Vive Flow was released.

In the future, AR contact lenses and virtual retinal display devices could be created. As see-through electronics and miniature display systems have evolved, AR contact lenses are an attractive option that can have many useful applications. Among the earliest attempts, in 2013 at the Consumer Electronics Show (CES), Innovega presented a contact lenses prototype that worked with AR glasses. In 2020 at CES, Mojo Vision presented a contact lenses prototype that worked without needing AR glasses. AR contact lenses that function with AR spectacles are known to be under development for the US military. However, an AR contact lenses product has not been officially released yet. In addition, virtual retinal display AR devices have been under development for a while, but a product has not been released yet. A virtual retinal display device will display an image directly onto the retina inside the user's eye. This technology could be used as a medical device that can help patients with visual disabilities (`https://en.wikipedia.org/wiki/Comparison_of_virtual_reality_headsets#Tethered_VR`).

Future metaverse systems are expected to evolve from the current VR-based interfaces into full XR-based systems, with hope that the content of this book will help to assist a successful and faster transition into XR-based metaverses. In the following section, details on metaverse and XR products and business are presented.

Metaverse XR Products and Business

The reason that metaverses are receiving much attention is not only due to the fun factor but also because there are many ways that a profit can be made, which include ownership, investments, events, device sales, creative design-based sales of virtual goods, platform usage fees, advertisement fees, and online store fees (`www.youtube.com/watch?v=OHqV1cJ1Bdw`). There are moneymaking methods suitable for large-scale and small-scale companies as well as methods that an individual can make a profit, which are explained in this section. Metaverses consist of multiple online virtual spaces that include virtual environments, buildings, infrastructure, transportation, and avatars, which each has its own individual value. These virtual objects can be designed, rented, sold, purchased, or invested through various forms of financial endeavors. For some virtual goods, if the original item has a unique value, then the original needs to be distinguishable to its duplicates/copies, and the buyer needs to be able to confirm that the purchasing object is an original, and its purchase needs to be verifiable and secure. This is where blockchain technology becomes very useful. Blockchain-based cryptocurrencies are commonly used to make purchases, with support of smart contracts and non-fungible tokens (NFTs).

Smart Contracts

A smart contract is a blockchain-based secure computer programmed contract that is capable of automatically managing and executing legal actions based on the contract terms (https://en.wikipedia.org/wiki/Smart_contract). Blockchains are used to secure the agreement of the contract terms which are unchangeable and confirmable through the blockchain records or a distributed ledger. Smart contracts are transparent and help to reduce the overhead cost of banks and legal fees needed to set up and execute contract terms. Without a smart contract, traditional financial contracts require trusted intermediators representing each company/firm, where fees for arbitrations and enforcement are significant and time-consuming. In addition, smart contracts rarely have any malicious or accidental exceptions occurring, and even if they occur, settlements are simpler because the contract execution process is easily traceable, and actions are transparent to the contracted users. The most popular smart contract platform is the Ethereum blockchain that was launched in 2015 (https://ethereum.org/en/). Most metaverse platforms use Ethereum for smart contract-based contracting and execution (https://en.wikipedia.org/wiki/Ethereum).

NFT

NFTs are blockchain-based financial securities of digital data recordings. The blockchain distributed ledger records all transactions of ownership of an NFT, allowing secure NFT selling and trading. Metaverse virtual objects are computer-based designs saved in a computer file format. Metaverse virtual objects are "fungible," which means that they can be replaced by another identical item and are mutually interchangeable with a digital copy of the original. Blockchains and securing smart contracts need to be used to make the original version "non-fungible" and have a

cryptocurrency-based token value. This is why the name non-fungible
token (NFT) is used. But unlike cryptocurrency, each NFT is uniquely
identifiable and secure through a blockchain platform, and smart
contracts are used to support the process. NFTs are not only for metaverse
virtual goods and property but are used for digital audio, video, art, and
photo files. Due to the versatility of investment worthy merchandise and
easy means of making a purchase/investment, the NFT market size grew
significantly during the COVID-19 pandemic period, where the total NFT
trading in 2020 were at the $82 million level, which grew to the $17 billion
level in 2021 (`https://en.wikipedia.org/wiki/Non-fungible_token`).

Metaverses can be visited using a computer monitor, laptop computer,
or tablet/pad computer. But the immersive presence of a metaverse is
best experienced when using HMDs (goggle-type devices) or glasses that
support XR, MR, VR, or AR services. In a metaverse, an infinite number of
things can be done which include going to a concert, having a meeting,
going on an exportation trip, exercising, education, playing games, etc. The
metaverse virtual space provides a platform for the user avatars to work,
study, explore, collaborate, and compete. Based on this definition, all
aspects of the metaverse are investment worthy.

A metaverse is based on an environment that is newly created, where
the entire virtual space can be sold for ownership. A virtual space can consist
of the virtual environment, buildings, infrastructure, and transportation
facilities, where each of these virtual entities is divided into purchasable
or investment worthy parts and is being sold through companies using
cryptocurrency tokens, blockchains, smart contracts, and NFTs. Some of
the representative companies include Decentraland (`https://
decentraland.org/`), Sandbox (`https://www.sandbox.game/en/`),
Axie Infinity (`https://axieinfinity.com/`), Illuvium (`https://www.
illuvium.io/`), and Roblox (`https://www.roblox.com/`). Commonly,
metaverse virtual investment and trade companies use Ethereum smart
contracts, and each has its own cryptocurrency tokens. For example,

Decentraland uses MANA, Sandbox uses SAND, Axie Infinity uses AXS,
Illuvium uses ILV, and Roblox uses ROBLOX as their cryptocurrency tokens
when making purchases, investments, or exchanges of virtual property.
Virtual real estate purchasing, exchanges, and investments can also be
conducted through companies like Metaverse Properties (`https://`
`metaverse.properties`). To support virtual real estate investments, this
company provides Metaverse Real Estate and Investment Trust (REIT)
services and a Metaverse Index (MVI). REIT and MVI provide detailed
information to assist and make virtual real estate investments. In addition,
virtual arts, avatars, wearables, rideable, property, and various goods of
the metaverse can be sold using NFTs on metaverse service platforms
such as Fiverr or Upwork. A profit can be made by selling property at a
price higher than purchased, renting property (and receiving rent fees),
and advertising on one's property (and receiving advertisement fees), or
various types of events could be held to make a profit. In addition, the
value of virtual property can be increased by virtual land improvement and
land amelioration, such as building useful facilities for avatars.

Alternatively, instead of virtual real estate, a metaverse investment
could be made by investing into the cryptocurrency tokens like MANA
(for Decentraland), SAND (for Sandbox), AXS (for Axie Infinity), ILV
(for Illuvium), ROBLOX (for Roblox), etc. Obviously selling tokens for a
price higher than the purchased price would be the objective. Instead of
investing into a few selected tokens, you can also invest by purchasing an
index of tokens using platforms such as Metaverse Index (MVI). An index
includes an expert selected group of metaverse tokens, where the tokens
to be included and their proportional amounts included in each index are
different. So careful index selection is needed.

The next type of metaverse merchandise focuses on the avatar and
its wearables and usable items, which can be made based on request
or can be designed and directly sold on platforms such as Upwork and
Fiverr. An avatar can resemble its user in detail (even can include live
expression details) or can be made to be more abstract and only slightly

resemble its user. Avatars can be beautified or made more handsome,
cute, ugly, monstrous, etc. using filters with various fashion, culture,
gender, or artistic preferences. The avatar's wearable and usable items
are very diverse and can easily be customized to one's preference. Avatar
wearables include clothes, shoes, sneakers, sandals, roller blades, ice
skates, snowboards, skiis, watches, jewelry, accessories, glasses, etc.
Avatar usable items include cars, trucks, buses, trains, tanks, motorcycles,
bicycles, scooters, skates, roller blades, roller boards, boats, yachts,
submarines, underground vehicles, blimps, combat jets, airplanes, rockets,
etc. Avatar wearables and usable items designed by world top brands are
very popular. Some of the top brands include Nike, Adidas, Gucci, Louis
Vuitton, Toyota, etc. In real life, a product from Gucci or Louis Vuitton may
be too expensive to buy for most customers, but in the metaverse world,
these luxury brand products are much more affordable (as they are virtual
goods) for one's avatar.

These luxury brand virtual goods can easily provide a surrogate
satisfaction by purchasing these for one's avatar, which is one of
the benefits of the metaverse. From the company business side, the
metaverse provides a great way to advertise their products and brand
name to a new generation of young metaverse users (`www.youtube.com/
watch?v=3U70-y-1NaM`).

Another method is to invest into metaverse related company stocks,
which include companies like Amazon, Microsoft, Meta/Facebook, Apple,
Nvidia, etc. This is the most traditional way of making an investment into
metaverse technology.

Wave

In 2016, the metaverse virtual entertainment platform Wave (`https://
wavexr.com`) was founded in Los Angeles, California, USA. The virtual
entertainment shows hosted are called "Waves" which support virtual
collaboration of artists and audience based on real-time live virtual

performances. An avatar of the artist is made with precision such that
the artist's voice, sound, motions, and emotions are accurately presented
in the metaverse event space. Waves are conducted at the same time
as the live concert in a location with or without a live audience. Wave
enables a live music concert to include additional virtual factors (such
as virtual games and shopping) for enhanced interaction with the
entertainer and other fans. Wave's real-time multicasting technology
enables entertainment events to be streamed live globally on wave.watch
(https://live.wavexr.com/home) and can be accessed using popular
social media (e.g., YouTube, Twitter, Twitch, TikTok, and Facebook)
and gaming platforms (e.g., Roblox). Some of the representative virtual
events hosted by Wave include concerts by DJ David Guetta, Travis
Scott, The Chainsmokers, Justin Bieber, Pentakill, Dillon Francis, Alison
Wonderland, Lindsey Stirling, The Weeknd, and John Legend (https://
metaverseinsider.tech/2022/05/01/metaverse-company-delivering-
the-best-of-live-music-gaming-broadcast-technology-to-fans/).

ZEPETTO

In August of 2018, ZEPETTO was first released and now has over 200
million users, where 80% of these users are Generation Z users. Generation
Z is defined as the generation after Millennials and before Generation
Alpha that have birthdays approximately in the range from 1997 to 2012.
One characteristic of Generation Z is that they were the first generation
to grow up in a society where Internet access, portable computers, and
smartphones were common and, therefore, have been called "digital
natives" as well (https://m.k-odyssey.com/news/newsview.php?nco
de=1065580437310285).

ZEPETTO enables avatars to be created based on a picture of its user,
where the avatar aspects and features can be modified to fit personal
desires. Various types of avatar clothing, footwear, accessories, and jewelry
can be purchased with the ZEPETTO currency ZEMs and coins. Houses,

buildings, gardens, and parks can be built and used to invite friends over for socializing activities. In addition, personal and group/team activities and games are commonly provided. ZEPETO opened a virtual art gallery which displayed some of the world's most famous art masterpieces.

ZEPETTO is also used as an entertainment platform. ZEPETTO is a product of NAVER Z, which is a subsidiary of the parent NAVER Corporation in South Korea. Major K-pop companies in South Korea like YG Entertainment, JYP Entertainment, and Big Hit Music have made investments into ZEPETTO.

In November of 2021, YG Entertainment launched "the SamE" metaverse space in ZEPETTO, which is the same as an actual fan project-space in front of YG Entertainment building in South Korea. Due to the COVID-19 pandemic, YG Entertainment made a duplicated virtual space in the metaverse. The SamE project-space and the café "MD shop" were popular locations for live musical events and exhibitions. But as it became difficult for the fans to visit these spaces due to the COVID-19 pandemic, the agency reproduced these spaces into the ZEPETTO metaverse. In the ZEPETTO MD shop, BLACKPINK's music videos are played, and YG artists' products are sold. Popular avatar items include BLACKPINK's 2019 Coachella Valley Music and Arts Festival costumes. In addition, when a new album was released, a special event that enabled fan avatars to take pictures with the BLACKPINK avatars was provided.

Likewise, JYP Entertainment is also active with K-pop entertainment events and fandom on ZEPETTO. JYP's K-pop groups TWICE and ITZY had released metaverse music videos specifically for ZEPETTO.

In addition, Big Hit Music is also very active on ZEPETTO, as it is the agency of BTS. BTS has held metaverse fan events on ZEPETTO. The BTS avatars in ZEPETTO are very popular, in which the ZEPETTO code names of the BTS avatars are commonly memorized by the BTS Adorable Representative M.C. for Youth (ARMY) fan club members. In addition, BTS released their metaverse music video and debuted their "Dynamite" choreography video in Fortnite.

In September of 2020, at the BLACKPINK signing event on ZEPETTO, approximately 50 million fans visited and took pictures and received signatures from BLACKPINK avatars. This example shows the massive accessibility of metaverse services, as participation of 50 million fans at a physical entertainment event is impossible. Currently, the main metaverse contents are online games and entertainment, where approximately 70% (or more) of the users are teenagers and Generation Z (`https://en.wikipedia.org/wiki/Generation_Z`). For these users, online services are very comfortable, and use of avatars in the metaverse has no awkwardness and is preferred in many cases.

Metaverse Global Market

Based on a Fortune Business Insights report, the forecast of the metaverse global market is expected to grow significantly. For the period from 2022 to 2029, a compound annual growth rate (CAGR) of 47.6% is predicted (`www.fortunebusinessinsights.com/metaverse-market-106574`). This growth rate of the metaverse global market will take the 2022 prediction level of $100.27 billion to the $1,527.55 billion level by 2029. Based on the "Metaverse Market Revenue Worldwide from 2021 to 2030" report from Statista, the worldwide metaverse market size in 2021 was $38.85 billion which grew to $47.48 billion in 2022 and is expected to reach $678.8 billion by 2030 (`www.statista.com/statistics/1295784/metaverse-market-size/`). These reports differ in criteria of metaverse market size evaluations, so the values are different, but it is evident that the metaverse market size will grow significantly over the next decade. Metaverse services require Internet platforms as well as significant software and hardware support. XR devices will play a significant role as these XR HMDs (or glasses) will serve as the main interface to metaverse worlds. Therefore, in the following, an analysis of metaverse market size of XR devices is provided.

Figure 1-1 shows the AR/VR Headset Market Share for 2020 (`www.idc.com/getdoc.jsp?containerId=prUS48969722`), and Figure 1-2 shows how the expected trend will change in 2024 (`www.businesswire.com/news/home/20200318005149/en/AR-and-VR-Headsets-Will-See-Shipments-Decline-in-the-Near-Term-Due-to-COVID-19-But-Long-term-Outlook-Is-Positive-According-to-IDC`). In 2020, VR standalone devices have the largest share of the market closely followed by VR tethered devices, where these two types of devices dominate the market consuming over 84%. However, the trend changes to VR standalone having the largest share but closely followed by AR standalone devices and AR tethered and VR tethered devices. The two most noticeable changes from 2020 to 2024 is the significant growth in AR devices and standalone devices (both VR and AR) becoming much more popular compared to tethered devices.

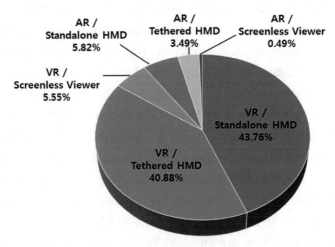

Figure 1-1. *AR/VR Headset Market Share for 2020*

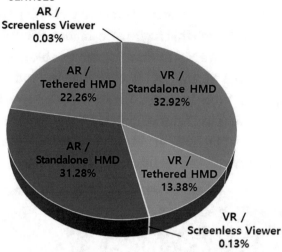

Figure 1-2. *Predicted AR/VR Headset Market Share for 2024*

Currently VR technology is well implemented in various types of
devices. But due to many difficulties in AR technology implementation, an
AR HMD is much more difficult to make and is therefore very expensive.
Future improvements in AR technology are expected to highly improve
the performance while reducing the power consumption such that AR
standalone devices will become more usable and popular. The big increase
in AR standalone devices in 2024 presented in Figure 1-2 reflects this
expected change.

One of the focuses of this book is to help AR development, which is
why Chapter 3 is focused on AR core technologies and Chapter 4 describes
deep learning technologies. Once AR technology reaches a higher level,
then MR devices (which combine AR and VR) can be developed at a higher
level, and with additional haptic interfaces added to MR devices, then true
XR devices can be made. So, there is still a long way to go to reach high-
performance XR metaverses.

Figure 1-3 shows the market trend of MR devices, which are expected
to grow approximately 44.7 times during an approximate 7-year period
from 2018 to 2025 (according to Statista report). Based on the preceding

discussion, Figure 1-3 seems to predict that MR technology will be
mature enough by 2025 such that high-performance MR devices will
be abundantly used. Future MR devices need to be able to support
continuous and smooth AR and VR domain switching and enable its user
to select among AR or VR only modes. By 2025, glasses-type lightweight
standalone MR products will be an important factor that could make MR
smart devices very popular (`www.statista.com/statistics/897595/`
`world-mixed-reality-market-value/`).

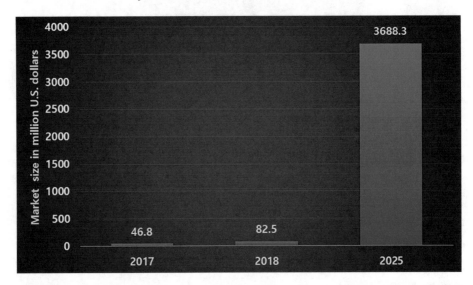

Figure 1-3. *MR Market Size Predictions*

Figure 1-4 shows the MR market share forecast by segment based on
2022 (`www.statista.com/statistics/610066/worldwide-forecast-`
`augmented-and-mixed-reality-software-assumptions/`). Percentage
wise, video games dominate by occupying 34%, and live events added
to video entertainment occupy 21%. This shows that the portion of
entertainment-related services are the most dominant MR service as they
add up to 55% overall. Video games and live events add up to 46% which
is significant. Online video games and live events are highly dependent

on real-time high-performance processing system technology as well as
broadband high-speed Internet and wireless communication services
(e.g., 5G, 6G, Wi-Fi, and Bluetooth).

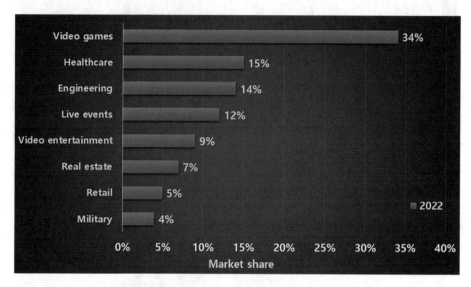

Figure 1-4. *MR Market Share Forecast by Segment*

Figure 1-5 shows the XR market size predictions up to 2025 (according
to Market Research Future report). The data shows that the XR market is
expected to grow approximately 14.56 times during an approximate 7-year
period from 2018 to 2025, reaching a $393 billion market size by 2025 (www.
marketresearchfuture.com/reports/extended-reality-market-8552).
Figure 1-5 clearly shows the need to study and invest in XR technology and
metaverse services, which is the focus of this book. Figure 1-6 shows the
XR headset global brands share for 2020 (www.counterpointresearch.
com/global-xr-ar-vr-headsets-market-share/).

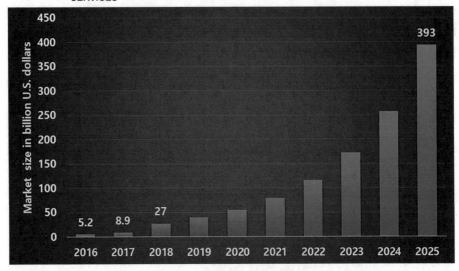

Figure 1-5. *XR Market Size Predictions*

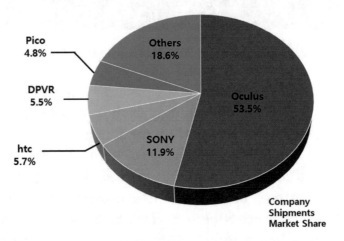

Figure 1-6. *XR Headset Global Brands Share for 2020*

This 2020 market trend radically changes, and by the fourth quarter
of 2021, Meta's Quest 2 occupied 80% of the global VR, AR, MR, and XR
headset market share based on product shipments. The second highest
was DPVR which occupied 8%, third was Pico which occupied 5%, and
other company products occupied a combined 7%.

Among XR devices, the most popular are Oculus Quest and Meta Quest 2 by a far margin. In May of 2019, the Oculus Quest VR HMD was released by Facebook. The Quest's introductory price was $399 for the 64 GB (gigabyte) storage memory device and $499 for the 128 GB storage memory device. In October of 2020, Oculus Quest 2 was released, and due to Facebook's company name change to Meta, the device was rebranded as Meta Quest 2 in November of 2021. Quest 2's initial price was $299 for the 64 GB storage memory model which was changed to 128 GB later and $399 for the 256 GB storage memory model.

DPVR's E3 VR headset was released on September 1st of 2019, which uses the SteamVR platform and has a retail price of $399 for the HMD. Pico was acquired by ByteDance in 2021 and has been improving its Neo standalone VR HMDs, in which the Pico Neo 3 was recently released on May 24, 2022.

Among AR and MR devices, the Microsoft HoloLens and HoloLens 2 are very popular. In March 2016, the Development Edition of Microsoft HoloLens was released by Microsoft at a list price of $3,000. Microsoft HoloLens is a MR smart glasses HMD device that runs on the Windows Mixed Reality platform and uses the Windows 10 operating system (OS). In February 2019, HoloLens 2 was introduced at the Mobile World Congress (MWC) and later became purchasable at a preorder price of $3,500.

The presented product release timeline and large difference in product cost of the VR-based Oculus Quest and Meta Quest 2 devices compared to the AR-based HoloLens and HoloLens 2 products show that AR technology is much harder to implement than VR devices. This is because AR devices have to overlay information and/or images onto the actual view of the user in real time, which is very difficult. The overlay of information and/or images onto the actual view of the user has to be instantaneous and comfortably viewable to the user and the user's surrounding environment in terms of color, brightness, and distance. Many additional XR field-of-view (FoV) aspects are described in Chapter 2.

Video Streaming Technology Introduction

Traditional multimedia was composed of text, audio, and video, which were delivered to users through broadcasting or unicasting. Except for the telephone, real-time interaction over traditional multimedia was not possible, and users could only passively receive the content and play it. Later as networks were built and networking technology evolved, multimedia content was able to be delivered to selected users through multicasting technology. Recently, the evolution of multimedia services is diversifying and speeding up due to the rapid development of the Internet and information technology and communications (ITC) systems and software. Multimedia now combines many content forms, and the delivery method has changed significantly. In addition, new ways to interact with multimedia content have been revolutionizing the way multimedia can be used.

Television (TV)

One reference point of multimedia technology is the black and white analog television (TV), which was used for approximately 30 years from 1936 to 1967. Black and white analog TV was replaced by color analog TV, which began broadcasting in 1954 in the United States. The three representative analog color TV standards are the National Television System Committee (NTSC), Phase Alternating Line (PAL), and the Electronic Color System with Memory (SECAM). NTSC was developed in North America and is the original analog color TV signal encoding system that was broadcasted since 1954. Western European countries wanted an analog color TV standard that was independent of NTSC and could perform better in Europe's geographical and weather conditions. This led to the development of PAL and SECAM. The United Kingdom was the first to broadcast analog color TV signals in 1967 using PAL. The first analog color TV broadcast using SECAM was conducted in France in 1967.

SECAM is originally written in French as SÉCAM, which is the acronym for *système électronique couleur avec mémoire* (`https://en.wikipedia.org/wiki/Television`).

Cable TV

In 1950, commercial services of cable television (TV) started in the United States. Cable TV has been abbreviated as "CATV" based on the acronym of the original 1948 technology "Community Access Television" or "Community Antenna Television" which is the origin of cable TV. CATV was needed because over-the-air broadcasted radio frequency (RF) TV reception has many limitations in areas far from TV transmitters or due to mountainous terrains. In such areas, a community antenna was constructed, and cables were connected to individual homes, which is how CATV was serviced. By 1968, only 6.4% of Americans used cable TV which expanded to 62.4% by 1994. Cable TV services became very popular in the United States, Canada, Europe, Australia, South Asia, East Asia, and South America. One of the common complaints consumers had with modern cable TV services was the bundling of channels that had to be purchased together, where in fact only a few desired channels were of interest. The cable TV bundling made cable TV services very expensive and gave users a feeling that they were wasting money. Based on cable TV technology, the first subscriber streaming service and the first "pay TV" service began with Home Box Office (HBO), which is discussed in the following (`https://en.wikipedia.org/wiki/Cable_television`).

HBO

HBO was the first to start "pay TV" services and subscriber video streaming services, which was brilliant and revolutionizing in both business and technology (`www.hbo.com/`). In November of 1972, HBO was launched by the parent company Home Box Office that is owned by Warner Bros.

Discovery, which has headquarters in New York City, New York, USA. HBO is the original subscription-based television service provided through cable TV and multipoint distribution service (MDS) providers to direct subscriber TVs. HBO's premium channels were provided to subscribers for an extra monthly fee (i.e., pay TV services). The media content on HBO's premium channels did not have advertisements, and many programs included objectionable material without editing. In 1976, HBO was the first television channel that used worldwide satellite program transmission. HBO was also the first streaming media company to create and release original program content. In May of 1983, HBO's first original television film "The Terry Fox Story" was released. Over the years, HBO has made numerous HBO Originals that cover the media genres of drama, comedy, miniseries, and docuseries. By September of 2018, HBO was available to approximately 35.656 million US households and had 34.939 million subscribers. As of 2018, HBO was globally available to at least 151 countries and had an estimated 140 million cumulative subscribers. As of 2017, an operating income of nearly $2 billion every year had been generated from HBO. In May of 2020, HBO Max was launched by Warner Bros. Discovery as a subscription-based VOD service that streams content from HBO, Warner Bros., and their related brands, which has been very successful (https://en.wikipedia.org/wiki/HBO).

Cinemax

In August of 1980, Cinemax was launched by HBO which is owned by Warner Bros. Discovery (www.cinemax.com/). Due to having the same parent company, HBO and Cinemax are sister companies. In August of 1991, HBO and Cinemax were the first two subscriber television services that offered complimentary multiplexed channels in the United States. The network service provided seven 24-hour, linear multiplex channels and the traditional HBO On Demand subscription video service. By September of 2018, Cinemax was available to approximately 21.736 million US households and had 21.284 million subscribers (https://en.wikipedia.org/wiki/Cinemax).

Blockbuster

In October of 1985, Blockbuster LLC was founded in Dallas, Texas, USA. Blockbuster provided home movies and video game rental services through its video rental shops, which expanded internationally throughout the 1990s due to its excellent business model. In 2004, Blockbuster had 9,094 stores and approximately 84,300 employees worldwide, where approximately 58,500 worked in the United States and 25,800 worked overseas. Blockbuster's business model revolutionized multimedia rental services and influenced many media companies. Blockbuster made rental fees cheap to encourage frequent and economic means to media sharing to the public but charged heavier on late return fees to discourage users from returning rented items late, which seriously hindered circulation of media sharing and made customer services and reservations very difficult. The success of Blockbuster's business model drew much attention, and many similar companies were established which also included some varied media rental business models.

In 1997, Netflix began postal mail-based DVD renting services that had no late return fees (further details on Netflix are described in the following section). In 2002, Tic Tok Easy Shop was created, which had Redbox automated retail kiosks (mostly installed in front of the shops for easy customer access) that enabled DVD rentals for $1 per day, which were very successful. Netflix's DVD mail delivery services, Redbox automated DVD rental kiosks, HBO's VoD services, and financial recessions in the economy resulted in many difficulties for Blockbuster. As a result, from 2005, Blockbuster's revenue began to decrease. In 2007, Netflix began streaming media and VoD services in the United States. Following Netflix's successful business model, many companies started OTT media streaming services. In 2010, Blockbuster filed for bankruptcy protection, and in 2014, the last remaining 300 Blockbuster owned stores all closed (`https://en.wikipedia.org/wiki/Blockbuster_LLC`).

IPTV

Internet Protocol television (IPTV) is the technology that enables
television content to be transmitted over the Internet. Because IPTV uses
the Internet Protocol (IP) and the Internet network, it is significantly more
versatile in user control compared to wireless broadcast TV, satellite TV,
and cable TV. IPTV is a core technology of streaming media. When using
IPTV, the user can begin viewing while the media content is progressively
being downloaded from the server. Media streaming provides many
advantages over media technologies that require a full file download
before viewing can start. Due to limitations in the supportable data rates
of the Internet, IPTV services were not possible until the 1990s. In 1995,
IPTV became possible with the company Precept Software releasing
"IP/TV" to provide video services over the Internet. IP/TV used Mbone
technology and was compatible with Windows and Unix-based systems
and applications (`https://en.wikipedia.org/wiki/Internet_Protocol_
television`).

Mbone is an abbreviated name for "multicast backbone" which is a
protocol developed in the early 1990s to enable Internet backbone and
virtual network services that can support Internet protocol version 4
(IPv4) multicast packet delivery. IP/TV could be used to deliver single and
multisource video and audio IPv4 packets over the Internet by using Real-
time Transport Protocol (RTP) and the RTP Control Protocol (RTCP). In
1998, Cisco acquired Precept and the IP/TV trademark.

As the Internet became faster and more reliable, IPTV services globally
spread quickly. Global market expectations in 2009 were $12 billion in
revenue based on 28 million subscribers, which reached $38 billion in
revenue based on having 83 million subscribers by 2013. The dominance
of IPTV technology and services has grown significantly ever since. Now
IPTV services are supported by SmartTVs which have smartphone-like
interfaces and control features as well as voice activation and control
technology support.

IPTV services are commonly supported by one (or a contracted group of) content service providers which use separate IPTV networks or virtual private networks (VPNs) over public networks. In addition, IPTV services are displayed on IPTVs or SmartTVs. IPTV services (and cable TV) use dedicated and controlled networks to provide video on demand (VoD) (or related) services. Due to the network service provider having full control over the network, Cable TV and IPTV streaming speeds are fast and reliable, such that channel changes can be made instantly. These aspects are what distinguish IPTV to over-the-top (OTT) services, which are described in more detail in the following.

China's Media Services

China has been a very successful early adopter in the media service domain, in which China's rich resources of high-quality engineers have driven rapid development. China's earliest video streaming and user created content (UCC) (i.e., also known as user generated content (UGC)) platforms were started by Youku in 2003 and Todou in 2005, and a few years later, companies like Tencent, Alibaba, and Baidu started to invest into this domain of business. In 2010, premium video streaming in China began with iQiyi being launched by Baidu, which was soon followed by Tencent Video (https://en.wikipedia.org/wiki/Mass_media_in_China).

YouTube

In February of 2005, former PayPal employees founded YouTube, which rapidly grew in popularity and content in North America (www.youtube.com/). In the following year in October of 2006, Google acquired YouTube for $1.65 billion, in which many considered it as an overpay at the time but it shows the remarkable business mind to realize valuable technology of the future by the Google leadership. YouTube has significantly contributed to expanding and improving the domain of UCC media content creation to include public users, which before it was mostly limited to the broadcast corporations and movie companies in the United States. In 2005, YouTube's Internet-based service model influenced many companies. YouTube's UCC revolution became even more influential due to Apple's iPhone (first launched in 2007) and other smartphone companies that followed (most of them launched in 2009), because smartphones enabled easy video recording and editing as well as direct uploading to YouTube wirelessly. YouTube TV is a very strong contender because its platform has some features that other big media streaming companies like Netflix, Prime Video, and Disney+ do not have. YouTube TV enables users to view TV programs from various channels live as they are being broadcasted in real time, or programs can be stored to a library and viewed later, where the library has near unlimited capacity. YouTube TV was the fastest growing live streaming service in 2019 and already has the largest market share among live streaming services. Other live streaming service platforms include Vue, Sling, DirectTV NOW, etc. YouTube TV includes many TV programs, and users can select to subscribe or view free with advertisements included. Because YouTube TV is not different from YouTube, and because most smartphone users have YouTube installed, the accessibility of YouTube TV is very convenient, and already almost everyone knows how to search and find the desired content and view it due to the familiarity of using the YouTube app on smartphones for a long time (https://en.wikipedia.org/wiki/YouTube).

Streaming OTT

Streaming media services are commonly provided using OTT media delivery technology. The US Federal Communications Commission (FCC) considers OTT services to be a linear video service provided over the public Internet in which cable operators do not manage the video services or the cable systems. The term "linear" refers to a video service that is scheduled and virtually playable simultaneously with transmission. The

Canadian Radio-Television and Telecommunications Commission (CRTC) considers OTT services to be a programming service provided over the Internet that is independent to the network (e.g., cable, satellite, etc.) and facilities used for its content delivery. The US FCC classifies OTT services into two types, multichannel video programming distributor (MVPD) or online video distributor (OVD). MVPD provides multiple channels of video programming through multichannel multipoint distribution services and direct broadcast satellite services, etc. Companies like YouTube TV, DirecTV Stream, Hulu + Live TV, FuboTV, and Sling TV can be considered as virtual MVPDs. An OVD provides video programming through the Internet in which the network does not include an MVPD nor is the network delivery path network (or a part of it) operated by that OVD. Companies like Netflix, Disney+, Amazon Prime Video, HBO Max, Hulu, Peacock, Discovery+, and Paramount+ can be considered as streaming OVDs. The term "streaming" commonly refers to media downloads that can start to be played before the full download of the media file is complete.

OTT streaming of media content is delivered directly to the viewers through the Internet in which users can receive OTT services on their computer, laptop, SmartTV, smartphone, and any other smart device (e.g., tablet, pad, etc.). In other words, unlike in IPTV services, OTT services can be accessed on a variety of receiving devices and are not limited to a specific Internet service provider. Users will commonly subscribe to multiple content providers (e.g., Netflix, Disney+, HBO Max, etc.) and stream media contents over the mobile/wireless Internet and view the content with the most convenient device based on their location and smart device availability and features. Therefore, OTT services can be broader in range and more diverse in content compared to IPTV services (`https://en.wikipedia.org/wiki/Over-the-top_media_service`).

Traditionally, video content was delivered by broadcast TV companies and later through cable and satellite TV companies. Therefore, the TV companies owned and operated most of the content creation, the film studios, and delivery platforms in the past. However, due to the revolution in Internet technology, computers, laptops, IPTV, SmartTVs, smartphones, tablet/pad smart devices, and the mobile Internet, new means of streaming media services that directly send to the users became more popular. Because streaming media services were delivered directly to the users bypassing (i.e., passing over) the traditionally mega TV companies and delivery platforms, the technology is called over-the-top (OTT).

Having to pay a subscription fee for streaming media services enabled the media content to be viewable at any time without any commercial interruptions. In addition, the media library included premium media content that could be viewed on demand based on a separate subscription and payment. Thus, newer, more valuable, or user exclusive content could be provided easily to the users, which helped to satisfy personal needs and desires. As the smartphone revolution began in 2007 with the Apple iPhone, and application (App) stores (e.g., Apple's App Store, Google's Play Store, AWS Appstore, etc.) became common along with online payment methods, subscription fee based streaming media services became widely acceptable to the public easily.

In the evolution of video streaming, file downloading was the earlier option of use by media platforms, in which the entire media file was downloaded before viewing could be started. This was the preferred option because networks were not as stable and did not have sufficient bandwidth and throughput to provide a reliable continuous streaming session for a long period of time. In addition, the download before viewing process (which uses a "push" based protocol) had some security issues (with network firewalls) that are explained in Chapter 6 when introducing the features of MPEG-DASH technology, which is the most commonly used modern video streaming network protocol. Additionally, former media players were not as capable of multitasking (i.e., progressively downloading while playing the media) as modern media devices are; thus, having a completely downloaded file in the player's memory before playing the media was the preferable method. The newer streaming media services commonly enable short previews of the content to assist the selection, and after content selection, the media begins to play even before the entire media file is downloaded to the user's device. In addition, streaming media companies have application stores that support software installations and upgrades when needed for the user's device. This is a necessity because smart devices have different hardware and software as well as frequent OS upgrades, and correspondingly the installed media streaming app will need to be upgraded and adjusted.

Brief History of Internet-Based Streaming Media

Internet-based streaming media has an interesting history that is closely tied with the evolution of video technology and the Internet. Some of the essential events are listed in the following in chronological order (https://en.wikipedia.org/wiki/Over-the-top_media_service).

- In May of 1993, the first video was streamed over the Internet at a one-twelfth lower frame rate (i.e., two frames per second) due to the Internet's small transmission bandwidth. The transmitted video was titled "Wax or the Discovery of Television Among the Bees" which had been originally released in 1991.

- In September of 1995, Real Networks enabled the first live streaming event over the Internet which was an ESPN SportsZone live radio broadcast of a Seattle Mariners and New York Yankees baseball game.

- In 1995, the Shockwave Player was released by
  Macromedia to provide media streaming functionality
  for the Netscape Navigator.

- In 1997, ShareYourWorld.com opened its video uploads
  and streaming services (closed in 2001).

- In 1999, the Microsoft Windows Media Player 6.4
  was released including the video streaming feature,
  Windows Media streaming protocols, and the ASF file
  format so multiple video and audio tracks could be
  stored in a single file.

- In January of 2005, Google Video was launched.

- In February of 2005, the Stickam website was launched
  to provide live video chatting.

- In March of 2005, the Dailymotion website was
  founded (in French) to provide Internet video-sharing.

- In April of 2005, YouTube opened its video uploads and
  streaming services.

- In May of 2006, Crunchyroll was founded to provide
  online East Asian media video streaming. Its
  streaming content included drama, music, electronic
  entertainment, auto racing, anime, manga, etc.

- In October of 2006, Justin.tv was founded to provide
  live video streaming services.

- In September of 2006, Amazon Unbox was launched in
  the United States.

- In October of 2006, YouTube merged with Google.

- In October of 2006, LiveLeak website was founded in the United Kingdom to provide Internet-based video-sharing.

- In December of 2006, Youku was founded in China to provide video streaming services.

- In January of 2007, Netflix started video streaming services.

- In September of 2007, Vevo was founded to provide music video streaming for the Universal Music Group and Sony Music Entertainment.

- In September of 2007, the Microsoft Silverlight application was introduced to support rich Internet applications.

- In March of 2008, Hulu was launched for public access in the United States providing online TV and movie streaming services. Its current owners are The Walt Disney Company (67%) and Comcast (33%) which is through NBC Universal.

- In September of 2008, Amazon Unbox was renamed to Amazon Video on Demand.

- In January of 2009, Google Video services were discontinued.

- In November of 2009, HTTP Live Streaming (HLS) adaptive bitrate streaming technology was introduced by Apple.

- In April of 2010, iQiyi was launched in China as a new online video platform.

- In December of 2010, Viki was founded, which is an international video website. Viki provides TV shows, movies, and premium videos.

- In April of 2011, Vudu launched online streaming services.

- In June of 2012, Vine was founded, which supports short-form (up to 6 seconds) video-sharing services.

- In December of 2012, Snapchat added on video send functionality in addition to photos.

- In June of 2013, Instagram added its video-sharing function.

- In 2014, Prime Video was added to Amazon's Prime subscription in the United Kingdom, Germany, and Austria.

- In March of 2015, the Periscope app was launched for live video streaming on iOS and Android smart devices.

- In May of 2015, the Meerkat app was released for live video streaming on iOS and Android smart devices.

- In 2015, Amazon Channels was launched which was Amazon's Streaming Partners Program.

- In January of 2016, Facebook Live was launched by Facebook.

- In April of 2016, Amazon Prime and Prime Video were separated (for services in the United States).

- In November of 2019, Disney+ was launched.

More details on the major OTT streaming services like Netflix, Hulu, Peacock, Disney+, Amazon Prime Video, and YouTube are provided in the following section.

Video Streaming Services and Business

Based on the "Video Streaming Market Share, 2022-2029" report from Fortune Business Insights, in 2021, the global video streaming market size was estimated to be worth $372.07 billion. The global video streaming market size in 2029 is projected to reach $1,690.35 billion based on a 19.9% compound annual growth rate (CAGR) for this forecast period. Alternatively, a report from Grand View Research estimates that the video streaming market size in 2022 has a value of $70.59 billion and the revenue forecast for 2030 reaches $330.51 billion based on a CAGR of 21.3% for the 2022 to 2030 period. CAGR represents the exponential growth rate over a multiple year period.

Forbes' "The World's Largest Media Companies 2022" ranking is based on company market value, where the top five on this list are (1) Comcast Corporation Class A, (2) Walt Disney Company, (3) Charter Communications, Inc. Class A, (4) Netflix, Inc., and (5) Paramount. There are additional factors that need to be considered beyond revenue and market share, which will be described in the following (`www.forbes.com/sites/abigailfreeman/2022/05/12/the-worlds-largest-media-companies-2022-netflix-falls-in-the-ranks-after-subscriber-loss-disney-climbs-to-no-2/`).

The United States has the largest video streaming companies that have the highest revenue per user. Figure 1-7 presents an overview of the video streaming revenue and projections for the United States, which shows a consistent growth and strong potential in the future (`www.businessofapps.com/data/video-streaming-app-market/`).

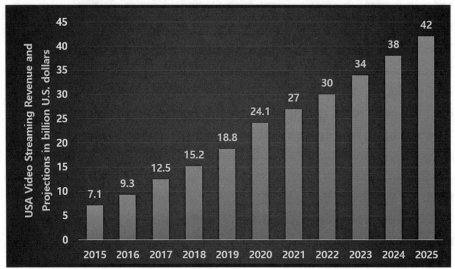

Figure 1-7. *US Video Streaming App Revenue and Projections*

In the graphs presented, the data related to Amazon Prime Video and Apple TV+ may be different compared to the number of subscribers because the data of Apple+ is influenced by free trial users and some Amazon Prime users are not Amazon Prime Video subscribers; therefore, parts of estimated data had to be used (based on Business of Apps report).

The profile of video streaming subscribers in the United States is presented in Figure 1-8 (based on the same report as Figure 1-7), where estimated values were used in the Amazon Prime Video and Apple TV+ subscription numbers.

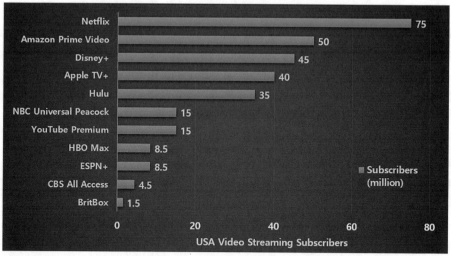

Figure 1-8. *US Video Streaming Subscribers*

Among Internet video streaming companies, the evolution of Netflix is of importance as several factors of its business model have highly influenced many other OTT video streaming companies. Therefore, more details on Netflix are provided in the following.

Netflix

In August of 1997, Netflix was founded in Scotts Valley, California, USA, with the business model of postal mail-based DVD renting services and selling DVDs. However, DVD sales were stopped the following year. The motive to create Netflix is related to Blockbuster. In 1997, Reed Hastings was charged a Blockbuster video late return fee of $40 which influenced him to create a new type of subscription-based rental company called Netflix later that year (on August 29) that enabled video rentals via mail orders which were delivered on DVDs and had no late fees. Because DVDs were easy to send and receive via postal mail, Netflix's service model became very popular. For a $20 monthly fee, Netflix users could make a list of DVD rentals using the netflix.com website, where up to four DVDs at a time could be subscribed, and when a DVD was returned, the next video in queue would be sent to the subscriber. The business model of Netflix was challenging as a significant amount of labor was involved. Production of DVDs took time which resulted in delays, especially for new video releases. The growing popularity of Netflix did influence the video rental business significantly. However, in 2000, when Netflix was having a challenging time in revenue, its cofounders Reed Hastings and Marc Randolph made an offer to sell Netflix at $50 million to Blockbuster. Although the Netflix business model had an influence on Blockbuster, Blockbuster's revenue was still significant, and especially the company was making a significant revenue (approximately $800 million) from late video returns, which was approximately 16% of Blockbuster's total revenue. Eventually Blockbuster's CEO John Antioco turned this offer down.

In 2007, Netflix began to provide streaming media and VoD services in the United States. Starting from 2010, Netflix expanded into Canada, Latin America, and the Caribbean. In February of 2013, Netflix debuted the company's first original series "House of Cards," which was followed by the original series "Orange Is the New Black" in the same year, which were great successes. Starting from 2016, Netflix expanded its services internationally. As of March 31, 2022, Netflix has 74.6 million subscribers in the United States and Canada and over 221.6 million subscribers worldwide.

Netflix's contributions to the OTT streaming media platform were significant in terms of technology and content creation. In recognition of this, in 2012, Netflix received its first Emmy Award, which was the "Emmy Engineering Award" for Netflix's profound influence on how the company changed the way television is watched. Additionally, Netflix original programs were receiving high accolades. In 2018, the number of Emmy nominations surpassed HBO. In 2019, Netflix received 14 Oscar nominations, which was the third most, following 20 total nominations for Fox (i.e., 15 for Fox Searchlight and 5 for 20th Century Fox) and 17 nominations for Walt Disney. In 2020, remarkably Netflix received 24 Oscar nominations, which was the most nominations among all film studios that year. This marked an evident point that the domain of high-quality original content creation had shifted, and platform exclusive content was equally acknowledged by the Academy of Motion Picture Arts and Sciences and the public.

Figure 1-9 shows the annual trend in Netflix's annual revenue. Figure 1-10 shows the annual profit (based on operating income) and content expenditure. Figure 1-11 shows Netflix's content expenditure (based on the same report as Figure 1-9).

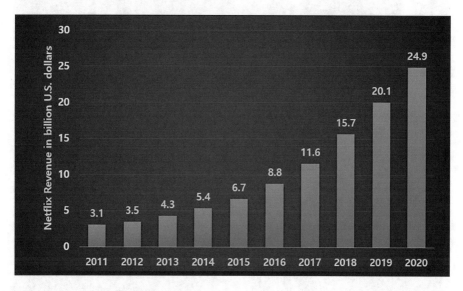

Figure 1-9. *Netflix Revenue*

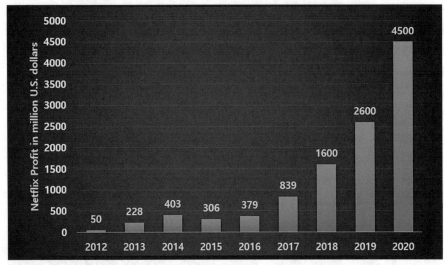

Figure 1-10. *Netflix Profit*

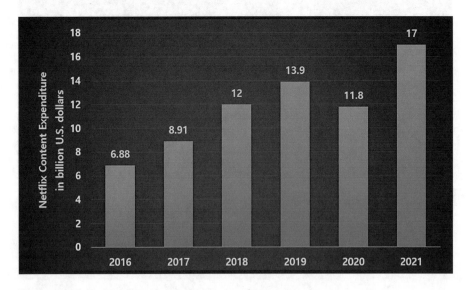

Figure 1-11. *Netflix Content Expenditure*

Netflix has a true global platform, as it is available and popular worldwide. As shown in Figure 1-9, in 2020, Netflix's revenue was $24.9

billion with an operating profit of $4.5 billion. Among this massive
revenue, the largest portion of $11.45 billion came from North America.
Netflix's profit was influenced by a $11.8 billion content expenditure
in 2020. In 2021, Netflix content expenditure reached $17 billion, which
was well enjoyed by its 209 million worldwide subscribers
(www.businessofapps.com/data/netflix-statistics/).

Disney+

Disney+ was launched in November of 2019, and within the first 24 hours,
it accumulated 10 million subscribers, which includes the users that
signed up during prerelease. Disney's media streaming business includes
ESPN+, Hulu, and India's most popular streaming service Hotstar. The
Disney library of content includes originals from Pixar, Lucasfilm, Marvel,
and the full catalog of The Simpsons. Before Disney+ opening, some of
these contents were available on other platforms but are now available
only on Disney+. In 2020, the most popular Disney+ show in the United
States was the Star Wars "The Mandalorian" (which also featured Baby
Yoda). In addition, programs like Marvel's WandaVision were extremely
popular. Figure 1-12 shows the revenue of Disney+ (based on the Business
of Apps report). Because Disney+ was launched in November of 2019, the
company's quarterly revenue is presented (www.businessofapps.com/
data/disney-plus-statistics/).

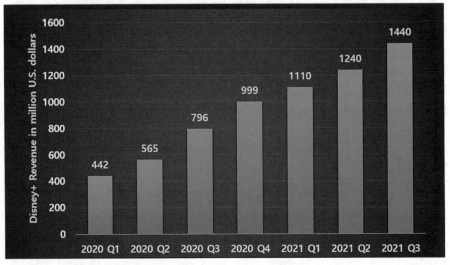

Figure 1-12. *Disney+ Revenue*

Amazon Prime Video

A strong competitor with Netflix and Disney+ is Amazon Prime Video. In the case of Amazon, the company wisely used its online sales platform to expand its OTT streaming services, including its subscribers. In 2011, Amazon Video on Demand was changed into Amazon Instant Videos, and its services were provided to all Amazon Prime subscribers. Amazon Instant Videos expanded its content range through a collaboration deal with Epix. A special feature of Amazon Instant Videos was that it allowed subscribers to purchase the rights to place the content in one's personal streaming library. In April of 2013, Amazon Prime Instant Video exclusively released its original programming comedy series "Betas," "Alpha House," and "Annedroids" which were very popular. Amazon Prime Video was launched worldwide in December of 2016, and as of April of 2021, the company had approximately 175 million users (https://en.wikipedia. org/wiki/Amazon_Prime_Video).

Hulu

In October of 2007, Hulu was co-launched by the News Corporation, NBC Universal, and Providence Equity Partners. In 2010, Hulu rebranded its company name to "Hulu Plus" and became the first media streaming company to use "Plus" in its name. Hulu's content library contains Hulu original programming as well as a diverse program list of content from ABC, Freeform, FX Networks, etc. Hulu began investing into original content creation, where in January of 2011, Hulu's first web series "The Morning After" was streamed. In February of 2012, Hulu premiered its first original scripted program "Battleground" which was a political documentary-style drama. In March of 2019, Disney obtained a 60% ownership of Hulu as 21st Century Fox was acquired by Disney. Currently, Hulu is owned 67% by The Walt Disney Company and 33% by Comcast through NBC Universal. As a result, Disney's media streaming services include Hulu, ESPN+, and Hotstar. As of April 2, 2022, Hulu has 45.6 million subscribers (based on Wikipedia) and ranks fifth among the US video streaming subscribers company rankings presented in Figure 1-8 (https://en.wikipedia.org/wiki/Hulu).

Peacock

In July of 2020, Peacock was launched by NBC Universal which is owned by Comcast. The name "Peacock" came from the NBC logo. Considering that Peacock is owned by NBC and Universal, evidently Peacock has an extensive library of movies and TV programs. In May of 2020, Peacock became available for the Apple TV on-launch and iOS devices. In July of 2020, Peacock became accessible through app access on the PlayStation 4. In September of 2020, Peacock became accessible on Roku digital media players. In June of 2021, Peacock became accessible through app access on Samsung smartTVs, Amazon Fire TV, and Amazon Fire tablets (e.g., Fire HD). As of 2021 late July, Peacock had accumulated more than 54 million signups, and by April of 2022, Peacock had 13 million paid subscribers and a total of 28 million monthly active accounts. Among the US video streaming subscribers company rankings in Figure 1-8, NBC Universal Peacock ranks sixth (`https://en.wikipedia.org/wiki/Peacock_ (streaming_service)`).

YouTube and YouTube Premium

Another very important measurement of platform influence is video streaming usage, in which YouTube dominates. Figure 1-13 presents the video streaming usage profile of the United States. Platform influence is related to household penetration rate and watch time, which are very important metrics used to describe the influence of streaming companies (based on Business of Apps report).

Household penetration rate is a common metric used to describe the market share of the streaming companies like Netflix, Prime Video, Disney+, etc. Comparing the recent US household penetration rates, Netflix is at 87%, Prime Video is at 53%, and Hulu is at 41.5%. Future projections of 2024 streaming subscribers show future expectations of Netflix at 235.6 million, Prime Video at 135 million, and Disney+ at 101.2 million. Household penetration rates are highly influenced by the quality and quantity of existing media content as well as expectations of future new content. This is why media streaming companies are investing into new exclusive content creation. In 2019 large investments into original program creation were made, where Netflix invested $15 billion, Prime Video invested $6 billion, Hulu invested $2.5 billion, and Disney+ invested $1 billion. Due to Netflix's massive investment, the company was able to provide more than one new show on average for every day in 2019. Based on the acquisition of ESPN+, Fox (which operates Hulu), and India's Hotstar, the streaming media content library of Disney+ has grown extensively.

In terms of watch time, YouTube dominates the competition. YouTube has 2 billion monthly users and has 250 million watch hours daily, which resulted in a $15 billion in advertisement revenue in 2019. YouTube TV had 2 million paying subscribers in 2020 (based on the Business of Apps report).

YouTube launched in April 2005 and was soon acquired by Google. In 2020, the revenue of YouTube reached $19.7 billion and YouTube Premium reached 30 million subscribers, which was accomplished in a short period since its launching in 2018. The power of YouTube is based on over 2.3 billion people accessing YouTube every month. In Figure 1-13, YouTube's annual revenue, number of users, and Premium subscribers are presented (based on the same report as Figure 1-7). Figure 1-14 shows the annual revenue of YouTube (`www.businessofapps.com/data/youtube-statistics/`). The trend of increase between 2010 and 2020 is significant and exponentially curved upward, which shows the effectiveness in the company's business and marketing strategy (`https://en.wikipedia.org/wiki/YouTube`).

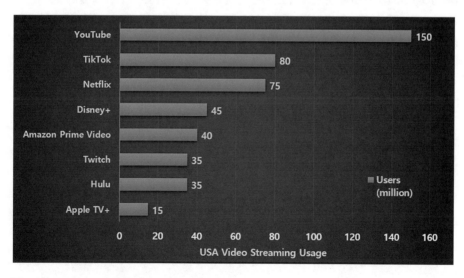

Figure 1-13. *US Video Streaming Usage*

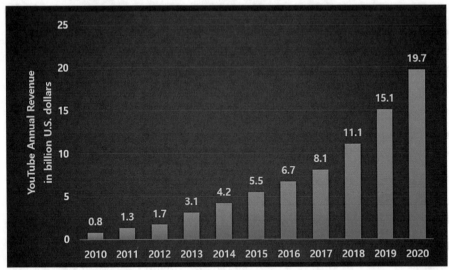

Figure 1-14. *YouTube Annual Revenue*

Figure 1-15 shows the number of YouTube users, which covers monthly active users (based on the same report as Figure 1-14). The number of YouTube users doubled in a 6-year period, as the number of users was 1 billion in 2013 which becomes 2 billion by 2019, which is an amazing accomplishment.

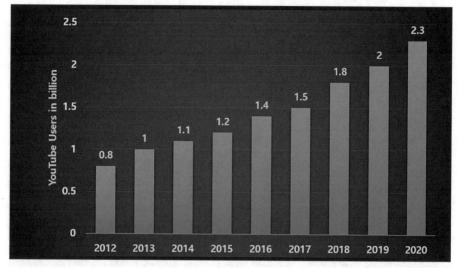

Figure 1-15. *YouTube Users (Covers Monthly Active Users)*

Figure 1-16 presents the changes in YouTube Premium subscribers (based on the same report as Figure 1-14). The number of YouTube Premium subscribers shows a significant increase as it increases 6.67 times in a 3-year period from 2015 to 2018 and triples from 10 million to 30 million in just 2 years from 2018 to 2020. YouTube Premium started as an advertisement-free music video streaming service under the name "Music Key" which was launched in November of 2014. In October of 2015, Music Key was changed to YouTube Red which provided advertisement-free access of all YouTube videos to its subscribers. In May of 2018, YouTube Red was rebranded into YouTube Premium, and YouTube Music was also launched as a separate subscription service.

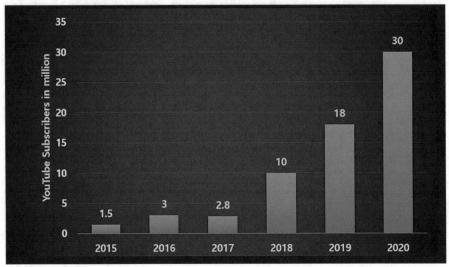

Figure 1-16. *YouTube Premium Subscribers*

Summary

This chapter provided an overview of the characteristics of metaverse, XR, and video streaming services. Details of the core technologies as well as business aspects were covered, and selected parts of history were included focusing on companies, products, and services that made a significant influence. In addition, the market's potential and future expectations were also introduced. In the following Chapter 2, details of metaverse XR technologies, which include metaverse platforms, XR devices, system components, workflow, hardware modules, software engines, as well as haptic devices, are introduced.

CHAPTER 2

Metaverse XR Components

The future market of XR devices is expected to grow significantly as technology evolves. These advancements in XR technology will drive metaverse services in new directions to become much more creative in designs and services. In addition, edge computing and mobile wireless technologies will significantly help the implementation of highly computational XR based metaverse and multimedia services in the future. More details on the current state-of-the-art in XR technology and future evolution directions will be introduced in this chapter as well as in Chapters 3 and 4 (`www.coursera.org/learn/ar-technologies-video-streaming`). Chapter 2 focuses on the core XR components, which include the following list of technologies:

- XR, MR, AR, and VR

- XR System Components and Workflow

- XR CPU and GPU Engines

- XR Software Engines and Platforms

- XR Lab Setup and Haptic Devices

- 3D Motion Treadmills

© Jong-Moon Chung 2023
J.-M. Chung, *Emerging Metaverse XR and Video Multimedia Technologies*,
https://doi.org/10.1007/978-1-4842-8928-0_2

XR, MR, AR, and VR

Virtual reality (VR) enables its user to immerse into an artificial virtual environment where the user will commonly use an avatar to exist and interact inside the VR space. The user's view in VR is different from the real environment, and therefore, fantasies and illusions are easy to create in the VR virtual environment. This unlimited design freedom is why VR is the most common platform for massively multiplayer online games (MMOGs) and metaverses.

Augmented reality (AR) is a mixture of real-life and VR parts, where users can obtain useful information about a location or objects and can interact with virtual contents in the real world. Commonly, an AR user can distinguish the superimposed virtual objects, augmented sounds, or haptic actions. AR users may be able to turn on or turn off selected AR functions (which may be related to certain objects, sounds, or haptics). In comparison with VR, AR users commonly feel less separated from the real world as they can see their actual environment in the background view. Virtual fantasies and illusions can be created and superimposed on a real-world view using AR.

Figure 2-1 presents the relation of AR, VR, and MR (`www. researchgate.net/publication/235093883_Some_Human_Factors_ Considerations_for_Designing_Mixed_Reality_Interfaces`). MR enables its user to cross over from the VR domain into the augmented realistic AR domain and vice versa. In order to create MR, both AR and VR domains have to be matched to become interconnectable. For this, AR and the augmented virtual domains have to be connected. AR is based on the real world with elements that are composed virtually based on reality. Augmented virtuality is created from the VR virtual environment which composes reality based on virtual components.

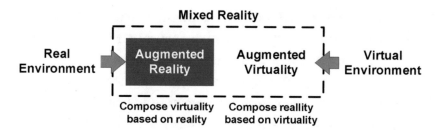

Figure 2-1. *A Definition of AR, VR, and MR (by Paul Milgram)*

Figure 2-2 shows the Venn diagram domain of AR technology, in which AR is the cross-domain of 3D technology, real-time interaction, and a combination of the real world and VR (`www.cs.unc.edu/~azuma/ARpresence.pdf`).

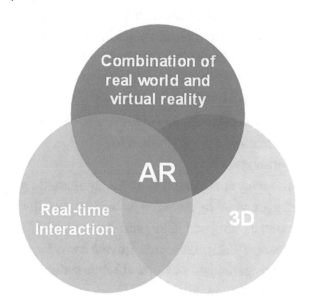

Figure 2-2. *A Definition of AR (by Ronald Azuma)*

Currently, most metaverse services are based on VR user environments. This is mainly because many types of video games and MMOGs have been using VR technology to enable player avatars to compete in virtual game environments, which may include multiple domains and universes. MMOGs are Internet connected online video games that enable many players to simultaneously participate, collaborate in teams, and compete in the same game environment.

MMOGs require high-quality networks, game servers, high-performance player computer terminals, as well as virtually created multiple game domains, dimensions, and/or universes. Thus, such MMOGs can be considered as the one of the original purposes to create and use a metaverse.

However, it is predicted that soon XR will be massively used in creating metaverse services. XR technology can enable users to experience both real and virtual environments by interpolating mixed reality (MR), AR, and VR with various haptic user interfaces to make the user's environment more interactive, realistic, broader, diverse, and immersive. New XR application programming interfaces (APIs) can enable various types of human-human, human-machine, and machine-machine interaction.

Future metaverse services will need advanced XR equipment as well as high-performance wired and wireless networks to support the required data rate, time delay, and reliability requirements. Advanced metaverse services require high levels of Quality of Service (QoS) and Quality of Experience (QoE) to enable the XR system to provide a satisfying level of immersive and virtual presence.

Based on this focus, new standards on XR equipment and networking services are being prepared by global organizations, like the 3rd Generation Partnership Project (3GPP) and the Institute of Electrical and Electronics Engineers (IEEE). Standards provide a way for new products and services to interoperate, safely be used, while satisfying the basic commonly required functionalities.

Just like MMOGs, metaverse systems can be supported by many types of networking platforms and be played using a personal computer (PC), video game console, smartphone, head mounted display (HMD), as well as various Internet of Things (IoT) devices. Therefore, metaverse applications have to be designed considering users in diverse environments using various interactive XR interfaces.

A full XR process is complex and hard to implement because XR requires accurate coordination of multiple cameras and sensors for acoustics, motion, and haptics to fit the user's senses such that the experience is immersive and comfortable. A full XR system will implement MR which will interconnect the real surroundings of the user through AR and access virtual domains using VR seamlessly. Evidently AR is more difficult to implement than VR, and MR technology is more difficult to implement than AR. Considering that XR is a combination of component technologies that include MR, speech-to-text (STT), voice recognition systems, special sound effects, as well as haptic and 3D motion user interfaces (UIs), XR technology is even more difficult to implement than MR technology. As a result, evolution toward XR metaverses will take several years in which significant technological breakthroughs are needed, which is why large research and development investments are needed.

XR System Components and Workflow

In order to express 3D visual effects on a XR system, various visual sensing and expression techniques have to be implemented, which are described in the following. XR systems are best when providing an "immersive presence." The term "immersion" refers to the feeling of being surrounded by an environment, which may be real, all virtual (in VR), or a combination of real and virtual (in AR and MR). When a XR user is immersed into a domain, then the user can feel one's physical and spatial existence and can act, react, and interact with surrounding beings, objects, and environment. This feeling is called "presence" which has different representations based on being in a real, all virtual (in VR), or a combination of real and virtual (in AR and MR) domain.

In order to explain the technical details, parts of the 3rd Generation Partnership Project (3GPP) standardization document "Technical Specification Group Services and System Aspects: Extended Reality

(XR) in 5G" (3GPP TR 26.928 V16.1.0) will be used in the following (https://portal.3gpp.org/desktopmodules/Specifications/ SpecificationDetails.aspx?specificationId=3534).

Right-Handed Coordinate

In Figure 2-3, the right-handed coordinate system is presented. The right-handed coordinate system is commonly used in 3D and graphics standards, specifications, designs, and systems, which include OpenXR, WebXR, 3GPP, IEEE, etc. Using one's right hand, by spreading the thumb, index finger, and middle finger out in a perpendicular form (which is uncomfortable), the right-hand thumb can represent the X axis, index finger represents the Y axis, and the middle finger can represent the Z axis, which is why this is called the "right-handed coordinate" or the "Cartesian right-handed coordinate." A location or position in the right-handed coordinate can be expressed using a point (x, y, z) where the reference center is the origin located at (0, 0, 0) in which x=0, y=0, and z=0. Directional movement in the right-handed coordinate is expressed using a vector which is based on a combination of 3D movement in the positive or negative X, Y, and Z axis directions. In reference to the origin of the right-handed coordinate, "right" is in the +X direction, "up" is in the +Y direction, and "forward" is in the -Z direction for direction changes and motion control. In addition, unless specified, all units are in meters.

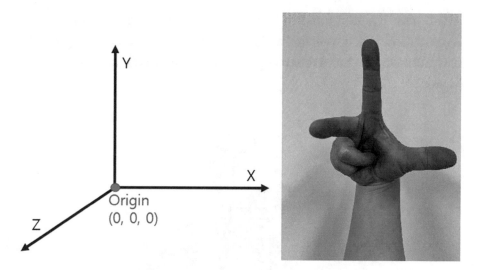

Figure 2-3. *Right-Handed Coordinate and My Right Hand*

3D Rotational Movement

Rotational movement of an object in a 3D domain is commonly expressed using roll, pitch, and yaw. These movements are commonly used in expressing motion of a flying object, like an airplane. For example, considering that the nose of an airplane is the front, changes in flight direction roll, pitch, and yaw can be defined as shown in Figure 2-4. Roll expresses clockwise or counterclockwise circular rotational movement of the airplane. Pitch expresses upward or downward rotational movement of the airplane. Yaw expresses the right or left rotational movement of the airplane.

Positions are represented using (x, y, z) coordinates (in 3D vector form) in reference to the origin (0, 0, 0) of the 3D space. In order to represent the orientation due to spatial rotational movement (i.e., roll, pitch, and yaw), an additional dimension has to be added, which makes the coordinates four dimensional (4D) resulting in a (x, y, z, w) vector coordinate called a "quaternion." Quaternions have been used in many 3D graphic platforms in the past, in which some limitations have been discovered (e.g., gimbal lock problems), so more reliable quaternion coordinates have been created.

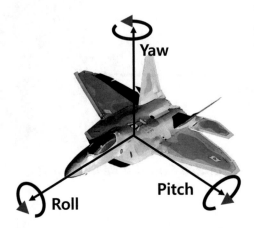

Figure 2-4. *3D Rotational Movement*

Degrees of Freedom (DoF)

DoF represents the amount and types of movement a XR user or avatar can conduct in a 3D space. DoF is expressed using multiple independent parameters that change based on the user's movement and changes in viewport within the 3D AR or VR space. A XR user will take actions and will interact with objects and the real/virtual environment, resulting in various movements, gestures, body reactions, expressions, and feelings (i.e., emotional and haptics).

In Figure 2-5, my avatar JM demonstrates the four types of XR based 3D DoF, which include 3DoF, 3DoF+, 6DoF, and constrained 6DoF movement that are described in the following (3GPP TR 26.928 V16.1.0).

3DoF movement commonly occurs when the XR user is sitting in a chair and can perform 3D movement around the X, Y, and Z axes as well as roll, pitch, yaw based rotational movement.

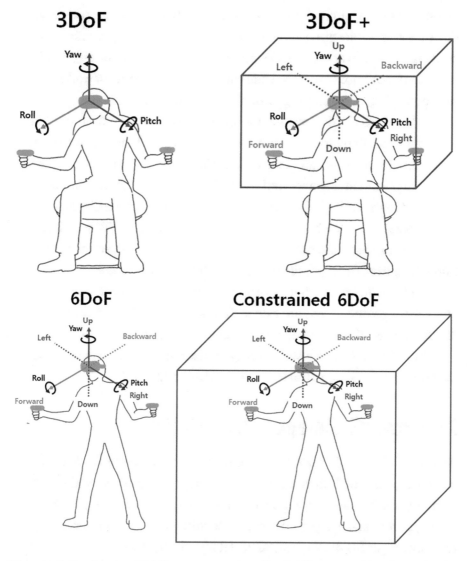

Figure 2-5. *Avatar JM Demonstrating the Difference of XR based 3D DoF Types*

3DoF+ movement enhances 3DoF by allowing additional translational movement along the X, Y, and Z axes for a limited range, which results from the XR HMD user's head movement while the user is sitting in a chair.

6DoF movement enhances 3DoF by allowing full translational movements along the X, Y, and Z axes to include movement upward and downward (e.g., elevating and heaving), left and right (e.g., strafing and swaying), and forward and backward (e.g., walking and surging). 6DoF movement commonly occurs when the XR user is capable of walking, running, flying, or swimming through the 3D XR environment.

Constrained 6DoF movement is 6DoF but with 3D constraints added to movements along the X, Y, and Z axes and may include roll, pitch, yaw based rotational movement constraints. Constrained 6DoF movement is very common in metaverses and MMOGs because avatar movement is restricted to the walls, buildings, environment, and various obstacles.

Constrained 6DoF has also been called "Room Scale VR" which defines the room or area where the XR user can work, play, or experience around mimicking the user's real-life motion in a limited virtual space.

3D environments with multi-rooms, spaces with uneven floor levels, and very large open areas are categorized as 6DoF or "unconstrained 6DoF," because these are beyond the scope of constrained 6DoF.

These DoF types are used to program user or avatar movement and describe the XR device's tracking sensors capabilities.

XR View, XR Viewport, and XR Pose

An XR view is a single 3D view of a scene or part of a scene. So, the XR view will change as the XR device's view direction changes, which will result from the user's head or eye movement. For 3D representation, the XR view displayed for each eye of the user may be different based on stereoscopic or monoscopic 3D displaying (3GPP TR 26.928 V16.1.0).

3D image rendering of the XR view needs to be accurately aligned with the user's viewing properties, which include the field-of-view (FoV), eye offset, etc. to create effects like occlusion and parallax. When a XR user moves in the 3D domain, the user's point of view will change, and objects and the environment will look different. In 3D visual domains, "occlusion" occurs when an object blocks the view of another object. In a 3D visual domain, the XR user will estimate the distance and size of objects when objects move relative to each other. This is based on "parallax" which is a phenomenon of relative movement of objects when the XR user's point of view changes. These aspects are critical in providing 3D immersive presence through the XR HMD system. In the 3D reference space, the position and orientation of the XR user's view defines the "view offset" amount, which will increase as the movement is larger and faster.

As presented in Figure 2-6, the XR Viewport (or viewport) is a flat rectangular 2D surface region (perpendicular to the viewing direction) of the XR view in which the target objects in the 3D space are displayed on the 2D surface of the XR device. Figure 2-6 is an example of a Microsoft HoloLens 2 user's inside view (viewport diagram). The XR Viewport is characterized by a rectangular dimension in terms of width and height. The view frustum is the region of 3D space that is displayed on the XR HMD's 2D screen. The view frustum is the region of space that starts at the near plane and extends to the far plane, which are both perpendicular to the viewing direction of the XR view. The view frustum is the region that defines the FoV of the XR HMD. The XR Viewport and the view frustum near plane are the same in many cases. In 6DoF cases with extensive environments (i.e., unconstrained 6DoF), the view frustum far plane may be set infinitely far away.

The XR Pose of the XR HMD user is called the "XR Viewer Pose." For proper XR Viewer Pose representation, the HMD has to accurately track the user's view and XR scene based on the XR Reference Space. A sequence of XR views can be used to form a views array, which can be used to describe a XR scene based on multiple viewpoints. A views array is constructed based on a XR Viewer Pose query to characterize the XR Reference Space.

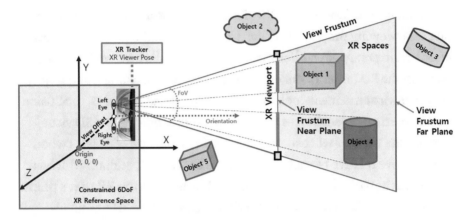

Figure 2-6. *XR Viewport, Field-of-View (FoV), and View Frustum. Only Object 1 and Object 4 Are in the View Frustum of the XR Device (Microsoft HoloLens 2)*

XR 3D Tracking Techniques

XR applications require fast and accurate 3D spatial tracking, which are enabled by the following techniques (3GPP TR 26.928 V16.1.0). The XR Viewer Pose is generated from continuous tracking of the user's movement in the XR Reference Space. The XR Viewer Pose is determined by the viewer's position and orientation. Very accurate positional tracking is needed for the XR application to work properly. 3D positional tracking methods include outside-in tracking, inside-out tracking, world tracking, and simultaneous localization and mapping (SLAM). These technologies are possible using the XR feature extraction and tracking technologies described in Chapter 3 and the artificial intelligence (AI) based deep learning technologies explained in Chapter 4.

Outside-in tracking is conducted by (multiple coordinated) tracking sensors (e.g., cameras) located at fixed locations in the XR facility (e.g., having motion detection sensors installed at all corners of the XR simulation room). Later shown in Figure 2-8, a Hikvision DS-2TD4166T-25 electro-optic (EO) and infrared (IR) dual camera is used to assist outside-in tracking as well as AR and VR automatic switching for continuous MR applications.

Outside-in tracking is possible only for a region that has preinstalled tracking sensors supporting it. Outside the preset tracking region, outside-in tracking cannot provide any information, and therefore, one (or multiple) of the following tracking methods needs to be used.

Inside-out tracking is conducted by multiple coordinated tracking sensors located on the XR HMD device. These sensors track the surroundings and identify the HMD's location and position based on internal processing of the sensed information. This is the most common tracking method applied on almost all XR HMDs, glasses, and headsets.

World tracking is conducted by one (or multiple coordinated) camera(s). The camera(s) determines the XR device's location and position as well as surrounding objects and the environment. World tracking is commonly used in AR devices and can be used in VR devices.

SLAM is used to create a map (or a territory picture) by combining multiple world tracking images from a XR HMD. SLAM connects multiple images and sensor data to create a map (or a territory picture) of a much wider region. SLAM could construct a more accurate and wider map (or territory picture) if images from multiple HMDs (and/or stationary cameras and sensors) can be used.

Localization Techniques

Localization is a technique to determine the location and position of users and objects in a 3D domain. Localization is used to create spatial maps for XR applications. Localization can be conducted using multiple sensors, cameras (e.g., monocular, stereo, and depth cameras), radio beacon signals, global positioning system (GPS), assisted-GPS (A-GPS), ultra-wideband (UWB), ultrasonic sensors, radio detection and ranging (RADAR), light detection and ranging (LIDAR), millimeter waves (mmWaves), gyroscope sensors, inertial sensors, etc. Signal analysis will be used on reference signal received power (RSRP), received signal strength indicator (RSSI), time of arrival (ToA), estimated ToA (ETA), variations in wavelength or phase, distortion of spectrum, etc.

More information used in the localization computations can help to increase the accuracy but will require more processing and memory. Some of the localization techniques are described in the following, which include spatial anchors and visual localization techniques (3GPP TR 26.928 V16.1.0).

Spatial anchors are reference points in the 3D domain that have known locations and can be used as references in calculating the position of other objects and users. Spatial anchors are known to provide accurate localization within a limited range. For example, in the Microsoft Mixed Reality Toolkit, the spatial anchoring has a 3 m radius. To increase the accuracy and range, coordination of multiple spatial anchors can be used. SLAM can also be used in the localization and tracking process. Visual localization uses visual SLAM (vSLAM), visual positioning system (VPS), and other visual imaging processing techniques as well as sensor data to conduct localization. More technical details are described in Chapter 3 in XR based detection technologies and Chapter 4 in deep learning technologies.

XR Experience

Immersive presence is a combination of two feelings: The feeling that you are surrounded by the metaverse/game environment (immersion) and the feeling that you are physically and spatially located in that environment (presence). There are two types of presence that the XR system needs to provide, which are "cognitive presence" and "perceptive presence."

Cognitive presence is the presence that is felt in the user's mind and is more content based (e.g., a good storyline) as it is triggered by imagination. Even without any XR device, cognitive presence can be felt by reading a good book or watching a good movie.

Perceptive presence is the presence that is felt through the user's five senses (i.e., eyesight, hearing, touch, taste, and smell) or a few of them. At the current technical level, perceptive presence based on eyesight and hearing is common in AR, VR, and MR devices. XR systems that can provide a perceptive presence based on three senses (i.e., eyesight, hearing, and touch) are possible using haptic devices (more details are in Chapter 3). However, the level of XR performance needs much more improvement, in which hopefully this book will help accomplish in the near future. Perceptive presence is a highly technical feature of XR systems as all of the introduced XR technologies (i.e., 3D coordinates, rotational movement, DoF, FoV, XR view, XR Viewport, XR Pose, tracking, localization, etc.) need to be used to create a high-quality XR perceptive presence (3GPP TR 26.928 V16.1.0).

XR Device and Network Performance Requirements

To create a high-level XR based immersive presence, a very low time delay and a very high-quality image and display performance are required. The time delay performance bound can be derived from the delay tolerance level, which is influenced by the round trip interaction delay. The image and display performance factors include the required image resolution, frame rate, and FoV. More details are described in the following (3GPP TR 26.928 V16.1.0).

Delay Tolerance

The round trip interaction delay is obtained by adding the User Interaction Delay to the Age of Content, which is described in the following.

User interaction delay is the length of time from the moment the user initiates an action until the time the content creation engine of the XR system has taken the action into account. User interaction delay is influenced by the sensor delay/cycle time, data processing time, communication/networking time, and queueing (memory) delay.

Age of content is the length of time from the moment the content is created until the time the content is presented to the XR user. Age of content is influenced by the content processing time, communication/networking time, queueing (memory) delay, and display time.

For XR systems, a total latency less than 20 ms is recommended. The total latency covers the time from the moment the XR user's head moves up to the time that changes on the XR device's display are complete. This is a very short time delay compared to MMOGs, which are also very high-speed systems.

Among various MMOGs, the first-person shooter (FPS), role playing game (RPG), and real-time strategy (RTS) types are most relevant to XR systems and metaverses. Shortened name-wise, an FPS-type MMOG is commonly called a "massively multiplayer online first-person shooter" (MMOFPS) game. Likewise, an RPG based MMOG is commonly called a MMORPG game, and an RTS based MMOG is commonly called a MMORTS game. MMOFPS games have a delay tolerance of 100 ms (i.e., 0.1 seconds), MMORPG games have a delay tolerance of 500 ms (i.e., 0.5 seconds), and MMORTS games have a delay tolerance of 1,000 ms (i.e., 1 second). However, to achieve a higher MMOG performance, a delay time much shorter than the delay tolerance level is recommended (3GPP TR 26.928 V16.1.0).

Image and Display Requirements

Image resolution is an important factor in deciding the quality of the immersive presence.

The FoV, frame rate, and image resolution are all important factors. Considering that the Meta Quest 2 is the leading XR HMD by a far margin, references to the Oculus specifications will be considered as a guideline.

The founder of Oculus Rift Palmer Luckey mentioned that at least an 8K resolution (i.e., 8196 × 4096 pixel image frame) per eye is needed to eliminate the pixelation effect. Pixelation occurs when the resolution is low such that the pixels forming the image are noticeable by the viewer. When pixelation occurs, it is hard for the XR user to feel an immersive presence, and the aspects of the animation and augmentation are noticeable. An image frame rate higher than 90 Hz (i.e., 90 frames/s) is recommended to create a comfortable and compelling virtual presence feel for the user (`https://developer.oculus.com/blog/asynchronous-timewarp-examined/`). Considering that most of the TV programs we watch have a fame rate in the range of 24 to 60 frames/s, the recommended 90 frames/s is a very high frame rate. In addition, a wide field-of-view (FOV) in the range of (at least) 100 to 110 degrees is recommended.

XR CPU and GPU Engines

The XR device's engine and software platform and operation relation between the central processing unit (CPU) and graphics processing unit (GPU) is illustrated in Figure 2-7 (3GPP TR 26.928 V16.1.0). The XR engine is in charge of the image rendering engine, audio engine, physics engine, and the artificial intelligence (AI) engine (`www.nrexplained.com/tr/26928/xreng`).

The rendering engine is in charge of all image and video rendering processes. Rendering is a computer process of creating an image from 2D or 3D models. The final image is called the "render" which may be photorealistic or non-photorealistic. Rendering requires computer graphic editing of the scene, object description, geometry, viewpoint, texture, lighting, transparentness, reflection, shading, information description, as well as augmented and virtual objects and domains. Rendering is the major final step in 2D and 3D computer graphics generation and is used in every image creation operation including XR, MR, AR, VR, video games, simulators, movies, TV, visual effects, animation, architecture, and design visualization (`https://en.wikipedia.org/wiki/Rendering_(computer_graphics)`).

The audio engine oversees the microphones and speakers and needs to assist the AI engine for voice control and speech-to-text (STT) processing. The audio engine processes the loading, modification, and balancing of speaker sound effects. Special acoustic effects using echoes, pitch and amplitude balancing, oscillation, and Doppler effects are essential in creating an immersive presence experience.

The physics engine reads and processes all sensor information and emulates realistic physical law based immersive presence effects. Accurate simulation of physical forces like collision, pressure, vibration, texture, heat, and chill are needed to enable the XR user to feel the air, wind, water, fluids, as well as solid objects. In the future, smell and taste physical effects could be added. By then the five basic human senses can all be influenced by the XR system, creating a full dimensional immersive presence experience.

The AI engine is used in everything and everywhere, including all XR devices, metaverses, MMOGs, and multimedia services. This is why Chapter 4 is separately dedicated to deep learning-based systems and their relations to processing audio, video, and sensor data as well as making optimized estimations and accurate predictions. So please refer to Chapter 4 for more details on the AI engine for XR devices, metaverses, MMOGs, and multimedia services.

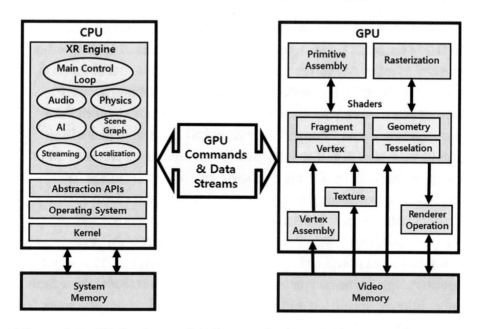

Figure 2-7. *XR Engine and Software Platform for CPU and GPU Operations*

The CPU is in charge of executing the XR engine, which includes accessing the system memory as well as controlling the application and management, scene graph, AI, audio, streaming, physics, and localization. The abstraction APIs like Vulkan, OpenGL, etc. are also processed by the CPU. XR devices use multicore CPUs in which the operating system (OS) and kernel will use to form directed acyclic graph (DAG) based processing sequences, in which multiple processing threads are executed over. The AI system of the CPU will process the deep learning algorithms that support the sensors, sound, and images of the XR system. The deep learning recurrent neural network (RNN) used for the sensors, physics, audio, and localization processing is an infinite impulse response process that has a DAG that cannot be unrolled. The deep learning convolutional neural network (CNN) used for video, image, scene graph, localization, feature detection, and feature tracking is a finite impulse response process that has a DAG that can be unrolled (https://en.wikipedia.org/wiki/Recurrent_neural_network).

The GPU will receive commands and data streams from the CPU. The GPU is in charge of video memory access as well as the image rendering pipeline process. The vertex shader is a programmable shader that is in charge of processing the vertices. Shaders are user-defined programs that are executed on selected stages of the GPU process. The primitive assembly function will convert a vertex stream into a sequence of base primitives. A base primitive is the processed result of the vertex stream's interpretation. The rasterization process will convert the image data and signals into projected images for video and graphics formation. Shader functions include fragmentation, vertex processing, geometry computations, and tessellation. The tessellation process assists arrangements of polygon shapes considering gapless close fittings and nonoverlapping repeated patterns. The shaders also consider the texture information of the objects and environment. (`www.khronos.org/opengl/wiki/Rendering_Pipeline_Overview`).

XR Software Engines and Platforms

The major XR software engines and platforms are introduced in chronological order of initial release, which include Lua (1993), Unreal (1998), Unity (2005), WebGL (2011), SteamVR (2014), WebVR (2016)/WebXR (2018), and OpenXR (2017).

Lua

Lua is a popular cross-platform OS programmed in ANSI C that was first released in 1993. Lua uses the filename extension ".lua" (`www.lua.org/`). Up to version 5.0, Lua was released under a license that is similar to the BSD license, but from version 5.0 it has been released under the MIT License. Lua means "moon" in Portuguese, which was named considering the programming platform SOL which means "sun" in Portuguese.

Lua uses parts of the SOL data-description syntax, parts of the control structures of Modula, parts of the multiple assignments and returns structure of CLU, as well as parts of C++, SNOBOL, and AWK. Lua was originally designed to be a general embeddable extension language that is easy to use and could enable software applications to be customized quicker by enhancing the speed, portability, and extensibility. Lua is a popular programming language for video games and applications because it is easy to learn and embed and enables fast execution. The representative games developed using Lua include Roblox, Garry's Mod, Payday 2, Phantasy Star Online 2, Dota 2, Angry Birds Space, Crysis, etc. In addition, Lua has been used by many applications such as Adobe Lightroom, Moho, iClone, Aerospike, etc. A poll conducted by GameDev. net revealed that Lua was the most popular scripting language for game programming in 2003 (`https://en.wikipedia.org/wiki/Lua_ (programming_language)`).

Unreal

The Unreal Engine (UE) was developed by Epic Games and was first released in the first-person shooter (FPS) game Unreal in 1998 (`www. unrealengine.com`). UE is a 3D computer graphics game engine that is programmed in C++ which has superior portability as it can be used on various computer OSs, smart device OSs, game consoles, and XR platforms. This is why UE has been used in development of films, television programs, and metaverses, in addition to video games. Unreal was also listed in the Guinness World Record as the "most successful video game engine" in 2014. A list of games made with UE can be found in Wikipedia (`https://en.wikipedia.org/wiki/List_of_Unreal_Engine_ games`). The source code of the Unreal Engine 5 is available on GitHub since April of 2022 (`https://github.com/EpicGames`) and can be used through a registered account. Commercial product use of UE with royalty is possible. Epic has waived the company's royalty margin until the game developers have accumulated a revenue of $1 million, and if the game is published on the Epic Games Store, the developer's fee is waived (but policies may change).

Unity

Unity was developed by Unity Technologies as a cross-platform game engine (https://unity.com). Unity was released in June of 2005 as a macOS X game engine at the Apple Worldwide Developers Conference. Although initially Unity was released for macOS X, its goal was set to democratize game development by providing an easy to learn and use game engine that works on many platforms (https://en.wikipedia. org/wiki/Unity_(game_engine)). Unity has been used in various computer and smartphone games and applications as it enables game engine development on over 19 platforms, where a list is provided in the following.

- Mobile platforms: iOS, Android (Android TV), tvOS

- Desktop platforms: Windows (Universal Windows Platform), macOS, Linux

- Web platforms: WebGL

- Console platforms: PlayStation (PS4, PS5), Xbox (Xbox One, Xbox Series X/S), Nintendo Switch, Stadia

- XR platforms: Oculus, PlayStation VR, Google's ARCore, Apple's ARKit, Windows Mixed Reality (HoloLens), Magic Leap, Unity XR SDK SteamVR, Google Cardboard

- Other platforms: Film, automotive, architecture, engineering, construction, and the US Armed Forces

Unity is written in C++ (runtime) and C# (Unity Scripting API) based on a proprietary license.

The Unity game engine can be used to develop 2D and 3D games as well as mobile apps, metaverses, interactive simulations, and XR applications. The Unity game engine is easy to learn and use because it provides a primary scripting API in C# using Mono that supports the Unity editor, which provides various plug-in options as well as drag and drop functionality. Unity provides the High-Definition Render Pipeline (HDRP), Universal Render Pipeline (URP), and the legacy built-in pipeline, which are incompatible with each other. Because Unity is easy to learn and use, many indie game developers have used it.

Indie games are video games made by an individual programmer or a team of programmers that do not belong to a game publisher. Indie games also include games that the programmer/designer has creative freedom in the game's development even though a game publisher is funding and distributing the game. Games developed and released by major game publishers are typically called triple A (i.e., AAA) games, which are different to indie games. The name "indie game" is an abbreviated term for "independent video game" (https://en.wikipedia.org/wiki/Indie_game).

WebGL

WebGL was initially released in March of 2011 by the Mozilla Foundation and was developed by the Khronos WebGL Working Group (https://get.webgl.org). WebGL supports highly accelerated GPU processing by supporting physics and image processing. The Khronos Group announced in February of 2022 that WebGL 2.0 is supported for all major browsers. WebGL is short for "Web Graphics Library" which is a library of JavaScript APIs for web browsers that can be used to render interactive 2D and 3D graphics. WebGL enables accelerated GPU processing of web browsers when it is fully integrated with other web applications (www.khronos.org/webgl/wiki/Main_Page).

SteamVR

SteamVR is a hardware and software platform for VR devices that was developed by the Valve Corporation (`www.steamvr.com/en/`). SteamVR was first applied on the Oculus Rift HMD in 2014 and since has been widely used to support many HMDs, which include the HTC Vive and Valve Index. SteamVR technology supports accurate positional tracking to enhance room-scale immersive presence experiences, which has significantly contributed to (constrained) 6DoF application development. SteamVR originates from the popular Steam video game technologies, digital distribution services, and storefront developed by the Valve Corporation which launched in September of 2003. Originally, SteamVR provided support for Windows, macOS, and Linux platforms, but in May of 2020, the support for macOS ended (`https://en.wikipedia.org/wiki/Steam_(service)#SteamVR`).

WebXR

The WebVR API was initiated in 2014, and in March of 2016 the WebVR API proposal version 1.0 was released by the Mozilla VR team and the Google Chrome team. In 2018, the WebXR Device API was released to supersede WebVR by extending the API to support XR applications which includes MR, AR, and VR. WebXR enables website access to the immersive content provided on XR devices (including MR, AR, and VR) which include HMDs, headsets, sensor information, tracking, and sound effects (`https://immersiveweb.dev/`). WebXR was designed to be easily integrable with various web browser tools and is commonly used with WebGL. WebXR provides a very versatile interface which enables various XR devices to access the WebXR content with very little modifications. The web browser access of XR applications significantly reduces development time and performance testing. However, there are many web browser types which can create interoperability issues, and web browsers have limitations in immersive expressions and user interaction compared to HMDs, so not every XR aspects can be developed in WebXR (`https://en.wikipedia.org/wiki/WebXR`). The technical details of WebXR are defined by the Immersive Web Group of the World Wide Web Consortium (W3C), where the specifications are made public on GitHub (`https://github.com/immersive-web/webxr`).

OpenXR

OpenXR is an open standard that supports XR platforms and device development that was developed and released by the Khronos Group in February of 2017 (`www.khronos.org/openxr/`). It is a cross-platform OS based royalty-free standard that is accessible in GitHub (`https://github.com/KhronosGroup/OpenXR-SDK-Source`). OpenXR's API has the following fundamental elements. "XrSpace" represents the 3D space, "XrInstance" represents the OpenXR runtime, "System" represents the XR devices, "XrSystemId" represents the XR controllers, "XrActions" helps to control user inputs, and "XrSession" assists the interaction session between the application and the user/runtime. OpenXR has been used for game and rendering engine support for the Unreal Engine (since September of 2019), Blender (since June of 2020), Unity (since December of 2020), Godot (since July of 2021), etc. OpenXR has been used to enable WebXR browser support on Google Chrome and Microsoft Edge. Some of the representative OpenXR conformant platforms include the Microsoft HoloLens 2, Windows Mixed Reality headsets, Oculus PC platform, Facebook Quest, Meta Quest 2, Valve SteamVR, VIVE Cosmos, and VIVE Focus 3 (`https://en.wikipedia.org/wiki/OpenXR`).

XR Lab Setup and Haptic Devices

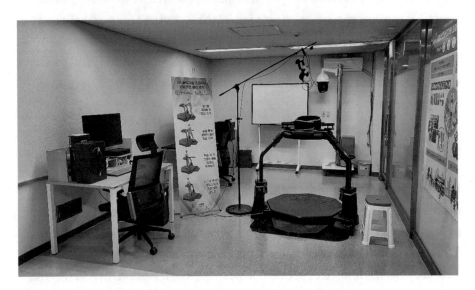

Figure 2-8. *A Part of My Metaverse XR System Research and Development Lab Which Includes a Virtuix Omni VR 3D Treadmill with a Meta Quest 2 HMD and a Hikvision DS-2TD4166T-25 Camera (in the Far Back on the Right Side of the Whiteboard)*

Figure 2-8 shows a part of my Metaverse XR system research and development lab (at Yonsei University, Seoul, South Korea) which shows a Virtuix Omni VR 3D treadmill with a Meta Quest 2 HMD and a Hikvision DS-2TD4166T-25 camera.

The Hikvision DS-2TD4166T-25 electro-optic (EO) and infrared (IR) dual camera is shown in the far back of the room. This camera can be used to control the AR and VR domain switching for MR applications, as the HoloLens 2 AR device can provide a constrained 6DoF (limited to the room size) where VR is needed to extend the limited room with doors that open up to different VR multiverses and metaverses. The IR camera helps the automated precision control especially when it is dark indoors or for outdoor XR experiments at night.

The Hikvision DS-2TD4166T-25 EO camera resolution is 1920×1080 (i.e., 2 MP level), and the IR camera resolution is 640 × 512 in support of a temperature range of -20 °C to 550 °C with a ±0.5°C error margin and a distance range of 200 m.

Figure 2-9 shows the Microsoft HoloLens 2, Manus Prime X Haptic VR gloves, and Meta Quest 2 in my Metaverse XR system research and development lab. More details on these systems are presented in the following.

Figure 2-9. *Microsoft HoloLens 2 (left), Manus Prime X Haptic VR Gloves (middle), and Meta Quest 2 (right) Systems in My Metaverse XR System Research and Development Lab*

The five basic human senses are sight, smell, touch, taste, and hearing, in which current MR, AR, or VR systems can commonly express sight and hearing effects, and a few XR systems can provide vibration-based touch effects in addition to the sight and hearing effects. Therefore, research and development of new XR technologies to express smell, touch, and taste effects need to be added. Some example haptic systems are described in the following.

Manus Prime X Haptic VR

Manus Prime X Haptic VR gloves are made of polyester (77%) and spandex (23%), and each glove has five flexible sensors and six inertial measurement units (IMUs) for movement sensing and includes programmable vibration motors inside the casings for haptic feedback and weighs 60 g. The IMU uses three types of sensors, which are the accelerometer, gyroscope, and magnetometer (`www.manus-meta.com/products/prime-x`). The gloves' accelerometers measure linear motion direction (i.e., X, Y, Z direction) acceleration. The gyroscopes detect roll, pitch, and yaw based rotational motion with a +/- 2.5 degrees orientation accuracy. The magnetometer finds the direction of the strongest magnetic force. The signal latency is less than 5 ms with a maximal range of 30 m. Prime X Haptic VR can be used for application development with Unity, SteamVR, Oculus, Vive, and other XR software platforms. Figure 2-10 shows the Manus Prime X Haptic VR gloves. The detection management user interface (with enhancements by Wonsik Yang) that includes an avatar robotic hand with sensor and IMU data displays is presented in Figure 2-11.

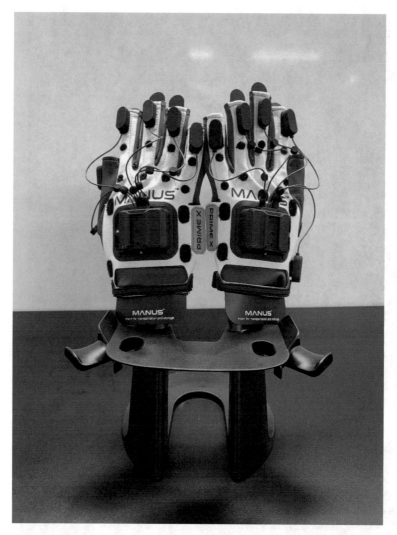

Figure 2-10. *Manus Prime X Haptic VR Gloves*

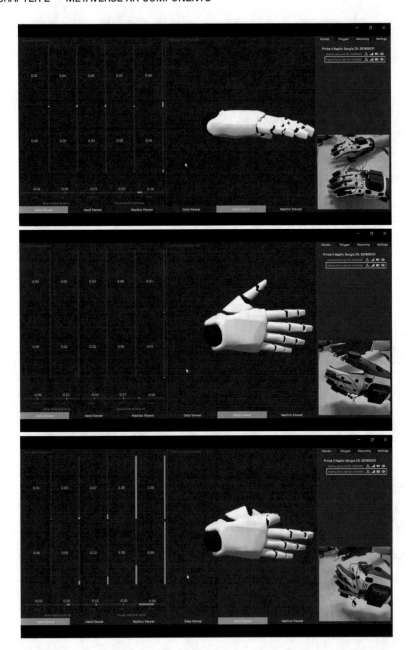

Figure 2-11. *Manus Prime X Haptic VR Gloves Detection Management Interface with Avatar Robotic Hand and Sensor and IMU Data Display*

Ultraleap Mid-Air Haptics

The STRATOS Inspire ultrasound speaker and STRATOS Explore from Ultraleap use programmable 3D sound sensor arrays, which can generate ultrasound waves that coincide to create mid-air haptic effects. These systems can generate a virtual touch feeling as well as a slight vibration feeling on the user's hand (`www.ultraleap.com/haptics/`).

HaptX Gloves DK2

HaptX DK2 are haptic gloves from HaptX that can provide force feedback to the user's hands. The feedback can be up to 40 pounds in the form of resistive force, so the user can feel and work with heavy objects in XR applications. The magnetic motion capture sensors conduct very accurate motion detection and enable the HaptX DK2 haptic gloves to have submillimeter precision sensing capability (`https://haptx.com/`).

Teslasuit

The haptic gloves and full body haptic suit from Teslasuit have some unique features that can enhance XR user experiences (`https://teslasuit.io/`). Teslasuit's haptic glove and suit can be used to monitor the heart rate, oxygen saturation, or other biometric information of the user, which can be used to analyze the mental state and stress level of the user in training or playing games. The haptic gloves can generate a feel of solid object texture using electric sensors with 45 channels and can generate a feel of virtual object resistance force. Using these gloves, the user can feel up to 9 N of feedback resistance force. For reference, the "N" stands for "Newton" which is the unit of force. To provide you with a feel of force, 1 N of force can accelerate an object with a mass of 1 kg to 1 m/s^2 (`www.britannica.com/science/newton-unit-of-measurement`). The haptic suit covers the user's full body, so full body sensing and feedback is possible. The haptic suit can provide near real-life sensations and feelings through electro muscle stimulations and transcutaneous electrical nerve stimulation.

3D Motion Treadmills

When using a XR HMD, glasses, or headset, the user is focused on the environment, objects, and events happening in the XR domain. Therefore, the user can easily lose balance, fall down, fall off, or bump into other people or various objects including walls, fences, doors, etc. All of these accidents can result in a physical injury (and in some cases death) as well as property damage.

In the preceding DoF description presented, the 3DoF and 3DoF+ are based on the user sitting in a chair while using the XR device. Even in these cases, many accidents have happened to XR users, but these accidents may not be as serious as the accidents that can occur to XR users of 6DoF and constrained 6DoF cases. This is because XR users of 6DoF and constrained 6DoF cases are standing up and moving around in the XR domain, where the actual room or location will have a different physical structure to the metaverse or MMOG environment viewed in the XR HMD, glasses, or headset. Especially, a higher level of immersive presence will result in a higher risk of an accident because the XR user will have a lesser amount of awareness of one's actual environment. This is why XR users of 6DoF and constrained 6DoF systems need a 3D motion treadmill. Selected 3D motion treadmills for XR applications are presented in the following.

Virtuix Omni Treadmill

Virtuix Omni is a VR treadmill device developed by Virtuix to assist 6DoF and constrained 6DoF VR gaming by enabling full body movement in VR environments (www.virtuix.com/). The Virtuix Omni was initially presented at the 2015 Consumer Electronics Show (CES) in Las Vegas. This 3D motion treadmill has a belt system that supports the user from falling while always keeping the user safely in the center of the treadmill. This 3D motion treadmill allows 360 degrees moving and running. The user's foot movement is tracked using the inertial measurement unit (IMU) tracking sensors attached to the custom shoes. The motion sensors on the custom shoes communicate wirelessly with an external computer providing movement information. The surface of the 3D motion treadmill has low friction coating applied, which makes it very slippery to minimize friction such that less resistance is felt during movement. The current price of a Virtuix Omni treadmill ranges from $1,995 to $2,295 (`https://en.wikipedia.org/wiki/Virtuix_Omni`).

Figure 2-12 shows the Virtuix Omni VR Treadmill in my Metaverse XR system research and development lab (at Yonsei University, Seoul, South Korea). Figure 2-13 shows the motion sensors (i.e., Pod 1 and Pod 2) used on the shoes of the Virtuix Omni VR Treadmill. These motion sensors need to be charged in advance and are installed on top of the special shoes as shown in Figure 2-14. The detected motion and status of the devices are transferred to the Virtuix Omni VR Treadmill control and management interface through the wireless sensors as shown in Figure 2-15.

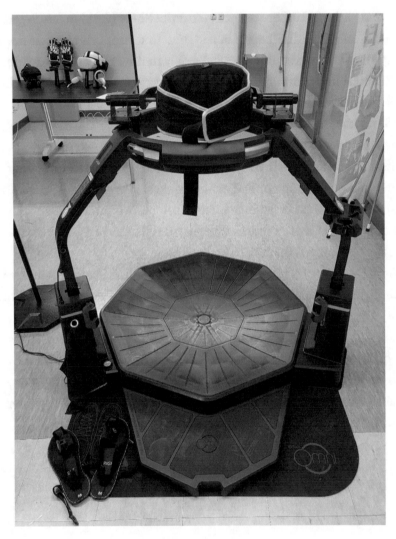

Figure 2-12. *Virtuix Omni VR Treadmill*

Figure 2-13. *Motion Sensors (Pod 1 and Pod 2) Used on the Shoes of the Virtuix Omni VR Treadmill*

Figure 2-14. *Shoes Used on the Virtuix Omni VR Treadmill with the Wireless Sensors (Pod 1 and Pod 2) Installed*

Figure 2-15. *Virtuix Omni VR Treadmill Control and Management Interface*

Cyberith Virtualizer

Cyberith Virtualizer is an omnidirectional treadmill developed by Cyberith that supports 360 degrees of walking and running in VR applications. The VR walking platform supports full movement by using six optical motion sensors as well as an optical rotation sensor and optical height sensor. The Cyberith Virtualizer has two versions, the Virtualizer ELITE 2 and the Virtualizer R&D Kit. The Virtualizer ELITE 2 is a powered walking platform. The Virtualizer R&D Kit supports higher precision and lower latency optical motion tracking (www.cyberith.com/?gclid=CjwKCAjwq5-WBhB7EiwAl-HEkj5rqxgnDK-uZx5AlhWBSL5QIzvJEcSuuEH1EH2qVIhyB2qwkF bE3BoCuAwQAvD_BwE).

KAT Walk C

KAT Walk C is an omnidirectional treadmill developed by KATVR that supports 360 degrees of walking, running, crouching, and jumping motion detection to support VR gaming. The system also provides real-time haptic response through vibration to the user. KAT Walk C was designed to be cost-effective while occupying a small space for comfortable use in private homes and small rooms. KAT Walk C provides diverse scenario support which includes sit-down interaction for vehicle control gaming (www.kat-vr.com/products/kat-walk-c2).

Spacewalker VR

Spacewalker VR treadmill is a VR treadmill in prototyping phase by SpaceWalkerVR that supports forward and backward (mono-directional) movement only. The system is equipped with a gyroscope that detects user movement such as walking, running, shooting, and picking up objects. The safety system uses integrated pressure sensors to automatically regulate speed such that it can prevent the user from falling (https://spacewalkervr.com/).

Infinadeck

Infinadeck is a VR application supportive 3D motion treadmill developed by Infinadeck. Infinadeck includes an active wireless control system and enables 360 degrees of movement through an omnidirectional moving floor (www.infinadeck.com/).

Summary

This chapter provided details on metaverse and XR systems, where the characteristics of XR, MR, AR, and VR were first described, followed by XR system components and the processing workflow. Then details on the hardware engines, software platforms, haptic devices, and 3D motion treadmills were provided. These advanced XR technologies will continue to evolve and drive metaverse XR services to improve significantly. In the following Chapter 3, XR head mounted display (HMD) technologies are introduced, which include XR device types, XR operation processes, as well as XR feature extraction and description algorithms.

CHAPTER 3

XR HMDs and Detection Technology

This chapter focuses on XR head mounted displays (HMDs), the XR operation process, and XR feature extraction and detection technologies. Details of the XR technologies applied in state-of-the-art devices (including HMDs) are introduced in this chapter. Among XR operations, the XR feature extraction and detection process is the most computation burdening as well as energy- and time-consuming procedure of the XR process. The most important XR feature extraction and detection schemes are introduced in this book, which include scale-invariant feature transform (SIFT), speeded-up robust feature (SURF), features from accelerated segment test (FAST), binary robust independent elementary features (BRIEF), oriented FAST and rotated BRIEF (ORB), and binary robust invariant scalable keypoints (BRISK) (www.coursera.org/learn/ar-technologies-video-streaming). This chapter consists of the following sections:

- XR HMDs

- XR Operation Process

- XR Feature Extraction and Description

© Jong-Moon Chung 2023
J.-M. Chung, *Emerging Metaverse XR and Video Multimedia Technologies*,
https://doi.org/10.1007/978-1-4842-8928-0_3

XR HMDs

For an XR experience, the HMDs can provide the best immersive presence effects. Thus, XR HMDs play a significant role in metaverse and game services. Therefore, in this section, some of the representative XR HMDs are presented, which include the Meta Quest 2, Microsoft HoloLens 2, HTC VIVE Pro 2, HTC VIVE Focus 3, Valve Index, Pimax Vision 8K X, and the PlayStation VR 2.

Meta Quest 2

The Facebook Oculus Quest is the preceding version of the Meta Quest 2. In May of 2019, the Oculus Quest VR HMD was released by Facebook. The Quest HMD had 4 GB of random-access memory (RAM) and was equipped with a Qualcomm Snapdragon 835 system on chip (SoC) with a 4 Kryo 280 Gold central processing unit (CPU) and an Adreno 540 graphics processing unit (GPU). The Quest's introductory price was $399 for the 64 GB storage memory device and $499 for the 128 GB storage memory device (`www.oculus.com/experiences/quest/`).

In October of 2020, Oculus Quest 2 was released, and due to Facebook's parent company name change to Meta, the device was rebranded as Meta Quest 2 in November of 2021. Quest 2 is a VR HMD equipped with a Qualcomm Snapdragon XR2 SoC with 6 GB RAM and an Adreno 650 GPU. Quest 2's initial price was $299 for the 64 GB storage memory model, which was changed to 128 GB later, and $399 for the 256 GB storage memory model.

The Meta Quest 2 software platform uses an Android operating system (OS). For first-time Quest 2 device setups, a smartphone running the Oculus app is needed. The Quest 2 software engine is Android 10 based which is processed with the help of the device's SoC, which is a Qualcomm Snapdragon XR2 and the Adreno 650 GPU which has an approximate speed of 1.2 TFLOPS. The platform allows up to three additional accounts to log onto a single Quest 2 headset, while sharing purchased software from the online Oculus Store is permitted. The platform supports the Oculus Touch controllers and recently included experimental Air Link wireless streaming as well as experimental Passthrough APIs for AR applications (`https://en.wikipedia.org/wiki/Oculus_Quest_2`).

Compared to the Facebook Oculus Quest, the Meta Quest 2 is about 10% lighter and has a more ergonomic controller. The device's power supply is based on a 3,640 mAh battery that supports approximately 2 hours for games and 3 hours for video watching. The full battery charging time through a USB-C power adapter takes about 2.5 hours. The display has a 1832×1920 pixel resolution per eye. The device supports 6DoF inside-out tracking using four infrared cameras along with an accelerometer and gyroscope inertial measurement units (IMUs). Metaverse, games, and multimedia applications need to run on the Quest OS which is based on an Android 10 source code. Hand tracking is conducted by a deep learning system based on four cameras for hand recognition and gesture recognition. More details on deep learning hand recognition and gesture recognition are provided in Chapter 4.

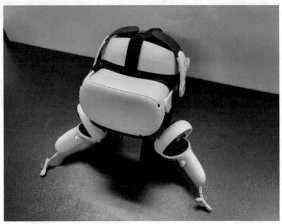

Figure 3-1. *Meta Quest 2*

Figure 3-1 presents the Meta Quest 2 headset (HMD) and controllers, where on the HMD, the motion (hand) sensors near the bottom of the device (which look like two black dots) can be seen. In Figure 3-2, the Meta Quest 2 inside view is presented (based on SIMNET graphics), where the views of the two eyes are presented in the top picture and the two eyes' combined view is presented in the bottom picture.

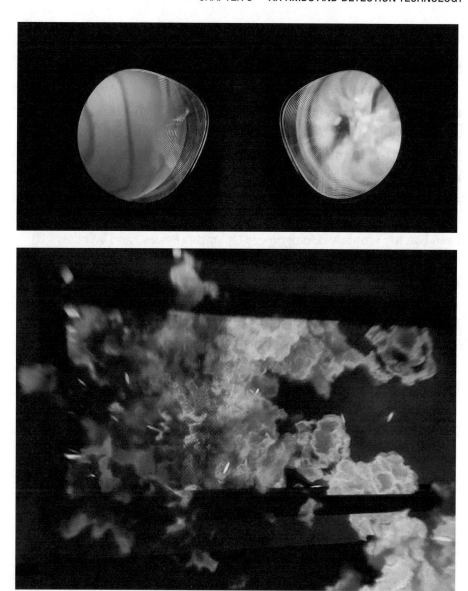

Figure 3-2. *Meta Quest 2 Inside View. Eyes Separate (Top) and Together (Bottom)*

Microsoft HoloLens 2

Microsoft HoloLens 2 was released in 2019. It is equipped with a Qualcomm Snapdragon 850 SoC with 4 GB DRAM memory with 64 GB storage. The device is equipped with IEEE 802.11ac Wi-Fi and Bluetooth 5.0 and USB Type-C. Microsoft HoloLens 2 uses a holographic processing unit that has a holographic resolution of 2K (1440×936) with a 3:2 display ratio that supports a holographic density above 2.5 k radiants (light points per radian). Head tracking is conducted through four visible light cameras, and two infrared (IR) cameras are used for eye tracking. The system is based on the Windows Holographic Operating System and Windows 10 with Microsoft Azure cloud computing support when needed. The two front mounted cameras are used to scan the surrounding area which are supported by the accelerometer, gyroscope, and magnetometer based IMUs to provide accurate 6DoF World-scale positional tracking. The onboard camera can provide 8 MP still pictures or video with 1080p (1980×1080) at a frame rate of 30 frames/s. The battery enables 2 to 3 hours of active use with up to 2 weeks of standby time. The power supply is an 18 W (i.e., 9 V at 2 A) charger but can charge with at least a 15 W charger. Microsoft HoloLens 2 includes a two-handed fully articulated hand tracking system and supports real-time eye tracking. The voice command and control on-device system is based on Cortana natural language.

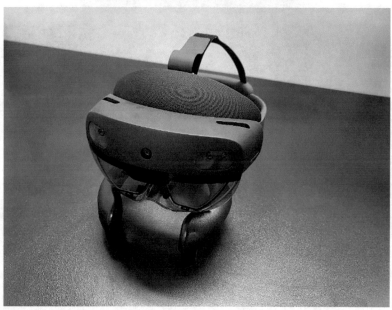

Figure 3-3. *Microsoft HoloLens 2*

Figure 3-4. Microsoft HoloLens 2 Inside View

Figure 3-5. *Microsoft HoloLens 2 Selection Menu Using AR*

Figure 3-3 shows the Microsoft HoloLens 2 device's front view (left picture) and the top view (right picture), Figure 3-4 shows the Microsoft HoloLens 2 inside view that has augmented objects imposed on the background view, and Figure 3-5 shows a Microsoft HoloLens 2 inside view selection menu using AR (based on HanbitSoft graphics).

The Microsoft Windows MR platform is a part of the Windows 10 OS which provides MR and AR services for compatible HMDs which include the HoloLens, HoloLens2, Lenovo Explorer, Acer AH101, Dell Visor, HP WMR headset, Samsung Odyssey, Asus HC102, Samsung Odyssey+, HP Reverb, Acer OJO, and the HP Reverb G2 (https://docs.microsoft. com/en-us/windows/mixed-reality/mrtk-unity/architecture/overvie w?view=mrtkunity-2021-05).

HTC VIVE Pro 2

HTC VIVE Pro 2 is a tethered (non-standalone) MR HMD developed by HTC VIVE that was released in June of 2021. HTC VIVE Pro 2 is a MR device; thus, it is equipped with AR and VR technologies. The VIVE PRO 2 costs $799 for the headset only and $1,399 for the full kit, which includes the Base Station 2.0 and controller (`www.vive.com/kr/product/vive-pro2-full-kit/overview/`). The HMD display has a 2448×2448 per eye resolution that supports a FoV up to 120 degrees and weighs 855 g. Tracking is conducted with SteamVR 2.0 based on its G-sensors, gyroscope, proximity, and interpupillary distance (IPD) sensors. IPD sensors are used to detect the distance between the center of the pupils. The device uses a proprietary cable, Link Xox cable, and USB 3.0 cable and enables connectivity through USB Type-C interfaces and Bluetooth wireless networking. The HTC VIVE Pro 2 5K resolution MR HMD is based on a Windows 10 OS supported by an Intel Core i5-4590 or AMD Ryzen 1500 CPU with a NVIDIA GeForce RTX 2060 or AMD Radeon RX 5700 GPU with 8 GB RAM or higher (`www.tomshardware.com/reviews/htc-vive-pro-2-review`). The Base Station 2.0 system in the VIVE PRO 2 Full Kit supports room-scale immersive presence VR applications. The system is supported by the VIVE Pro series or Cosmos Elite headsets, and the controllers assist exact location tracking. The non-standalone needs to be tethered to a high-performance Windows OS computer. The tethered computer's minimum requirements include a Windows 10 OS supported by an Intel Core i5-4590 or AMD Ryzen 1500 CPU with a NVIDIA GeForce GTX 1060 or AMD Radeon RX 480 GPU with 8 GB RAM.

HTC VIVE Focus 3

HTC VIVE Focus 3 is a standalone VR HMD developed by HTC VIVE that was released in August of 2021. The HMD is equipped with a Qualcomm Snapdragon XR2 (Snapdragon 865) SoC and runs on an Android OS (www.vive.com/kr/product/vive-focus3/overview/). The HMD display has a 2448×2448 per eye resolution that supports a 120 degree FoV and is equipped with 8 GB RAM and 128 GB storage memory. Tracking is conducted with the HTC VIVE inside-out tracking system based on its Hall sensors, capacitive sensors, G-sensors, and gyroscope sensors (www.tomshardware.com/reviews/vive-focus-3-vr-headset).

Valve Index

Valve Index is a VR HMD developed by Valve that was first introduced in 2019 (www.valvesoftware.com/en/index). The HMD requires a high-performance computer equipped with Windows OS or Linux OS that supports SteamVR to be tethered to the device (tethered cable with DisplayPort 1.2 and USB 3.0). The device conducts motion tracking with SteamVR 2.0 sensors. The HMD weighs 809 g and costs $499 for the headset only and $999 for the full kit, which includes the headset, controller, and Base Station 2.0 (www.valvesoftware.com/ko/index). The HMD display has a 1440×1600 per eye resolution that supports an adjustable FoV up to 130 degrees and is equipped with a 960×960 pixel camera (www.tomshardware.com/reviews/valve-index-vr-headset-controllers,6205.html).

Pimax Vision 8K X

The Pimax Vision 8K X is a high-resolution HMD developed by Pimax. The HMD was first introduced at CES 2020 and weighs 997.9 g and costs $1,387 (https://pimax.com/ko/product/vision-8k-x/). The HMD display has a 3840×2160 per eye resolution for the native display and a 2560×1440 per eye resolution for the upscaled display that supports a FoV up to 170 degrees. The device uses SteamVR tracking technology with a nine-axis accelerometer sensor (www.tomshardware.com/reviews/pimax-vision-8k-x-review-ultrawide-gaming-with-incredible-clarity). The Pimax Vision 8K X HMD needs to be tethered to a high-performance Windows OS computer in which the USB 3.0 connection will be used for data communication and the USB 2.0 connection can be used for power supply. The tethered computer needs to be equipped with Windows 10 Pro/Enterprise 64 bits (version 1809 or higher) OS supported by an Intel I5-9400 CPU (or higher) with a NVIDIA GeForce RTX 2080 (or at least RTX 2060 or higher) with at least 16 GB of RAM.

PlayStation VR 2

PlayStation VR 2 is an HMD developed by Sony Interactive Entertainment for VR games, especially for the PlayStation 5 VR Games (www.playstation.com/ko-kr/ps-vr2/). The device was first introduced at CES 2022. PlayStation VR 2 needs to be tethered (via USB Type-C wire connection) to a PlayStation 5 player. The HMD weighs less than 600 g. The PlayStation VR 2 has a 2000×2040 per eye panel resolution display with a FoV of approximately 110 degrees. Four cameras are used for tracking of the headset and controller, and IR cameras are used for eye tracking. The HMD can provide vibration haptic effects and is equipped with a built-in microphone and stereo headphones.

XR Operation Process

XR is a combination of MR, AR, VR, and haptic technologies. XR uses AR to enable virtual text or images to be superimposed on selected objects in the real-world view of the user, in which the AR generated superimposed virtual text or image is related to the selected object. AR technology is a special type of visual based context aware computing. For an AR user, the real-world and virtual information and objects need to coexist on the same view in harmony without disturbing the user's view, comfort, or safety. However, AR technology is very difficult to implement as the computer-generated virtual text or image needs to be superimposed on the XR user's real-world view within a few milliseconds. The details of AR processing are described in the following section. The AR process is very complicated, and its operation process is time-consuming. So, accurately completing the AR process within the time limit of a few milliseconds is very difficult. If the XR user changes head or eye directions, the focus of sight will change, and the entire process has to be continuously updated and refreshed within the time limit of a few milliseconds. This is why AR development is so much more difficult and slower compared to VR system development.

The AR operation process includes image acquisition, feature extraction, feature matching, geometric verification, associated information retrieval, and imposing the associated information/object on the XR device's display. These processes can be conducted without artificial intelligence (AI) technology (i.e., "non-AI" methods) or using AI technology. There are a variety of non-AI based AR feature detection and description algorithms, in which SIFT, SURF, FAST, BRIEF, ORB, and BRISK schemes are described in this chapter. AI based AR technologies commonly use deep learning systems with convolutional neural network (CNN) image processing engines, which are described in Chapter 4.

AR user interface (UI) types include TV screens, computer monitors, helmets, facemask, glasses, goggles, HMDs, windows, and windshields.

Among handheld AR displays, smartphones were the easiest platform to begin commercial services. Powerful computing capability, good camera and display, and portability make smartphones a great platform for AR. Figure 3-6 shows a smartphone-based AR display example, and Figure 3-7 presents an AR research and development environment in my lab at Yonsei University (Seoul, South Korea) connected to a smartphone.

AR eyeglass products include the Google Glass, Vuzix M100, Optinvent, Meta Space Glasses, Telepathy, Recon Jet, and Glass Up. However, the large amount of image and data processing that AR devices have to conduct requires a significant amount of electronic hardware to execute long software program codes. As a result, AR eyeglasses are a significant challenge as there is very little space to implement the AR system within the small eyeglass frame. In the near future, XR smart eyeglasses will become significantly popular products, but much more technical advancements are required to reach that level. Hopefully, this book will help you and your company reach this goal faster.

AR HMD is a mobile AR device that can provide an immersive AR experience. The earliest examples include HMDs for aircraft maintenance and aviation assistance.

Figure 3-6. *Smartphone Based AR Process Example*

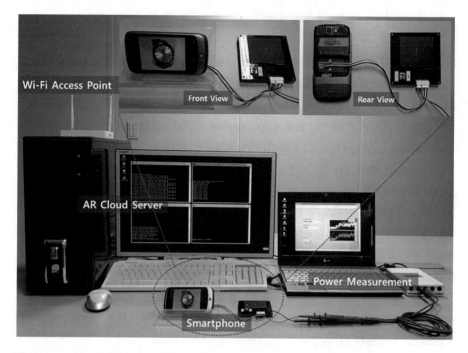

Figure 3-7. *Example AR Development Setup in My Lab*

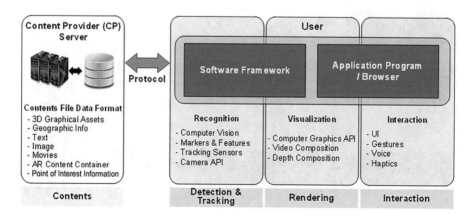

Figure 3-8. *AR Technological Components*

AR Technology

As presented in Figure 3-8, AR services need to be supported by the user's XR device and the content provider (CP) server. In standalone XR devices, the CP server is on the XR device. In tethered non-standalone XR devices, the CP server is commonly located in a local computer or edge cloud. The CP server may include 3D graphical assets, geographic information, text, image and movie libraries, AR content container, and point of interest information. The user's XR device contains recognition functions, visualization functions, and interactions functions that are based on the software framework, application programs, and browser. The recognition functions support the computer vision, markers and features, sensor tracking, and the camera application programming interface (API). The visualization functions support the computer graphics API, video composition, and depth composition. The interactions functions support the user interface (UI), gestures, voice, and haptics.

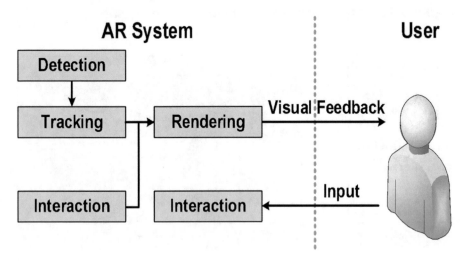

Figure 3-9. *AR Workflow*

Figure 3-9 shows the AR workflow, which starts with detection of the environment as well as the objects and people within the image. Based on the application's objective, the AR system will select objects and people within the image and continuously track them. Even though the objects and people may not move, because the XR device's user view changes often (through head and eye movement), the objects and people within the user's view will change, which is why tracking is always needed. Based on user interaction and interaction of the application, the augmented information/image needs to be generated and included into the display image of the AR user through the image rendering process. Visual feedback of the rendered image (which includes the augmented information/image) is displayed on the user's screen (www.researchgate.net/publication/224266199_Online_user_survey_on_current_mobile_augmented_reality_applications).

AR Feature Detection and Description Technology

AR feature detection requires the characteristic primitives of an image to be accurately identified. The identified objects need to be highlighted using unique visual cues so the user can notice them. Various feature detection techniques exist, where the common objective is to conduct efficient and effective extraction of stable visual features. AR feature detection influencing factors include the environment, changes in viewpoint, image scale, resolution, lighting, etc. AR feature detector requirements include robustness against changing imaging conditions and satisfaction of the application's Quality of Service (QoS) requirements (www.researchgate.net/publication/220634788_Mobile_Visual_Search_Architectures_Technologies_and_the_Emerging_MPEG_Standard).

During the Interest Point Detection (IPD) process, the detected interest points can be used to obtain feature descriptors, in which circular or square regions centered at the detected interest points are added where the size of the (circular or square) regions are determined by the scale. Figure 3-10 shows a feature detection and IPD example.

Figure 3-10. *AR Feature Detection and IPD Example*

Feature Detection and Feature Description

Feature detection is a process where features in an image with unique interest points are detected. The feature descriptors characterize an image's features using a sampling region. Figure 3-10 shows a feature detection example in which a circular image patch is applied around detected interest points.

There are AR algorithms that are capable of feature detection or feature description, and some can do both. For example, binary robust independent elementary features (BRIEF) is a feature descriptor scheme, and features from accelerated segment test (FAST) is a feature detector scheme. Schemes that do both feature detection and description include scale-invariant feature transform (SIFT), speeded-up robust features (SURF), oriented FAST and rotated BRIEF (ORB), and binary robust invariant scalable keypoints (BRISK).

There are two methods to conduct feature detection without using AI technology. Method-1 uses spectra descriptors that are generated by considering the local image region gradients. A "gradient" is a multivariable (vector) generalization of the derivative, where derivatives are applied on a single variable (scalar) in a function. Method-1 base algorithms include SIFT and SURF. Method-2 uses local binary features that are identified using simple point-pair pixel intensity comparisons. Method-2 based algorithms include BRIEF, ORB, and BRISK.

AR schemes that mix and match feature detection and feature description algorithms are commonly applied. Feature detection results in a specific set of pixels at specific scales identified as interest points. Different feature description schemes can be applied to different interest points to generate unique feature descriptions. Application and interest points characteristic based scheme selection is possible.

AR System Process

The AR process consists of five steps, which include image acquisition, feature extraction, feature matching, geometric verification, and associated information retrieval, as presented in Figure 3-11. Image acquisition is the process of retrieving an image from the AR camera. Feature extraction is based on an initial set of measured data, where the extraction process generates informative nonredundant values to facilitate the subsequent feature learning and generalization steps. Feature matching is the process of computing abstractions of image information and to make a local decision if there is an image feature (or not), which is conducted for all image points. Feature matching needs support from the database. Geometric verification is the identification process of finding geometrically related images in the image dataset (which are a subset of the overall AR image database). Associated information retrieval is the process of searching and retrieving metadata, text, and content-based indexing information of the identified object. The associated information is used for display on the XR device's screen near (or overlapping) the corresponding object.

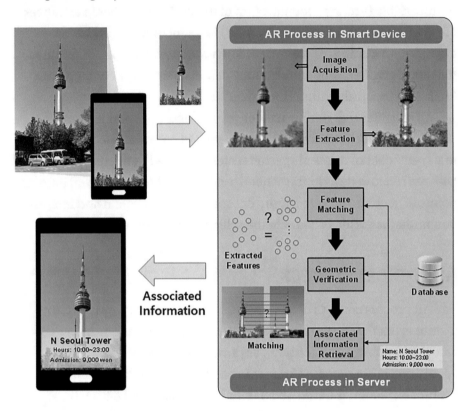

Figure 3-11. *AR Process*

AR Cloud Cooperative Computation

As presented in the details above, the AR process is complicated and requires a large database and a lot of image and data processing. This is the same for both the AI based AR processes (using convolutional neural network (CNN) deep learning described in Chapter 4) and the non-AI based AR processes (e.g., SIFT, SURF, FAST, BRIEF, ORB, BRISK).

Some of the main issues with the AR process are listed in the following. First, all object information cannot be stored on the XR device, which is why an external AR database is commonly needed. Second, XR requires a large amount of computation to complete its task, and the amount of XR processing directly influences the battery power consumption of the XR device. If more processing is conducted on the XR device, then the operation time of the device will become shorter (`www.itiis.org/digital-library/manuscript/1835`). Third, more processing on the XR device will cause the device to warm up faster, and a larger battery will be needed making the XR device heavier. Fourth, the device will become much more expensive if more processing is conducted on the XR device, because a higher performing CPU and GPU and more memory will be needed. Therefore, to share the processing load and overcome database limitations of the XR device, XR cloud computation offloading can be used. Figure 3-12 presents an example of the AR process (the feature matching, geometric verification, and associated information retrieval part) conducted using a cloud offloading server.

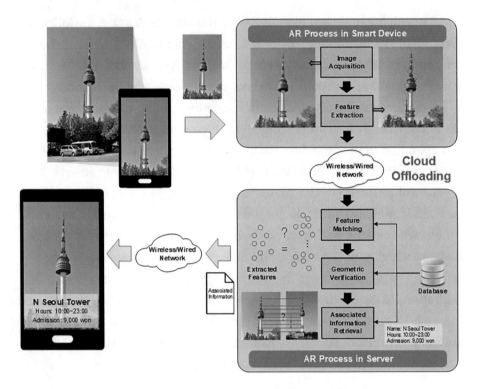

Figure 3-12. *Example of an AR Process Using a Cloud Offloading Server*

Cloud cooperative computation is also called "cloud offloading" because a part of the required computing process is offloaded to be computed by the main cloud server or the local edge cloud system (www.cs.purdue.edu/homes/bb/cs590/handouts/computer.pdf).

More details on cloud offloading, edge computing, and content delivery network (CDN) support for XR, metaverse, and multimedia streaming services are provided in Chapters 7 and 8.

Virtualization allows cloud server vendors to run arbitrary applications (from different customers) on virtual machines (VMs), in which VM processing is based on the infrastructure as a service (IaaS) cloud computing operations (where more details are provided in Chapter 8).

Cloud server vendors provide computing cycles, in which XR devices can use these computing cycles to reduce their computation load. Cloud computing (offloading) can help save energy and enhance the response speed of the XR service. However, unconditional offloading may result in excessive delay, which is why adaptive control is needed. To conduct adaptive control, the cloud server load and network congestion status monitoring is needed. Adaptive cloud offloading parameters include network condition, cloud server status, energy status of the XR device, and target Quality of Experience (QoE) level (`www.itiis.org/digital-library/manuscript/1093`).

XR Detection Process

Feature extraction is the process of finding the interest points from the image or video. The system needs to detect the descriptors from interest points and compare the descriptors with data in the database. In the feature extraction process, the qualification of the descriptors is selected based on the invariability from noise, scale, rotation, and other accuracy degrading factors. The kinds of descriptors that are used include corner, blob, region, etc. Figure 3-13 shows an example of an AR description generation process.

Original Image   Gray Scale   Interest Point   Descriptors

Figure 3-13. *Example of an AR Description Generation Process*

Among these methods, blob detection is very popular. Blob detection is the process of detecting blobs in an image. A blob is a region of an image that has constant (or approximately constant) image properties. All the points in a blob are considered to be similar to each other. These image properties (i.e., brightness, color, etc.) are used in the comparison process to the surrounding regions. Figure 3-14 presents a blob detection example conducted on a field of sunflowers. In mathematical formula terms, blob detection is based on the image's Laplacian of Gaussian (LoG) which uses the Hessian matrix **H**, which is obtained by the second-order derivative. The Hessian is the determinant of matrix **H,** and the Laplacian is the trace of matrix **H**.

Figure 3-14. *Blob Detection Example*

Popular feature extraction techniques include the Haar feature that was developed by P. Viola et al. in 2001, scale-invariant feature transform (SIFT) was developed by D. G. Lowe in 2004, histogram of oriented gradient (HOG) was developed by N. Dalal et al. in 2005, speeded-up robust features (SURF) was developed by H. Bay et al. in 2006, and oriented FAST and rotated BRIEF (ORB) were developed by E. Rublee et al. in 2011.

In the AR system process, feature extraction needs to be conducted accurately but is among the most difficult and computationally burdening AR processes. AR feature extraction has a significant influence on the accuracy of the AR process, so more technical details are described in the following.

As presented in Figure 3-15, the AR feature extraction process is based on the following six steps: grayscale image generation (GIG), integral image generation (IIG), response map generation (RMG), interest point detection (IDP), orientation assignment (OA), and descriptor extraction (DE).

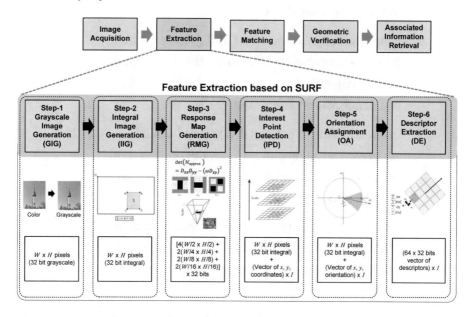

Figure 3-15. *AR Feature Extraction Process*

A description of the AR feature extraction step procedures is provided in the following.

1. Grayscale Image Generation (GIG): Original image captured by the AR device is changed into a grayscale valued image in order to make it robust to color modifications.

2. Integral Image Generation (IIG): Process of building an integral image from the grayscale image. This procedure enables fast calculation of summations over image subregions.

3. Response Map Generation (RMG): In order to detect interest points (IPs) using the determinant of the image's Hessian matrix **H**, the RMG process constructs the scale space of the image.

4. Interest Point Detection (IPD): Based on the generated scale response maps, the maxima and minima (i.e., extrema) are detected and used as the IPs.

5. Orientation Assignment (OA): Each detected IP is assigned a reproducible orientation to provide rotation invariance (i.e., invariance to image rotation).

6. Descriptor Extraction (DE): Process of uniquely identifying an IP, such that it is distinguished from other IPs.

XR Feature Extraction and Description

In this section, XR feature extraction and detection algorithms are described. Figures 3-16 through 3-24 present the process details of SIFT, SURF, FAST, BRIEF, ORB, and BRISK, and Tables 3-1 and 3-2 provide a comparison of AR feature detection and description methods (Y.-S. Park, Ph.D. Dissertation, Yonsei Univ., 2018). Table 3-1 presents an AR feature detection and description method comparison based on year, feature detector, spectra, and orientation. Table 3-2 summarizes the distance function, robustness, pros and cons of AR feature detection, and description methods.

Table 3-1. *AR feature detection and description method comparison based on proposed year, feature detector, spectra, and orientation*

Categories	SIFT	SURF	FAST	BRIEF	ORB	BRISK
Year	1999	2006	2006	2010	2011	2011
Feature detector	Difference of Gaussian	Fast Hessian	Binary comparison	N/A	FAST	FAST or AGAST
Spectra	Local gradient magnitude	Integral box filter	N/A	Local binary	Local binary	Local binary
Orientation	Yes	Yes	N/A	No	Yes	Yes
Feature shape	Square	HAAR rectangles	N/A	Square	Square	Square
Feature pattern	Square	Dense	N/A	Random point-pair pixel compares	Trained point-pair pixel compares	Trained point-pair pixel compares

Table 3-2. *AR feature detection and description method comparison based on distance function, robustness, and pros and cons*

Categories	SIFT	SURF	FAST	BRIEF	ORB	BRISK
Distance function	Euclidean	Euclidean	N/A	Hamming	Hamming	Hamming
Robustness	6 Brightness, rotation, contrast, affine transform, scale, noise	4 Scale, rotation, illumination, noise	N/A	2 Brightness, contrast	3 Brightness, contrast, rotation, limited, scale	4 Brightness, contrast, rotation, scale
Pros	Accurate	Accurate	Fast, real-time applicable	Fast, real-time applicable	Fast, real-time applicable	Fast, real-time applicable
Cons	Slow, compute-intensive, patented	Slow, patented	Large number of interest points	Scale and rotation-invariant	Less scale invariant	Less scale invariant

SIFT

Scale-invariant feature transform (SIFT) is one of the first feature detector schemes proposed. The SIFT software source code and user guidelines are provided in GitHub (https://github.com/OpenGenus/ SIFT-Scale-Invariant-Feature-Transform#:~:text=Scale%20 Invariant%2DFeature%20Transform%20(SIFT),-This%20 repository%20contains&text=D.,these%20features%20for%20 object%20recognition). SIFT uses image transformations in the feature detection matching process. SIFT is highly accurate; however, it does have a large computational complexity which limits its use in real-time applications. Figure 3-16 shows the SIFT feature extraction process.

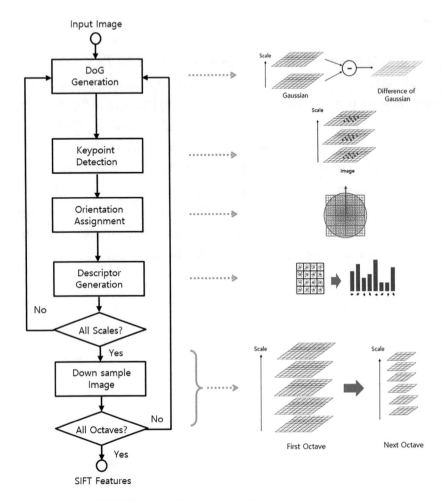

Figure 3-16. *SIFT Feature Extraction Process*

SIFT processing steps begins with the Difference of Gaussian (DoG) generation, which builds a scale space using an approximation based on DoG techniques (`https://en.wikipedia.org/wiki/Scale-invariant_ feature_transform`). The local extrema of the DoG images (at varying scales) are the selected interest points. DoG images are produced by image convolving or blurring with Gaussians at each octave of the scale space in the Gaussian pyramid. Gaussian image (based on set number of octaves) is down-sampled after each iteration of an octave. DoG is used because it is a Laplacian of Gaussian (LoG) approximation method that has low computational complexity compared to LoG and does not need partial derivative computations like LoG does. In addition, DoG obtains local extrema of images with difference of the Gaussians.

Interest point detection (IPD) classical methods use LoG because it is scale invariant when applied at multiple image scales, which makes it a popular approach to improve the performance. Gaussian scale-space pyramid and kernel techniques are frequently used in IPD. Figure 3-17 shows an example SIFT IPD process applying Gaussian scale-space pyramid and kernels. SIFT uses an approximation of the Laplacian of Gaussian (LoG) because the Laplacian is a differential operator of a function on the Euclidean space. The second-order Gaussian scale-space derivatives are very sensitive to noise and require significant computation.

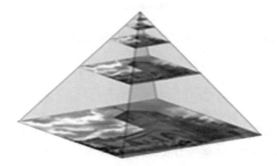

Figure 3-17. *SIFT IPD Process Applying Gaussian Scale-Space Pyramid and Kernels*

Keypoint detection starts with the keypoint localization process in which each pixel in the DoG image is compared to its neighboring pixels. The comparison is processed on the current scale and two scales above and below. The candidate keypoints are pixels that are local maximums or local minimums (i.e., extrema). The final set of keypoints excludes low contrast points. Next, orientation assignment is conducted using the keypoint orientation determination process. The orientation of a keypoint is the local image gradient histogram in the neighborhood of the keypoint. The peaks in the histogram are selected as the dominant orientations.

The SIFT descriptor generation process computes the feature descriptor for each keypoint. The feature descriptor consists of 128 orientation histograms. Figure 3-18 shows a SIFT descriptor generation example.

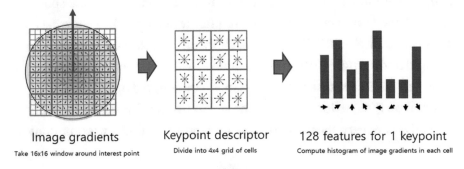

Image gradients
Take 16x16 window around interest point

Keypoint descriptor
Divide into 4x4 grid of cells

128 features for 1 keypoint
Compute histogram of image gradients in each cell

Figure 3-18. *SIFT Descriptor Generation Example*

SURF

Speeded-up robust feature (SURF) approximation techniques are used to get faster yet similarly accurate IPD results compared to SIFT. The SURF software source code and user guidelines are provided in GitHub (https://github.com/herbertbay/SURF). SURF uses the determinant of Hessian (DoH) matrix in the IPD process, where box filters are used in approximating the DoH (https://en.wikipedia.org/wiki/Speeded_up_robust_features). The Hessian matrix is a square matrix with second-order partial derivative elements that are used to characterize the level of surface curvature of the image, which is important in keypoint detection. Figure 3-19 presents the SURF feature extraction process.

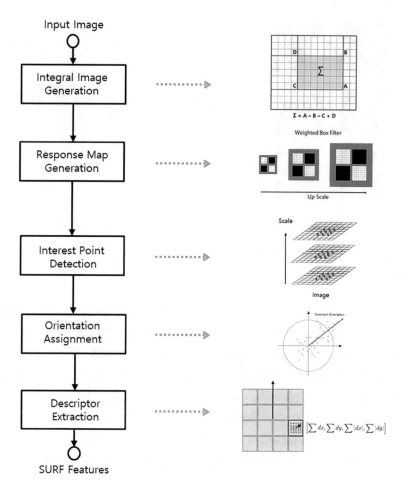

Figure 3-19. *SURF Feature Extraction Process*

The SURF approximation process is applied to SIFT's DoG with a box filtering process. The square box filters are used for approximation instead of Gaussian averaging of the image because it enables fast approximation and box area calculation. An example of box filters and an integral image used in SURF is shown in Figure 3-20 along with an integral image example.

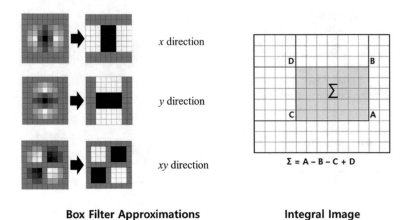

x direction

y direction

xy direction

Σ = A – B – C + D

Box Filter Approximations   **Integral Image**

Figure 3-20. *SURF Box Filter Approximation and Integral Image Example*

Integral image generation is used to generate integral images that are used for fast convolution computation. Multiple parallel processing of box filtering on different scale images is used to approximate the LoG process. Then the IPD process uses a Hessian matrix-based Blob detection. The feature descriptor scheme processes the interest point's neighboring pixels by dividing them into subregions. The SURF descriptor describes the pixel intensity distribution based on a scale independent neighborhood. Each subregion's wavelet response is used (e.g., regular 4×4 subregions).

FAST

Features from accelerated segment test (FAST) have fast matching and low computation characteristics, which enable FAST to detect a greater number of interest points at the given scale compared to scale-space detector methods SIFT and SURF. The FAST software source code and user guidelines are provided in GitHub (https://github.com/soh534/fast). FAST uses a template-based corner detector scheme, in which a "corner" is a fixed scale interest point. Figure 3-21 presents the FAST feature detection process.

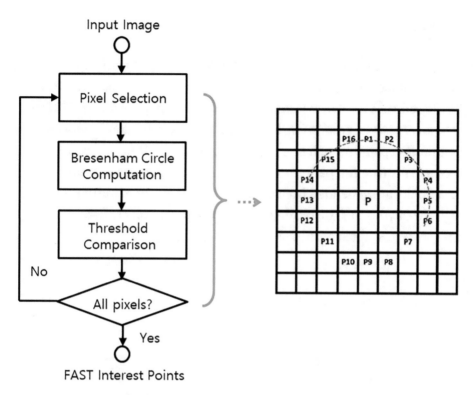

Figure 3-21. *FAST Feature Detection Process*

In the Bresenham circle computations, each corner has a point with two dominant and distinct gradient orientations. The center pixel is compared with surrounding pixels in a circular pattern based on the Bresenham circle. The circular template is used to detect corners based on intensity comparison. The size of the connected pixel region is commonly 9 (FAST9) or 10 (FAST10) out of a possible 16 pixels. Next, threshold comparison of each pixel is compared to a preset threshold value, which determines whether the pixel value is greater or lesser than the center pixel. A decision tree is used to quickly determine the comparison order of pixels. The FAST descriptor output has an adjoining bit vector form (https://en.wikipedia.org/wiki/Features_from_accelerated_segment_test).

BRIEF

Binary robust independent elementary features (BRIEF) is a popular binary feature descriptor technology used in robotic applications. The BRIEF software source code and user guidelines are provided in GitHub (`https://github.com/lafin/brief`). BRIEF uses a randomly generated distribution pattern, such as a patch form of 31×31 pixels, where an example distribution pattern could consist of 256 pixel point-pairs. The descriptors are generated from the binary comparison of the point-pairs. Figure 3-22 presents the BRIEF feature description process (`www.cs.ubc.ca/~lowe/525/papers/calonder_eccv10.pdf`).

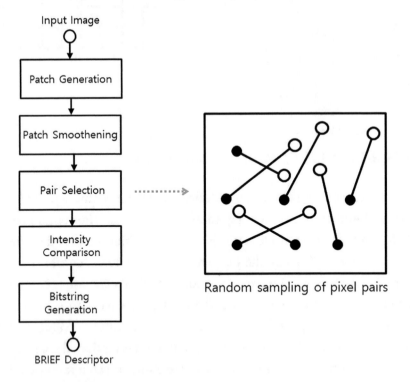

Figure 3-22. BRIEF Feature Description Process

The BRIEF binary descriptor process applies sampling patterns to sample points in the region around the descriptors. In the orientation compensation process, the keypoint orientation is determined by the size of the orientation compensation that is needed to compensate for rotational changes. Then sampling pairs are formed. The final descriptor is made by pairs based on comparing sampling pairs. BRIEF compares random point-pairs within the local region and does not have an intricate sampling pattern or mechanism for orientation compensation.

In terms of noise sensitivity, the BRIEF descriptors use information based on single pixel locations, which makes it sensitive to noise. Gaussian filters are used to relieve the noise sensitivity.

ORB

Oriented FAST and rotated BRIEF is a hybrid scheme that combines features of FAST and BRIEF for feature extraction and description. The ORB software source code and user guidelines are provided in GitHub (`https://github.com/Garima13a/ORB`). ORB has fast computation speed; it is highly efficient in memory usage and has a high matching accuracy. This is why ORB is used instead of SIFT and SURF for feature extraction in many cases. Figure 3-23 presents the ORB feature extraction process (`https://en.wikipedia.org/wiki/Oriented_FAST_and_rotated_BRIEF`).

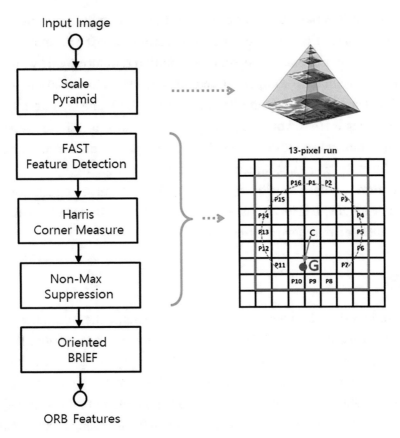

Figure 3-23. *ORB Feature Extraction Process*

ORB uses a multi-scale feature-based image pyramid, where FAST and rBRIEF (which is a rotated version of BRIEF) are applied to each scale of the image pyramid. FAST feature detection uses a corner detector to detect keypoints. Harris corner measure is applied on the keypoints to select the top N points with the strongest FAST responses. The center of gravity (centroid) G of an image patch is computed with moments to improve rotation invariance. In the oriented BRIEF process, the orientation is computed based on the direction of the vector from the keypoint to G. BRIEF features use the orientation information to be rotation-invariant, where rBRIEF is used as the binary descriptor. The search and matching process is based on a correspondence search that uses multi-probe locally sensitive hashing (MP-LSH). When a match fail occurs, neighboring buckets are searched for matches. MP-LSH uses fewer hash tables to save memory consumption and generates more consistent hash bucket sizes compared to BRIEF.

BRISK

Binary robust invariant scalable keypoints (BRISK) is a low computational feature detector scheme that is known to provide a better performance than SURF with comparable accuracy. The BRISK software source code and user guidelines are provided in GitHub (`https://github.com/kornerc/brisk`). Figure 3-24 shows the BRISK feature extraction process.

BRISK conducts candidate IPD using a corner detect algorithm called adaptive and generic corner detection based on the accelerated segment test (AGAST), which is an extension to the FAST algorithm. AGAST uses a circular-symmetric pattern region shape with 60 point-pairs and uses point-pair line segments arranged in 4 concentric rings (`www.researchgate.net/publication/221110715_BRISK_Binary_Robust_invariant_scalable_keypoints`).

BRISK uses scale-space keypoint detection, which is a scale-space technology that creates octaves and intra-octaves, where each octave is half-sampled from the previous octave. The intra-octave is down-sampled to be placed in between octaves, and non-maximal suppression is conducted on each octave and intra-octave. Sub-pixel maximum is computed across the patch, and continuous maximum is computed across scales.

BRISK also applies sample point Gaussian smoothing to the patch area around each sampling point. As a result, red circles represent the size of the standard deviation of the Gaussian filter. In the BRISK pair generation process, point-pairs of pixels are separated into two groups. The long segment pairs are used in coarse resolutions, and the short segment pairs are used in fine resolutions. The short and long segment pair separation is used to represent the scale invariance. The gradient computation is computed on the long segment pairs first to determine the feature orientation. Next the gradient is computed on the short segment pairs to find the amount of rotation in reference to the orientation. The BRISK descriptor generation process makes a binary descriptor from the rotated short segment pairs.

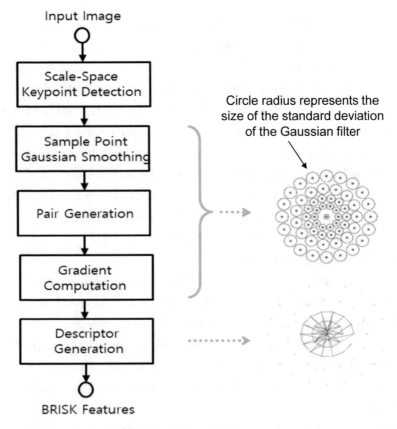

Figure 3-24. *BRISK Feature Extraction Process*

Summary

This chapter provided details of XR devices and feature extraction and detection schemes, which include SIFT, SURF, FAST, BRIEF, ORB, and BRISK. Without feature extraction and description of sensor and image data, XR devices cannot provide any functions or features. Because these processes are very computationally burdening as well as energy- and time-consuming, process offloading methods are also described. In the following Chapter 4, details of artificial intelligence (AI) and deep learning technologies used in metaverses, XR, and multimedia systems are introduced.

CHAPTER 4

Deep Learning for Metaverse XR and Multimedia Systems

Metaverse and XR systems use a lot of artificial intelligence (AI) technology in every aspect of the systems and services. For example, AI, machine learning (ML), and deep learning (DL) are used for computer vision, feature extraction and tracking, avatar and robotic control, user eye and motion tracking, speech recognition, natural language processing, sensor signal tracking, computational creativity, and future predictions (www.coursera.org/learn/deep-learning-business).

Multimedia systems also use AI technology everywhere, which include user recommendation systems, enterprise resource planning (ERP) and management, server streaming speed control, video and audio adaptive quality control, illegal image or information automatic detection, automated privacy protection, as well as automated network and cloud security monitoring and cyberattack defense control.

DL enables extreme levels of precision and reliable automated control and is self-learning and adaptable to changes, which is why metaverse XR and multimedia services use DL abundantly.

© Jong-Moon Chung 2023
J.-M. Chung, *Emerging Metaverse XR and Video Multimedia Technologies*,
https://doi.org/10.1007/978-1-4842-8928-0_4

In order to thoroughly cover all details of deep learning-based AI technologies, Chapter 4 is formed of the following sections:

- Backpropagation Supervised Learning

- Deep Learning with Recurrent Neural Network (RNN)

- Deep Learning with Convolutional Neural Network (CNN)

- Performance of AI Systems

- Performance of CNN at the ImageNet Challenge

- Performance of RNN in Amazon's Echo and Alexa

- Advanced RNN and CNN Models and Datasets

Before we start on how DL is implemented in metaverse XR and multimedia systems, first let's define AI, ML, and DL so they can be distinguished. Figure 4-1 illustrates the relation between AI, ML, and DL (https://blogs.nvidia.com/blog/2016/07/29/whats-difference-artificial-intelligence-machine-learning-deep-learning-ai/).

AI is intelligence performed by a computing system. AI systems are designed to mimic natural intelligence, which is intelligence performed by a living being, such as a human or animal (https://en.wikipedia.org/wiki/Artificial_intelligence). Modern AI systems are able to exceed the performance of human intelligence in specific tasks, as explained with examples in later sections of this chapter. AI technology enables a computing system to make an intelligent decision or action and enables an intelligent agent (e.g., hardware, software, robot, application) to cognitively perceive its environment and correspondingly attempt to maximize its probability of success of a target action. AI has been used in making optimal decisions (or faster suboptimal decisions) for many types of control systems. Various forms of AI technology can be found in optimization theory, game theory, fuzzy logic, simulated annealing, Monte Carlo experiments and simulation, complex theory, etc.

ML is an AI technique that can enable a computer to learn without being explicitly programmed. ML has evolved from pattern recognition and computational learning theory in AI. ML provides the functionality to learn and make predictions from data.

DL is a ML technique that uses multiple internal layers (hidden layers) of nonlinear processing units (artificial neurons) to conduct supervised or unsupervised learning from data. DL is commonly implemented using an artificial neural network (NN).

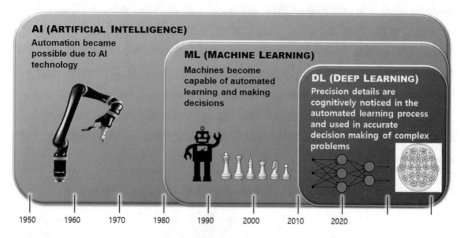

Figure 4-1. *Relation Between AI, ML, and DL*

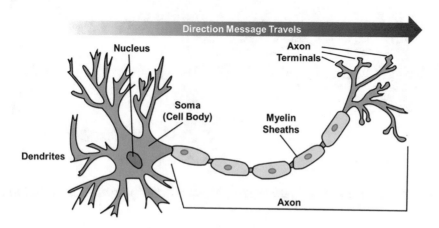

Figure 4-2. *Neuron (i.e., Nerve Cell)*

Figure 4-2 presents a model of a neuron (i.e., nerve cell). The dendrites serve as the input terminals of the neuron. The dendrites are connected to the soma (i.e., cell body) which has a nucleus in the center. The soma is connected to the axon terminals through the axon, which has multiple myelin sheaths. A neuron signal is an electrical signal created from biochemical activity. The neuron signal is detected by the dendrites and transferred to the axon terminals. As shown in Figure 4-3, the axon terminals of one neuron are connected to the dendrites of multiple neurons that will relay the signal throughout the human body. The connecting parts of the axon terminals of one neuron with the dendrites of multiple neighboring neurons are called the synaptic connections. A human's brain has approximately 100 billion (i.e., 10^{11}) neurons and 10,000 (i.e., 10^4) connections per neuron, resulting in 1 quadrillion (i.e., 10^{15}) synaptic connections. The synaptic connections are where human knowledge and intelligence is created as well as information and memories are stored.

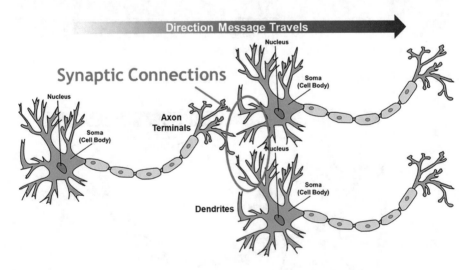

Figure 4-3. Neurons Transferring Signals over Synaptic Connections

DL systems use artificial NNs which are built using artificial neurons (i.e., nerve cells). One of the earliest neuron models uses a threshold logic unit, which was designed by W. McCulloch and W. Pitts in 1943, which is presented in Figure 4-4 (`https://link.springer.com/article/10.1007/BF02478259`).

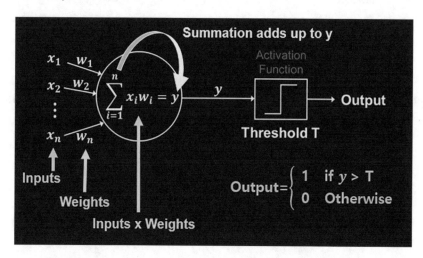

Figure 4-4. *Artificial Neuron (i.e., Nerve Cell) Used in DL and Artificial NNs*

The threshold logic unit-based neuron model has a part that multiplies each input (i.e., $x_1, x_2,..., x_n$) with a weight value (i.e., $w_1, w_2,..., w_n$) and adds all values up (i.e., $y = (x_1w_1 + x_2w_2 + ... + x_nw_n)$, and then the added value (y) is compared in the activation function to decide the output value. The activation function can be a hard output or soft output type. Hard outputs are easier to compute than soft outputs. Figure 4-4 uses the hard output binary values (0 or 1) that result from y compared to the threshold T in the activation function defined in the following:

$$Output = \begin{cases} 1 & if \ y > T \\ 0 & otherwise \end{cases}$$

Soft output values can be created by using one of the following activation functions (instead of the threshold T):

- Logistic sigmoid $\qquad\qquad \sigma(y)=\dfrac{1}{1+exp(-y)}$

- Softplus $\qquad\qquad\qquad \zeta(y) = log\,(1 + \ exp\,(y))$

- Rectified linear unit (ReLU) $g(y) = \ max\,(0, y)$

These three are the representative soft output activation functions, but more exist. The logistic sigmoid activation function is presented in Figure 4-5, the Softplus activation function is presented in Figure 4-6, and the ReLU activation function is presented in Figure 4-7.

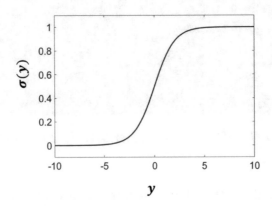

Figure 4-5. *Logistic Sigmoid Activation Function*

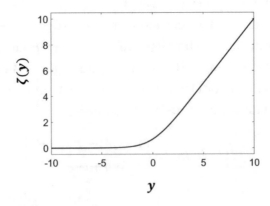

Figure 4-6. *Softplus Activation Function*

146

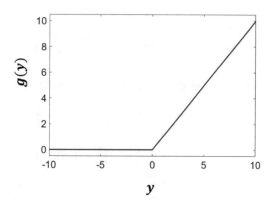

Figure 4-7. *ReLU Activation Function*

DL NNs are formed using perceptrons and multilayer perceptrons (MLPs). A perceptron is a ML algorithm that conducts supervised learning of linear (binary) classification. Perceptrons are trained to determine if an input (tensor, vector, or scalar value) belongs to one class or another. A MLP is a feed forward NN that is formed of multiple layers of perceptrons, where each layer may use multiple perceptrons in parallel. MLPs use backpropagation based supervised learning to train the outputs (to accurately conduct nonlinear classification). More details on backpropagation supervised learning are described in the following section.

DL NNs often use the Softmax function to enhance the accuracy of the classification process. Softmax is a logistic function that maps a K dimensional vector (e.g., a set of K data inputs) of real values to values in the range of 0–1 such that all values of the vector add up to 1. The following is a Softmax transfer example for three original inputs, three Softmax outputs, and the applied constraint.

- Original inputs a_1, a_2, a_3

- Softmax outputs $\widetilde{a}_1 = \dfrac{e^{a_1}}{e^{a_1} + e^{a_2} + e^{a_3}},$

$$\widetilde{a}_2 = \dfrac{e^{a_2}}{e^{a_1} + e^{a_2} + e^{a_3}}, \widetilde{a}_3 = \dfrac{e^{a_3}}{e^{a_1} + e^{a_2} + e^{a_3}}$$

- Constraint satisfied $\left(\widetilde{a_1}+\widetilde{a_2}+\widetilde{a_3}\right)=1$

A Softmax transfer example is provided in the following using numbers. For example, based on $\left(\widetilde{a_1}+\widetilde{a_2}+\widetilde{a_3}\right)=1$

$$\begin{array}{c}\left.\begin{array}{l}a_1 = 9\\a_2 = 20\\a_3 = 25\end{array}\right\} \rightarrow \left\{\begin{array}{l}\widetilde{a_1} = 0.00000011178\\\widetilde{a_2} = 0.00669285018\\\widetilde{a_3} = 0.99330703804\end{array}\right.\end{array}$$

The weights (w_1, w_2 w_3) and Softmax values ($\widetilde{a_1}+\widetilde{a_2}+\widetilde{a_3}$) combined in the following form of

$$w_1\widetilde{a_1} + w_2\widetilde{a_2} + w_3\widetilde{a_3}.$$

ML and DL systems also use AutoEncoders. An AutoEncoder (or AutoAssociator) is a NN used to learn the characteristics of a dataset such that the representation (encoding) dimensionality can be reduced. The simplest form of an AutoEncoder is a feedforward nonrecurrent neural network (non-RNN).

Backpropagation Supervised Learning

When designing a DL system to achieve a certain level of intelligence, the number of neurons to include in the NN needs to be considered. This is because one neuron can only make a very simple one-dimensional decision. So, for more complex intelligence, we need more neurons working together. Therefore, we need to understand what neurons can do and how to form a NN structure that can perform well. Starting with the simplest example, an artificial neuron with two inputs and two weights is presented in Figure 4-8, where the weights need to be properly trained.

The single neuron (single layer) in Figure 4-8 has two inputs and two weights (i.e., w_1, w_2) and the achievable decision boundaries (on the right side). Figure 4-9 shows a two-layer NN using three neurons with four weights (i.e., w_1, w_2, w_3, w_4) and the achievable decision boundaries (on the right side). Figure 4-10 shows a three-layer NN using five neurons with eight weights (i.e., w_1, w_2, w_3, w_4, w_5, w_6, w_7, w_8) and the achievable decision boundaries (on the right side). As illustrated in these figures, as the number of layers and neurons and weights increases, the level of achievable decision boundaries becomes more sophisticated.

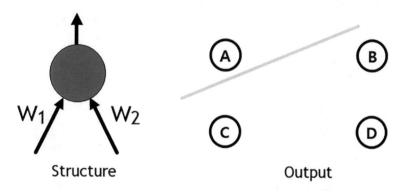

Figure 4-8. *Neuron (Single Layer) with Two Inputs and Two Weights (i.e., w_1, w_2) (Left Side) and the Achievable Decision Boundaries (Right Side)*

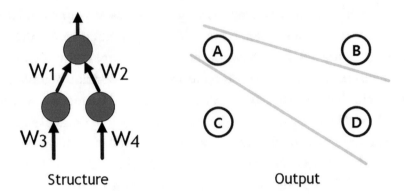

Figure 4-9. *Two-Layer NN Using Three Neurons with Four Weights (i.e., w_1, w_2, w_3, w_4) (Left Side) and the Achievable Decision Boundaries (Right Side)*

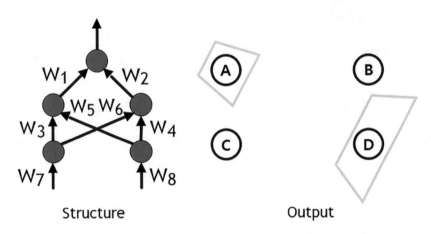

Figure 4-10. *Three-Layer NN Using Five Neurons with Eight Weights (i.e., w_1, w_2, w_3, w_4, w_5, w_6, w_7, w_8) (Left Side) and the Achievable Decision Boundaries (Right Side)*

A DL based general NN model and its weight training region are presented in Figure 4-11. Generalized NNs have an input layer and an output layer and one or more hidden layers. All connections with the hidden layer neurons have weights that need to be trained. The most common training method is backpropagation based supervised learning.

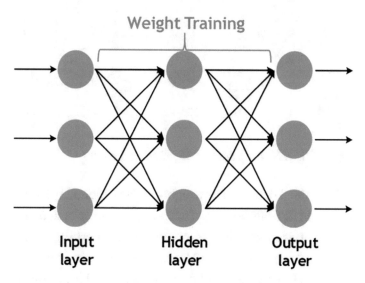

Figure 4-11. *Generalized NN Model and Weight Training Region*

The input layer is where the input to the NN comes in. The output layer is where the output of the NN goes out and is used. The hidden layer contains the intelligence in a distributed fashion using many neurons, interconnections, weights, biases, activation functions, etc. As shown in Figure 4-12, DL NNs may use many hidden layers to conduct precise learning (by accurately training the weights) and precision control, which is where the name "deep learning" came from.

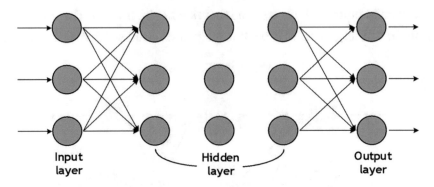

Figure 4-12. *DL NN with Multiple Hidden Layers*

Learning is how DL trains the weights of the hidden layers to make the NN intelligent. DL NN learning (training) methods include supervised learning, unsupervised learning, semi-supervised learning, and reinforcement learning. Supervised learning is a training method that uses labeled data. Labeled data is input data that has the desired output value included. This is like an exam problem where the answer is used with the problem to educate (train) the student (NN). Unsupervised learning is a training method that uses unlabeled data (no desired outputs are used). Semi-supervised learning is a training method that uses both labeled data and unlabeled data (`www.deeplearningbook.org/`). Reinforcement learning is a training method that uses feedback (reward) of the output to make optimal decisions but does not use any labeled data.

Among these learning methods, supervised learning using backpropagation training is used the most for metaverse XR and multimedia systems, so we will focus on this DL technique. Backpropagation is used to train the perceptrons and MLPs. Backpropagation uses training iterations where the error size as well as the variation direction and speed are used to determine the update value of each weight of the NN.

Figure 4-13 shows the backpropagation training process based on supervised learning. The backpropagation learning algorithm steps are summarized in the following:

1. Forward propagate the training pattern's input data through the NN.

2. NN generates initial output values.

3. Use the output value and labeled data desired output value to compute the error value. Use the error value and input value to derive the gradient of the weights (size and +/- direction of change) of the output layer and hidden layer neurons.

4. Scale down the gradient of the weights (i.e., reduce the learning rate), because the learning rate determines the learning speed and resolution.

5. Update weights in the opposite direction of the +/- sign of the gradient, because the +/- sign of the gradient indicates +/- direction of the error.

6. Repeat all steps until the desired input-to-output performance is satisfactory.

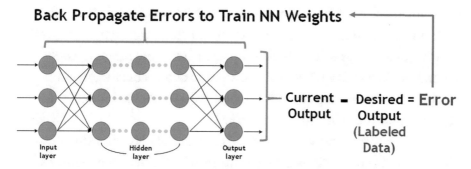

Figure 4-13. Supervised Learning Using Backpropagation Training

Backpropagation learning uses the gradient to control the weight values. Gradient is the derivative of a multivariable (vector) function. Gradients point in the direction of the greatest rate of increase of the multivariable function, and the magnitude of the gradient represents the slope (rate of change) in that direction. So, updating the hidden layer weight values considering the direction and magnitude of the current gradient can significantly help to minimize the error output. However, because each weight of the NN is used in the calculation of various other inputs, the size of a weight update has to be small in each training iteration. This is because a big change in one weight may mess up the weights that were properly trained to match the other input to output values.

Deep Learning with RNN

Recurrent neural network (RNN) deep learning is the most powerful AI technology for speech recognition, speech-to-text (STT) systems, as well as sensor data sequence analysis and future predicting. Therefore, almost all XR, game, metaverse, and multimedia systems use RNN technology. A few representative examples of smartphone apps that use RNN speech recognition and STT technology include Apple Siri, Amazon Alexa, Google Assistant and Voice Search, and Samsung Bixby and S Voice. In addition, RNN is used for handwriting recognition and almost any type of sequential or string data analysis. RNN is also capable of software program code generation, in which a RNN system is used to automatically generate computer programming codes that can serve a predefined functional objective (www.deeplearningbook.org/).

The RNN system structure is based on a neural network with directed cyclic connections between the (artificial electronic) neurons. Directed cyclic connections create internal states with dynamic temporal characteristics. The RNN internal memory is used to process arbitrary input data sequences. Sequence modeling is used for data sequence classification and clustering. A sequence modeling structure based on sequence-to-sequence (S2S) learning is shown in Figure 4-14. RNN S2S learning systems have N inputs that are transformed into M outputs, in which N and M can be different numbers.

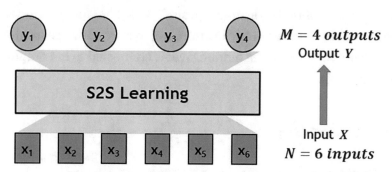

Figure 4-14. *RNN S2S Learning System Example with Six Inputs and Four Outputs*

The RNN data analysis process is based on the five following steps:

1. Data enters the input layer.

2. Representation of the data in the input layer is computed and sent to the hidden layer.

3. Hidden layer conducts sequence modeling and training in forward and/or backward directions.

4. Multiple hidden layers using forward or backward direction sequence modeling and training can be used.

5. Final hidden layer sends the processed result to the output layer.

Figure 4-15 presents a forward RNN example that is composed of an input layer, output layer, and a hidden layer in the middle. Correlation of the data sequence in the forward direction is analyzed in forward RNNs. The sequential data input that enters the input layer has a processing sequence direction as shown by the arrows in Figure 4-15. Sequence modeling of the input data symbols (from X_1 to X_4) has the same direction as the hidden layer processing direction, which is why it is called a forward RNN. Related memory of the hidden layer is connected to the output layer for data analysis.

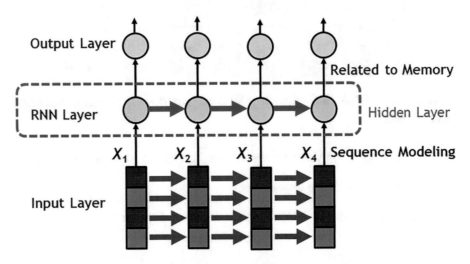

Figure 4-15. *Forward RNN System Example*

Figure 4-16 presents a backward RNN example where the hidden layer operates in a sequence direction that is opposite to the forward RNN, which is why it is called a backward RNN. Correlation of the data sequence in the backward direction is analyzed in backward RNNs.

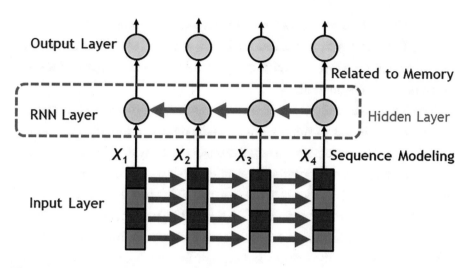

Figure 4-16. *Backward RNN System Example*

RNNs may use multiple hidden layers and more input and output layer nodes for more complex data analysis. Figure 4-17 shows a S2S deep learning RNN example, in which the hidden layers may be in the form of a forward RNN or backward RNN.

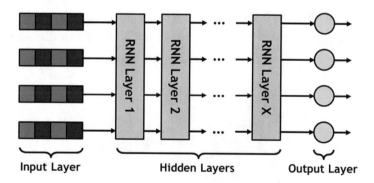

Figure 4-17. *S2S Deep Learning RNN Example*

Because RNNs and CNNs use many hidden layers in their NNs for data analysis, they are called deep neural networks (DNNs), and because deep neural networks are used to learn the data pattern and semantics (and much more) through training, the overall technology is called deep learning (DL). The number of hidden layers required as well as the input, output, and hidden layer structures are based on the data type and target application results needed.

The RNN data analysis applies a representation process to the input data, which is similar to subsampling. As the data sequentially enters the RNN through the input layer, a small dataset (in array or matrix form) is formed, and data representation is applied to extract the important data that characterizes the dataset in the best way. This process is repeated as the data continuously enters the RNN input layer. Representation is a nonlinear down-sampling process that is effective in reducing the data size and filtering out the noise and irregular factors that the data may have. The RNN "representation" process is similar to the "subsampling" and "pooling" process used in CNN, which will be described in the following section of this chapter when describing XR image processing techniques using deep learning. Some examples of representation are presented in the following.

Figure 4-18 shows an RNN "center" representation example. The center method chooses the center value of a dataset. For example, among the nine numbers in the dataset, the number 5 is in the middle, so it is selected to be the representation of the input dataset.

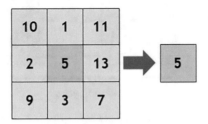

Figure 4-18. *RNN "Center" Representation Example, Where the Center Value of the DataSet Is Selected*

Figure 4-19 shows a RNN "median" representation example.

The median method first lines up the dataset values in order of the largest to the smallest and then selects the value in the middle. For example, in Figure 4-19, if we line up the numbers in the dataset from largest to the smallest, then we get 13, 11, 10, 9, 7, 5, 3, 2, 1 in which 7 is in the middle of the number sequence, so the median value is 7.

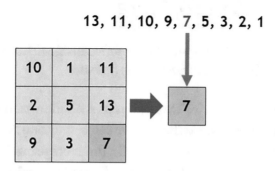

Figure 4-19. *RNN "Median" Representation Example, Where the Median Value of the DataSet Is Selected*

Figure 4-20 shows a RNN "max pooling" representation example. Among the 9 numbers in the dataset, the largest number is 13, so 13 is selected as the representation value.

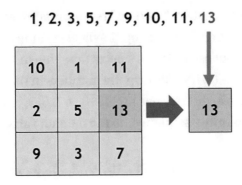

Figure 4-20. *RNN "Max Pooling" Representation Example, Where the Maximum Value of the DataSet Is Selected*

Figure 4-21 shows a RNN "average" representation example. The representation methods described above select only one number among the dataset. Unlike these methods, the average method uses all values of the dataset, so no value is discarded without influencing the representation value. In the average representation example of Figure 4-21, all numbers in the dataset are added and then divided by 9 (because we have nine numbers in the dataset) to obtain the average value 6.7 which becomes the representation value.

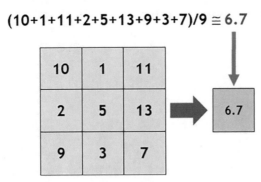

Figure 4-21. *RNN "Average" Representation Example, Where the Average Value of the DataSet Is Selected*

Figure 4-22 shows a RNN "weighted sum" representation example. The dataset values d_1, d_2, ..., d_9 are individually multiplied by the weights w_1, w_2, ..., w_9 in the weight set (in array or matrix form) to create the weighted sum $v = (w_1d_1 + w_2d_2 + ... + w_9d_9)$. Because there are nine values in this dataset example, if all the weights are equal to 1/9 (i.e., $w_1 = w_2 = ... = w_9 = 1/9$), then the weighted sum value v would be the same as the average representation value. Therefore, the RNN "weighted sum" representation is a generalized form of the RNN "average" representation.

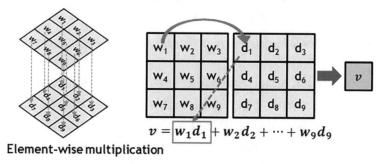

Element-wise multiplication

Figure 4-22. *RNN "Weighted Sum" Representation Example, Where the Resulting Weighted Sum Value Is v*

The next procedure is "context-based projection" which is conducted in the hidden layer. This process uses assisting data in the representation process. The assisting data is called the "context." Context data may be the original data input, or it may be a biased version of the data or transformed data. For example, in Figure 4-23, the context dataset is multiplied to weight set (in array or matrix form) $\mathbf{W^c}$, and the representation is multiplied to the $\mathbf{W}$ weight set (in array or matrix form) using the element-wise multiplication method shown in Figure 4-23. Each value of the context data and representation is multiplied to a weight value and then enters the hidden layer for forward or backward direction RNN processing.

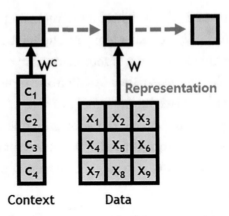

Figure 4-23. *RNN Hidden Layer Context-Based Projection Example*

A context-based projection example using a larger structure hidden layer process is shown in Figure 4-24. In this example, three sets of data (i.e., Data 1, Data 2, Data 3) are processed together using the representation weight set (in array or matrix form) **W** with context weight set **W**ᶜ based context-based projection sequentially applied.

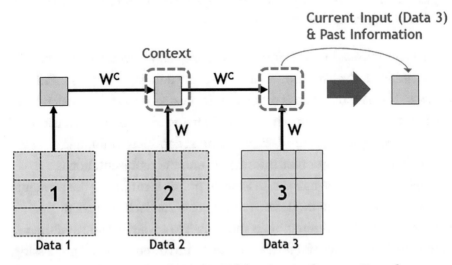

Figure 4-24. *Larger-Scale RNN Hidden Layer Context-Based Projection Example*

RNN hidden layer processes frequently use the "attention" function with the representation process, as presented in Figure 4-25. Attention enables the decoder to attend to different parts of the source data segment at various steps of the output generation. For example, in language translation systems, the RNN will attend to sequential input states, multiple words simultaneously, and words in different orders when producing the output translated language.

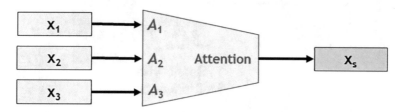

Figure 4-25. *RNN Softmax Transfer with Attention Data Processing Example, Where the Attention Values A_1, A_2, and A_3 Represent the Importance of the DataSet*

In the RNN process of representation with attention, the Softmax transfer is used frequently to transfer the values a_1, a_2, and a_3, respectively, into $\widetilde{a_1}$, $\widetilde{a_2}$, and $\widetilde{a_3}$.

The attention values A_1, A_2, and A_3 represent the importance of the input datasets X_1, X_2, and X_3.

Then weight values w_1, w_2, and w_3 are, respectively, applied to the Softmax output values resulting in $w_1\widetilde{a_1}$, $w_2\widetilde{a_2}$, and $w_3\widetilde{a_3}$ to transform each dataset, where an element-wise multiplication is applied to the outputs 1', 2', and 3' that are shown in Figure 4-26.

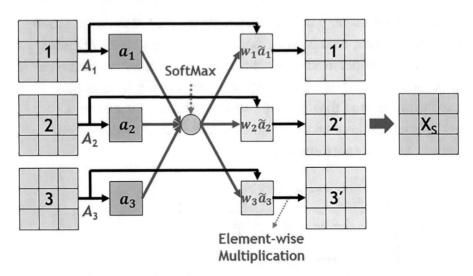

Figure 4-26. *RNN Softmax Transfer with Attention and Element-Wise Multiplication Data Processing Example*

RNN types include the fully recurrent neural network (FRNN) and the long short-term memory (LSTM). In FRNNs, all neurons have connections to other neurons with modifiable weights. The neurons are used to form the input, hidden, and output layers. LSTMs are currently the most popular RNN model. LSTM cells have an input gate, output gate, forget gate(s), and self-loop(s), and they may have many more gates (https://en.wikipedia.org/wiki/Long_short-term_memory). Self-loop(s) in the LSTM cells provides data sequence memory effects. Figure 4-27 shows a LSTM RNN example, where the input at time t is x_t. The input signal x_t is fed into the input, input gate, output gate, and forget gate which are combined into the state that has a self-loop feedback (red arrowed line). The state value is fed back (blue arrowed lines) into the input gate, forget gate, and output gate.

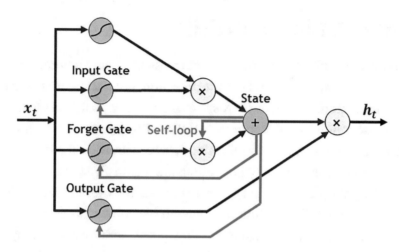

Figure 4-27. *RNN LSTM System Example*

The RNN forget gate (which is also called the recurrent gate) helps to prevent backpropagated errors from vanishing (called the vanishing gradient problem) or exploding (called the divergence problem). In addition, it enables errors to flow backward through an unlimited number of virtual layers (VLs) extending the memory characteristics.

LSTM RNN systems are very effective on data sequences that require memory of far past events (e.g., thousands of discrete time steps ago) and perform well on data sequences with long delays and mixed signals with high and low frequency components.

LSTM RNN applications are extensive, which include XR system sensor analysis, STT, speech recognition, large-vocabulary speech recognition, pattern recognition, connected handwriting recognition, text-to-speech synthesis, recognition of context sensitive languages, machine translation, language modeling, multilingual language processing, automatic image captioning (using LSTM RNN + CNN), etc.

Deep Learning with CNN

Deep learning with convolutional neural network (CNN) is commonly used in image processing and feature detection and tracking in metaverse XR and multimedia systems. CNN systems are based on a feed forward NN and use multilayer perceptrons (MLP) for this process. CNN was designed based on animal visual cortexes, where individual vision neurons progressively focus on overlapping tile shape regions. Vision tile regions sequentially shift (convolution process) to cover the overall visual field.

Deep learning CNN techniques became well known based on an outstanding (winning) performance of image recognition at the ImageNet Challenge 2012 by Krizhevsky and Hinton from the University of Toronto, which is described in further details in a following section of this chapter (www.image-net.org/challenges/LSVRC/). CNNs need a minimal amount of preprocessing and use rectified linear units (ReLU) activation functions more often (i.e., $g(y) = max\,(0, y)$). CNNs are used in image/video recognition, recommender systems, natural language processing, Chess, Go, as well as metaverse XR devices and multimedia systems.

Figure 4-28 presents a CNN structure. CNNs are composed of convolutional layers and feature maps as well as subsampling, local contrast normalization (LCN), dropout, ensemble, bagging, and pooling processes.

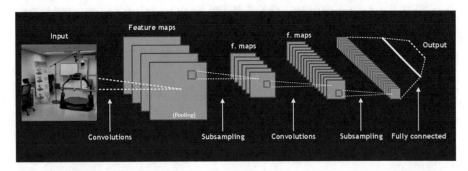

Figure 4-28. *CNN Structure*

The convolutional layer executes the convolution process to find the same feature in different places of an image. Convolution is conducted using learnable filters/kernels (that have small receptive fields) that are passed (convoluted) through the input data/image. Each filter moves sequentially across (convolved) the input data/image to make a two-dimensional activation map based on each filter. Figure 4-29 shows an example of the CNN convolution process used in making feature map (f. map) data, as shown in Figure 4-28.

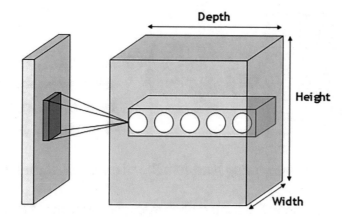

Figure 4-29. *Example of the CNN Convolution Process*

Feature maps are made from the activation maps of the filters. The number of learnable filters/kernels (and how the data, weight training, bias values, etc. are used) in the convolution process determines how many feature maps are generated after convolution.

Subsampling uses a selecting operation (pooling) on the feature maps. Subsampling is a nonlinear down-sampling process that results in smaller feature maps. The CNN subsampling process is similar to the RNN representation process. The most popular subsampling schemes (many exist) include median value, average value, and max pooling.

Subsampling based on "median value" is illustrated in Figure 4-30, where for each subregion the median value (middle value) is selected as the representative sample. When a subregion has an odd number of values, the value in the middle will become the median value. When the subregion has an even number of values, the average of the two middle values becomes the median value. For example, in Figure 4-30, in the boxed region, there are an even number of values. When lined up in order of value size, the sequence of 2, 4, 6, and 9 is obtained, where the two middle values are 4 and 6, and the average of these two values is 5. So, the median value for this subregion is 5.

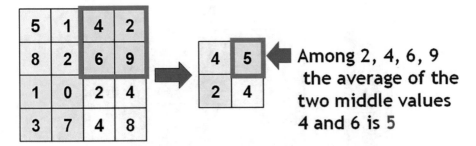

Figure 4-30. *Subsampling Example Based on the Median Value*

Figure 4-31 shows the subsampling example based on the average value, where for each subregion, the average value is used as the representative value.

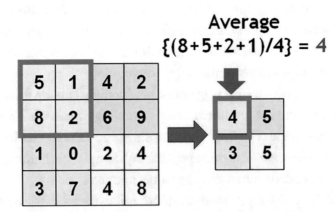

Figure 4-31. *Subsampling Example Based on the Average Value*

Figure 4-32 shows an example of subsampling based on the maximum (max) value, where each subregion selects its max value as its representative value.

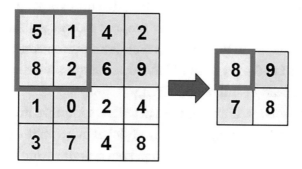

Figure 4-32. *Subsampling Example Based on the Maximum Value*

The local contrast normalization (LCN) process is used after the convolution process to improve the optimization results and the image's invariance (i.e., characteristic of not changing after transformation or processing). The LCN is commonly used on the image after convolution and before pooling (subsampling), as shown in Figure 4-33. As the convolution layer increases the number of feature maps, the pooling (subsampling) layer is used to decrease the spatial resolution.

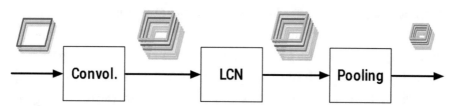

Figure 4-33. *Example of the LCN and Pooling Process Following the Convolution Process*

Additional techniques used in CNNs include the dropout, ensemble, bagging, and pooling processes, which are explained in the following.

The dropout process helps in training neurons to properly work even when other neurons may not exist (neuron failure). Therefore, the dropout process makes the CNN more robust to noise and erroneous data. In the dropout process, on each iteration, selected neurons are randomly turned off based on a probability model. The dropout process is applied to the output layer which is in the form of a multilayer perceptron (MLP) that is fully connected to the previous hidden layer. Outputs are computed with a matrix multiplication and biased offset.

Ensemble models are often used in CNNs to improve the accuracy and reliability by providing an improved global image of the data's actual statistics. Ensembles are created by repeated random sampling of the training (labeled) data.

Bagging uses multiple iterations of training the CNN with training/labeled data that has random sample replacements. After training, the results of all trained models of all iterations are combined.

Performance of AI Systems

AI technology has radically evolved, such that on specific tasks an AI system can outperform humans, even the best experts. A representative example of humans competing with AI started with IBM's Deep Blue. In 1996, Deep Blue lost in a six-game match to the chess world champion Garry Kasparov. After being upgraded, Deep Blue won its second match (i.e., three games won with one draw) with Garry Kasparov in 1997. The estimated processing capability of IBM's Deep Blue is 11.4 GFLOPS. Afterward, the technology of AI computers evolved such that AI computers commonly beat chess Grand Masters. As a result, separate from the World Chess Federation (FIDE) Ratings (for chess Grand Masters), the Computer Chess Rating Lists (CCRL) was formed in 2006 so chess fans and AI programmers could compare the performance of various AI engines in chess competitions (https://en.wikipedia.org/wiki/Deep_Blue_(chess_computer)).

Another representative example of an open-domain Question-Answering (QA) AI system beating the best human contestants happened on the television quiz show "Jeopardy!" on January 14th of 2011, when the IBM Watson QA AI system beats two Jeopardy! top champions in a two-game competition (https://en.wikipedia.org/wiki/IBM_Watson). Jeopardy! is a television quiz show in the United States that debuted on March 30th of 1964 and is still very popular. For this competition, the IBM Watson QA system went through over 8,000 independent experiments that were iteratively processed on more than 200 8-core servers that were conducted by 25 full-time researchers/engineers for this Jeopardy! match (www.ibm.com/support/pages/what-watson-ibm-takes-jeopardy).

Watson is an open-domain QA problem solving AI system made by IBM. Watson uses the deep learning QA (DeepQA) architecture for QA processing. The QA system requirements include information retrieval (IR), natural language processing (NLP), knowledge representation and reasoning (KR&R), machine learning (ML), and human-computer interface (HCI). DeepQA is a combination of numerous analysis algorithms, which include type classification, time, geography, popularity, passage support, source reliability, and semantic relatedness.

A more recent example of humans competing against DL computers is the Google's DeepMind AlphaGo system that beats the world top ranking Go players during 2015 to 2017. The AlphaGo Master system (used in 2017) was equipped with a second generation (2G) tensor processing unit (TPU) that has a processing capability of 11.5 PFLOPS (i.e., 11.5×10^{15} FLOPS). A TPU is a more advanced hybrid system form of multiple central processing units (CPUs) and graphics processing units (GPUs) combined for advanced DL processing (www.nature.com/articles/nature16961).

CPUs are used to execute computations and instructions for a computer or smartphone, which are designed to support all process types. A GPU is a custom-made (graphics) processor for high-speed and low power operations. GPUs are commonly embedded in computers and smartphone video cards, motherboards, and inside system on chips (SoCs).

When describing IBM's Deep Blue or Watson, the term FLOPS was used, which is a unit that is used to measure a computer's performance. FLOPS stands for "FLoating-Point Operations Per Second" which represents the number of floating-point computations that a computer can complete in a second. For modern computers of smartphones, the unit GFLOPS is commonly used, which stands for Giga FLOPS, in which a Giga=Billion=10^9. Another unit that is used to measure a computer's performance is IPS which stands for "Instructions per Second" which represents the number of operations that a computer can complete in a second. For modern computers or smartphones, the unit MIPS is commonly used, which stands for Millions of IPS. Humans are extremely versatile, but are not good in FLOPS performance, only reaching an average of 0.01 FLOPS = 1/100 FLOPS of a performance. 0.01 FLOPS means that it will take an average of 100 seconds to conduct one floating-point calculation. This may be shocking to you because this is too slow, but in your head without using any writing tools or calculator, try to compute the addition of two simple floating-point numbers "1.2345 + 0.6789" which results in 1.9134. You may have been able to complete this quickly, but for an average person, it is expected to take an average of 100 seconds to complete this floating-point calculation. Other numbers that can be used to approximately characterize the human brain includes 2.5 PB (i.e., 2.5×10^{15} Bytes) of memory running on 20 W of power.

In terms of FLOPS comparison, approximately humans can perform at a 0.01 FLOPS level, modern smartphones and computers are in the range of 10~300 GFLOPS, and TPU 2G (which was used in the Google's DeepMind AlphaGo Master system in 2017) can provide an approximate 11.5 PFLOPS (i.e., 11.5×10^{15} FLOPS) performance.

Performance of CNN at the ImageNet Challenge

The performance level of CNN image technology is explained in this section, where the ImageNet Large Scale Visual Recognition Challenge (ILSVRC) is the original and best example. ILSVRC was an annual contest that started in 2010 focused on object category classification and detection. ILSVRC was called the "ImageNet Challenge" for short. There were three main challenges used to benchmark large-scale object recognition capability. There was one "Object Localization (top-5)" competition and two "Object Detection challenges" where one was for image detection and the other was for video detection. The "Object Localization (top-5)" was the original competition of ILSVRC. The other two Object Detection challenges were included into ILSVRC later.

The ILSVRC used a training dataset size of 1.2 million images and 1,000 categories of labeled objects. The test image set consisted of 150,000 photographs. For the Object Localization (top-5) contest, each competing AI program lists its top 5 confident labels based on each test image in decreasing order of confidence and bounding boxes for each class label. Each competing program was evaluated based on accuracy of the program's localization labeling results, the test image's ground truth labels, and object in the bounding boxes. The program with the minimum average error was selected as the winner (https://en.wikipedia.org/wiki/ImageNet).

As the amount of training will influence the level of learning, there were very strict participant's program requirements. Based on the program requirements, each team (participating AI program) is allowed two submissions per week, where there is no regulation on the number of neural network layers that can be used in a contestant's AI program. The learning scheme and parameters had to be based only on the training set.

Figure 4-34 presents the ILSVRC "Object Localization (top-5)" competition annual winners and accuracy performance. Deep learning CNN technology became globally acknowledged based on the 2012 ILSVRC performance results. The 2012 winner was AlexNet, which was created by Alex Krizhevsky, Ilya Sutskever, and Geoffrey Hinton from the University of Toronto. AlexNet achieved a 83.6% accuracy in the Object Localization (top-5) competition. This was a 9.4% improvement in the performance in the Object Localization (top-5) competition compared to the 74.2% accuracy achieved by Xerox in 2011. AlexNet used deep learning (DL) for the first time, which was based on a 8-layer DL neural network that used 5 convolution layers, 3 fully connected layers, and 60 million parameters. AlexNet trained for 6 days using two Nvidia GTX-580 GPUs with 3 GB of memory.

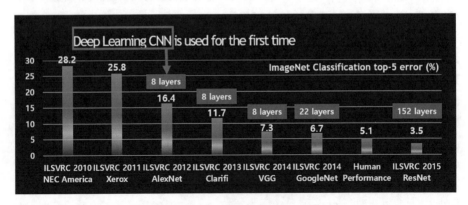

Figure 4-34. *ILSVRC ImageNet "Object Localization (Top-5)" Competition Annual Winners and Accuracy Performance. The Numbers in the Graph Are the Average Error Percentage Values. The Average 5.1% Human Error Performance Was Included in the Figure as a Reference. During ILSVRC 2015, Microsoft's ResNet Exceeded the Human Average Performance for the First Time*

The 2014 winner was Google's GoogleNet (Inception-v1) which achieved a 93.3% accuracy in the Object Localization (top-5) competition. This was the first time a computer was able to exceed the 90% accuracy level. GoogleNet used a 22-layer DL neural network with 5 million parameters and trained for 1 week on the Google DistBelief cluster.

The 2015 winner was Microsoft's ResNet, which achieved a 96.5% accuracy in the Object Localization (top-5) competition. This is the first time a computer program was able to exceed the 94.9% human accuracy level. ResNet used a 152-layer DL neural network that was trained for approximately 3 weeks on 4 NVIDIA Tesla K80 GPUs using a combined processing capability of 11.3 BFLOPs. By 2017, among the 38 competing teams, 29 teams achieved an accuracy exceeding 95%.

Performance of RNN in Amazon's Echo and Alexa

In order to demonstrate how deep learning RNN can be used, the operations of the Echo and Alexa are described in the following. Amazon Echo is a voice controlled intelligent personal virtual assistant, where Alexa is accessible through the Echo smart speaker. Alexa is a cloud-based AI personal assistant developed by Amazon that requires network connection to the Amazon cloud, which is a cloud offloading system. Alexa is used in the Echo and Echo Dot products. More recent Echo product information can be found at `www.amazon.com/smart-home-devices/b?ie=UTF8&node=9818047011`.

In November of 2014, the Amazon Echo was released along with Alexa services at a price of $199 for invitation and $99 for Amazon Prime members. A smaller version of the Amazon Echo device is the Echo Dot device, where the first-generation device was released in March of 2016 and the second-generation device was released in October of 2016. The Echo system uses a seven-microphone array built on the top of the device, and acoustic beamforming and noise cancellation is applied for improved voice recognition capability. The seven-microphone array enables high-quality natural language processing (NLP), which is used to match the user's voice or text as input, so the Alexa system could provide automated services requested by the user. The Alexa virtual assistant is always-on and always-listening to support the voice activated questions and answering (QA) system.

Figure 4-35 shows the Alexa operations initiated by the user's voice through the Echo device. Alexa uses DL and ML to continuously get smarter and conduct automated speech recognition (ASR) and natural language understanding (NLU). Alexa's voice is generated by a long short-term memory (LSTM) RNN system.

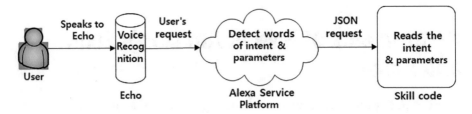

Figure 4-35. *Alexa Operations Initiated by the User's Voice Through the Echo Device*

Alexa's Skills include a library of AI based functions that can assist in finding product information (type, volume, profit), marketing progress, and results search. The Alexa Skills Kit (ASK) is a developer kit used to create new custom Skills for Echo and Echo Dot.

The DL speech recognition system is triggered when the user speaks into the Echo system. The Echo's voice recognition system detects trigger words and required Skills.

The Echo sends the user's request to the Alexa Service Platform (ASP). The ASP uses its DL RNN speech recognition engine to detect words of intent and parameters.

The ASP sends a JavaScript Object Notation (JSON) text document (including the intent and parameters) to the corresponding Skill on the Alexa Cloud using a Hypertext Transfer Protocol (HTTP) request.

Figure 4-36 shows the procedures of how the Skill code works with the ASP and Echo to complete the user's request. The Skill code parses the JSON and reads the intent and parameters, and then it retrieves necessary data and then executes required action(s).

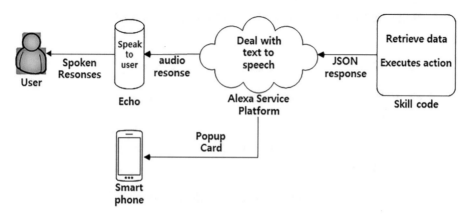

Figure 4-36. *Skill Code Working with the ASP and Echo to Complete the user's Request, and Smartphone Notices (Popup Cards) Can Be Received as an Option*

Next, Alexa makes a Response JSON document and sends it to the ASP. This Response JSON document includes the text of Alexa's reply to the user. As an option, the smartphone app Popup Card info can be used, in which the Popup Card includes the markup text and image URL. The ASP voice replies to the user. Optional settings can make the smartphone app popup card show up on the user's smartphone.

Advanced RNN and CNN Models and Datasets

More advanced RNN and CNN models as well as benchmarkable deep learning datasets exist. However, due to space limitations of this chapter, a list of the advanced algorithms and datasets as well as their website links is provided to enable the reader to study more.

Popular deep learning benchmarkable datasets are listed in the following:

- MSCOCO (https://cocodataset.org/#home)

- PASCAL VOC (http://host.robots.ox.ac.uk/pascal/VOC/)

- CIFAR-10, CIFAR-100 (www.cs.toronto.edu/~kriz/cifar.html)

- ImageNet (https://image-net.org/index.php)

- MNIST (http://yann.lecun.com/exdb/mnist/)

Advanced speech, sensors, and acoustic recognition deep learning (RNN related) algorithms are listed in the following:

- End-to-end speech recognition with RNN (https://proceedings.mlr.press/v32/graves14.html).

- Deep speech 2 (http://proceedings.mlr.press/v48/amodei16.pdf).

- Listen, attend, and spell (https://arxiv.org/abs/1508.01211).

- Sequence transduction with RNN (https://arxiv.org/abs/1211.3711).

- Streaming end-to-end speech recognition (https://
  storage.googleapis.com/pub-tools-public-
  publication-data/pdf/9dde68cba3289370709cee41e9
  bd4e966e4113f2.pdf).

- Neural transducer (https://arxiv.org/
  pdf/1511.04868.pdf).

- Monotonic Chunkwise Attention (https://arxiv.org/
  abs/1712.05382).

Advanced image recognition deep learning algorithms (CNN related) are listed in the following:

- You Only Look Once (YOLO) algorithms

  - YOLOv1 (https://arxiv.org/abs/1506.02640)

  - YOLOv2 (https://arxiv.org/abs/1612.08242?c
    ontext=cs)

  - YOLOv3 (https://arxiv.org/abs/1804.02767)

  - YOLOv4 (https://arxiv.org/abs/2004.10934)

  - Scaled-YOLOv4 (https://ieeexplore.ieee.org/
    stamp/stamp.jsp?tp=&arnumber=9577489&tag=1)

- Region with CNN (R-CNN) algorithms

  - R-CNN (https://ieeexplore.ieee.org/
    document/6909475)

  - Fast R-CNN (https://dl.acm.org/doi/10.1109/
    ICCV.2015.169)

  - Faster R-CNN (https://ieeexplore.ieee.org/
    document/7485869)

- Cascade R-CNN (`https://ieeexplore.ieee.org/document/8578742`)

- Libra R-CNN (`https://openaccess.thecvf.com/content_CVPR_2019/papers/Pang_Libra_R-CNN_Towards_Balanced_Learning_for_Object_Detection_CVPR_2019_paper.pdf`)

- Single Shot MultiBox Detector (SSD) (`https://arxiv.org/pdf/1512.02325.pdf`)

- RefineDet (`https://arxiv.org/abs/1711.06897`)

- RetinaNet (`https://ieeexplore.ieee.org/document/8237586`)

- FPN (`https://arxiv.org/abs/1612.03144`)

Software architecture- and processing method-wise, image recognition deep learning algorithms can be divided into one-stage methods and two-stage methods. One-stage methods include SSD, RetinaNet, YOLOv1, YOLOv2, YOLOv3, YOLOv4, and Scaled-YOLOv4 (`www.jeremyjordan.me/object-detection-one-stage`). Two-stage methods include FPN, R-CNN, Fast R-CNN, Faster R-CNN, Mask R-CNN, Cascade R-CNN, and Libra R-CNN (`https://medium.com/codex/a-guide-to-two-stage-object-detection-r-cnn-fpn-mask-r-cnn-and-more-54c2e168438c`).

Summary

This chapter introduces AI and deep learning technologies, including the internal functions of RNN and CNN systems. The history of AI and deep learning system achievements is described, including the more recent ImageNet Challenge (for CNN technology) and Amazon's Echo and Alexa (for RNN technology). The chapter also includes a list of advanced RNN and CNN models and datasets. AI and deep learning technologies will continue to be extensively used in metaverse services, XR devices, and multimedia streaming systems, which include sensor/image signal analysis, video/audio adaptive quality control, recommendation systems, enterprise resource planning (ERP), automated management, server control, security, as well as privacy protection. In the following Chapter 5, details of video technologies used in metaverse XR and multimedia systems are introduced, which include the H.264 Advanced Video Coding (AVC), H.265 High Efficiency Video Coding (HEVC), H.266 Versatile Video Coding (VVC) standards, and holography technology.

CHAPTER 5

XR and Multimedia Video Technologies

This chapter focuses on the core video encoding and decoding technologies used in XR services like Meta Quest 2 and Microsoft HoloLens 2 and the popular over-the-top (OTT) video services like Netflix, Disney+, and YouTube. The sections cover the history of Skype (as it is one of the earliest video conferencing and Voice over IP (VoIP) applications in the world) and YouTube and the evolution of their video and audio codec technologies. In addition, details of the H.264 Advanced Video Coding (AVC), H.265 High Efficiency Video Coding (HEVC), H.266 Versatile Video Coding (VVC) standards, and futuristic holography technology are introduced.

- XR Device Video Codecs (Meta Quest 2, Pico G2, and DPVR P1)

- Multimedia Codecs (Skype, YouTube, Netflix, and Disney+)

- H.264 AVC Video Technology

- H.265 HEVC Video Technology

- H.266 VVC Video Technology

- Holography Technology

© Jong-Moon Chung 2023
J.-M. Chung, *Emerging Metaverse XR and Video Multimedia Technologies*,
https://doi.org/10.1007/978-1-4842-8928-0_5

XR Device Video Codecs

Among XR headsets and HMDs, the Meta Quest 2, Pico, and DPVR have the largest market share. These headsets all use H.264 and H.265 video codecs in their core display technologies. As described in this chapter, there are many video profiles in H.264 and H.265 where the XR device conducts auto detection and automatically selects the highest-quality multimedia format based on the XR device's hardware and software capabilities as well as the network conditions. The XR device's capabilities depend on the CPU, GPU, SoC, battery status, memory, display resolution, and platform software type and condition. Network status factors like delay and throughput are also considered.

The Meta Quest 2 maximum VR video resolutions all use the H.265 HEVC video codec. The Quest 2's monoscopic highest (width×height) pixel resolution 8192×4096 at 60 fps (fps = frames/s = frames per second), stereoscopic highest pixel resolution 5760×5760 at 60 fps, and the 180 Side by Side highest pixel resolution 5760×5760 at 60 fps all use the H.265 HEVC video codec.

The Pico G2 4K maximum video resolutions use the H.264 AVC or the H.265 HEVC video codecs. The Pico G2's 4K monoscopic highest pixel resolution 5760×2880 at 30 fps uses the H.264 codec, the stereoscopic highest pixel resolution 4096×4096 at 30 fps uses the H.264 or H.265 codec, and the 180 Side by Side highest pixel resolution 5760×2880 at 30 fps uses the H.264 codec (https://headjack.io/knowledge-base/best-video-resolution-for-pico-headsets/).

In addition, the DPVR P1 4K VR Glasses VR headsets support the 3GP, H.264, H.265, and MP4 video codecs (www.estoreschina.com/dpvr-p1-4k-vr-glasses-virtual-reality-headset-milk-white-p-11477.html).

Multimedia Codecs

Skype, YouTube, Netflix, and Disney+ systems conduct auto detection and automatically select the highest-quality multimedia format based on the receiving OTT device's capabilities and network conditions. OTT device capabilities include video codec and audio codec, processing capability, memory, and especially the display resolution and platform software. Network status factors like delay and throughput are considered.

Considering that Skype was founded in 2003, YouTube was founded in 2005, Netflix started multimedia streaming in 2007, and Disney Streaming was announced in 2021, based on this chronological order of establishment, the multimedia codecs used by these companies are introduced in the following. By observing the video and audio codec changes made by these companies, we can easily see what were the best options for each time period.

Skype Multimedia Codecs

Skype supports video chat and voice call services. The name "Skype" was derived from "sky" and "peer-to-peer." Skype communication uses a microphone, speaker, video webcam, and Internet services. Skype was founded by Niklas Zennström (Sweden) and Janus Friis (Denmark) based on the software created by Ahti Heinla, Priit Kasesalu, and Jaan Tallinn (Estonia) in 2003. On August 29, 2003, the first public beta version of Skype was released. In June 2005, Skype made an agreement with the Polish web portal Onet.pl which enabled integration into the Polish market. On September 12, 2005, eBay, Inc. agreed to acquire Skype Technologies SA for approximately $2.5 billion, and on September 1, 2009, based on Skype's value of $2.75 billion, eBay announced it was selling 65% of Skype (to Silver Lake, Andreessen Horowitz, and the Canada Pension Plan Investment Board) for $1.9 billion. By 2010, Skype had 663 million registered users. On May 10, 2011, Microsoft acquired Skype for $8.5 billion and began to integrate Skype services into Microsoft products. On February 27, 2013, Microsoft introduced Office 2013 which included 60 Skype world minutes per month in the Office 365 consumer plans, which was for home and personal use as well as universities. On April 8–30, 2013, the Windows Live Messenger instant messaging service was phased out in favor of promoting Skype (but Messenger use continued in mainland China). On November 11, 2014, Microsoft announced that Lync would be replaced by Skype for Business in 2015, where later versions included combined features of Lync and the consumer Skype software. E–organizations were given the option to switch their users from the default Skype for Business interface to the Skype for Business (Lync) interface (`https://en.wikipedia.org/wiki/Skype`).

Skype is based on a hybrid peer-to-peer model and uses a client and server system architecture. Supporting applications include VoIP, video conferencing, instant messaging, and file transfer. Skype video conference calls can be made from various platforms using smartphones, tablets, and PCs. Desktop Client Operating Systems (OSs) including Windows and HoloLens as well as other desktop OSs which include OS X (10.6 or newer) and Linux (Ubuntu and others) support Skype.

Other mobile device OSs that support Skype include iOS (for Apple's iPhone and iPad), Android (for various Android smart devices), BlackBerry 10, Fire OS, Nokia X, and many more (including support for selected Symbian and BlackBerry OS devices). Skype calls to other Skype users within the Skype services are free. Skype could also be used to make traditional phone calls to landline telephones and mobile phones using debit-based user account charges based on Skype Credit or by subscription. Similar technologies that support VoIP and video conferencing include Session Initiation Protocol (SIP) and H.323 based services which are used by companies like Linphone and Google Hangouts.

Skype video codecs before Skype 5.5 used VP7 as the video codec, but after 2005, Skype started to use the True Motion VP7 codec. In early 2011, Skype 5.5 moved to VP8. The video codecs True Motion VP7 and VP8 were developed by On2 Technologies for Google. Skype 5.7 uses VP8 for both group and one-on-one standard definition video chatting. But after Microsoft acquired Skype in 2011, the video codec was replaced to H.264.

The Skype video call quality is based on the mode being used. The standard mode has a video resolution of 320×240 pixels with 15 fps; high-quality mode has a resolution of 640×480 pixels with 30 fps. High definition (HD) mode has the highest resolution of 1280×720 pixels with 30 fps. Other H.264 codecs are also used in group and peer-to-peer (one-on-one) video chatting.

Skype initially used G.729 and SVOPC as its VoIP audio codec. Skype added SILK to Skype 4.0 for Windows and other Skype clients. SILK is a lightweight and embeddable audio codec created by Skype, where more details are provided in the following. Skype's Opus is an open source codec that can integrate the SILK codec for voice transmission with Constrained Energy Lapped Transform (CELT) codecs for higher-quality audio transmissions (e.g., live music performances).

SILK is an audio compression format and audio codec that was developed by Skype Limited to replace the SVOPC codec. SILK was initially released in March 2009, and its latest software development kit (SDK) version 1.0.9 was released in 2012. SILK operation specs include the audio sampling frequencies of 8, 12, 16, and 24 kHz (i.e., 24,000 samples/s) resulting in a bitrate range of 6~40 kbps (bps = bits/s = bits per second). SILK has a low algorithmic delay of 25 ms, which is based on a 20 ms frame duration plus a 5 ms look-ahead duration. The reference programming of SILK is in C language, and the codec is based on linear predictive coding (LPC).

Skype also uses Opus as its audio codec. Opus was developed by Xiph and is standardized as RFC 6716 by the Internet Engineering Task Force (IETF). It was designed as a lossy audio coding format to efficiently encode speech and general audio into a single format. Opus was designed to combine SILK with CELT, in which switching between or combining SILK and CELT could be conducted as needed for maximum efficiency. Opus maintains low-latency sufficient for real-time interactive communications and was designed to have low complexity to run on low end ARM3 processors.

CELT is an open royalty-free lossy audio compression codec software algorithm format used by Skype. CELT has very low algorithmic delay, which is very beneficial in supporting low-latency audio communications. CELT was designed using lower latency Modified Discrete Cosine Transform (MDCT) technology.

YouTube Multimedia Codecs

YouTube is a global video-sharing website that uses H.264/MPEG-4 AVC, WebM, and Adobe Flash Video technology. Three former PayPal employees (Chad Hurley, Steve Chen, and Jawed Karim) created YouTube in February 2005. The cofounder Karim said that the inspiration for YouTube first came from the difficult experience in finding online videos of Justin Timberlake and Janet Jackson's 2004 Super Bowl halftime performance exposing incident and later the 2004 Indian Ocean tsunami, where the need of a video-sharing site was realized. Cofounders Hurley and Chen said that the original idea for YouTube was an online dating service based on videos. On February 14, 2005, the domain name www.youtube.com was activated and on April 23, 2005, the first YouTube video titled "Me at the Zoo" was uploaded, which shows cofounder Karim at the San Diego Zoo (https://en.wikipedia.org/wiki/YouTube).

In September 2005, a Nike advertisement featuring Ronaldinho reached one million views for the first time. In November 2005 to April 2006, YouTube received a $11.5 million venture investment from Sequoia Capital, and on December 15, 2005, the www.youtube.com site was officially launched. In July 2006, YouTube announced that every day there were more than 65,000 new videos uploaded. In November 2006, YouTube was bought by Google, Inc. for $1.65 billion. In 2010, the company headquarters was moved to San Bruno, California, USA. In April 2011, YouTube software engineer James Zern revealed that 30% of videos accounted for 99% of YouTube's views. In 2014, YouTube announced that every minute, 300 hours of new videos were uploaded. In 2015, YouTube was ranked as the third most visited website in the world (based on Alexa and SimilarWeb). In 2015, YouTube was attracting more than 15 billion visitors per month making it the world's top TV and video website (based on SimilarWeb). In January 2016, the San Bruno headquarters (CA, USA) was expanded to an office park that could support up to 2,800 employees based on a facility investment of $215 million.

YouTube is a representative Internet video OTT service, which enabled user-generated content (UGC) video uploading. UGC is also called user created content (UCC), which is a video that is made and uploaded mostly by amateurs. This broke the traditional video service model of professionally generated content (e.g., TV programs or videos made in studios and broadcasting companies) and direct movie/video sales (e.g., video streaming companies like Netflix, Disney+, etc.). Now, video streaming companies also use OTT service models.

YouTube video technology used to require an Adobe Flash Player plug-in to be installed in the Internet browser of the user's computer to view YouTube videos. In January 2010, YouTube's experimental site used the built-in multimedia capabilities of HTML5 web browsers to enable YouTube videos to be viewed without requiring an Adobe Flash Player or any other plug-in to be installed. On January 27, 2015, HTML5 was announced as the default playback method. HTML5 video streaming uses

MPEG Dynamic Adaptive Streaming over HTTP (DASH), which supports adaptive bit-rate HTTP based streaming by controlling the video and audio quality based on the status of the player device and network.

The preferred video format on YouTube is H.264 because older smart devices can easily decode H.264 videos more easily with less power consumption. Some older smart devices may not have a H.265 decoder installed, and even if it may be installed the power consumption and processing load may be too burdening for an older smart device. Therefore, if the wireless network (e.g., Wi-Fi, 5G, or LTE) is sufficiently good, H.264 could be the preferred video codec to use. This is why in some cases, when a user tries to upload a high-quality H.265 video to YouTube, the uploading YouTube interface may convert the H.265 video into a lower-quality H.264 format or multiple H.264 formats, which are used in MPEG-DASH. More details on MPEG-DASH are described in Chapter 6, and the technical details on YouTube recommended upload encoding settings can be found at https://support.google.com/youtube/answer/1722171?hl=en.

Netflix Multimedia Codecs

Netflix started multimedia streaming in 2007 using the Microsoft video codec VC-1 and audio codec Windows Media Audio (WMA). Currently, Netflix uses H.264 AVC and H.265 HEVC. H.264 AVC is used to support the CE3-DASH, iOS1, and iOS2 Netflix profiles. H.265 HEVC is used to support the CE4-DASH Netflix profile for UltraHD devices. CE3-DASH and CE4-DASH commonly use HE-AAC and Dolby Digital Plus for audio codecs, and iOS1 and iOS2 both use HE-AAC and Dolby Digital for audio codecs (https://en.wikipedia.org/wiki/Technical_details_of_Netflix).

Among existing Netflix encoding profiles, the following are deprecated (which means that although they are available, they are not recommended): CE1, CE2, and Silverlight use VC-1 for video and WMA for the audio codec; Link and Kirby-PIFF use H.263 for video and Ogg Vorbis for the audio codec; and Vega uses H.264 AVC for video and AC3 for the audio codec.

Table 5-1 summarizes the Netflix profile types (that are not deprecated) and corresponding video and audio codec types, multimedia container, digital rights management, and supported device types.

Table 5-1. *Netflix profile types and video and audio codec types used*

Netflix profile types	Video codec	Audio codec	Multimedia container	Digital rights management	Supported devices
CE3-DASH	H.264 AVC	HE-AAC, Dolby Digital Plus, Ogg Vorbis	Unmuxed FMP4	PlayReady, Widevine	Android devices, Roku 2, Xbox, PS3, Wii, Wii U
iOS1	H.264 AVC	HE-AAC, Dolby Digital	Muxed M2TS	PlayReady, NFKE	iPhone, iPad
iOS2	H.264 AVC	HE-AAC, Dolby Digital	Unmuxed M2TS	PlayReady, NFKE	iPhone, iPad
CE4-DASH	H.265 HEVC, VP9	HE-AAC, Dolby Digital Plus	Unmuxed FMP4	PlayReady, Widevine	UltraHD devices

Netflix uses the multimedia container file formats of fragmented MP4 (FMP4) and the MPEG-2 transport stream (M2TS). Multimedia containers enable multiple multimedia data streams to be combined into a single file which commonly includes the metadata that helps to identify the combined multimedia streams. This is why multimedia containers are also called "metafiles" or informally "wrappers" (https://en.wikipedia.org/wiki/Container_format). More details on containers, Dockers, and Kubernetes will be provided in Chapter 8.

For digital rights management (DRM), CE3-DASH and CE4-DASH use PlayReady or Widevine, and iOS1 and iOS2 use PlayReady or NFKE. DRM enables control and policy enforcement of digital multimedia legal access and is based on licensing agreements and encryption technology. DRM technologies help monitor, report, and control use, modification, and distribution of copyrighted multimedia and software. There are various technological protection measures (TPM) that enable digital rights management for multimedia content, copyrighted works, and proprietary software and hardware (`https://en.wikipedia.org/wiki/Digital_rights_management`).

Disney+ Multimedia Technology

Disney Streaming started off as BAMTech in February 2015, which was founded through MLB Advanced Media. In August 2016, one-third of the company was acquired by the Walt Disney Company for $1 billion. In October 2018, BAMTech was internally renamed to Disney Streaming Services, and in August 2021, via Twitter, it was announced that the company was renamed to Disney Streaming (`https://en.wikipedia.org/wiki/Disney_Streaming`).

Disney+ makes automatic adjustments and delivers the best multimedia quality based on device capability and network conditions. Disney+ supports the video formats of Full HD, 4K Ultra HD, HDR10, Dolby Vision, and (limited) IMAX Enhanced (`https://help.disneyplus.com/csp?id=csp_article_content&sys_kb_id=543d7f68dbbf78d01830269ed3961932`).

- **Full HD** video resolution is 1080p (higher than HD 720p).

- **4K Ultra HD** video resolution is 3840×2160 (higher than Full HD).

- **HDR10** provides a broader range of colors and brightness display and is the default High Dynamic Range (HDR) format.

- **Dolby Vision** adds screen based optimized colors and brightness dynamic control to HDR.

- **IMAX Enhanced** supports the 1.90:1 display expanded aspect ratio so the picture can cover the full height of the screen, but the other IMAX Enhanced features and functionalities are not supported yet.

H.264/MPEG-4 AVC Video Technology

H.264 is also called MPEG-4 Part 10 Advanced Video Coding (AVC), which was developed by the project partnership Joint Video Team (JVT) of ITU-T Video Coding Experts Group (VCEG) and ISO/IEC JTC1 Moving Picture Experts Group (MPEG)[1]. Worldwide, H.264 and H.265 are the two most popular standards for video recording, compression, and distribution, in which details on H.265 are provided in the following section. The ITU-T standards for H.264 AVC for generic audiovisual services can be found at `www.itu.int/rec/T-REC-H.264`.

H.264 was designed to have half or a lesser bitrate compared to MPEG-2, H.263, or MPEG-4 Part 2 without increasing the complexity too much. H.264 uses block-oriented motion compensation compression, similar to former standards like H.262 and H.263. The increased

---

[1] ITU-T stands for the "International Telecommunication Union-Telecommunication Standardization Sector," ISO/IEC JTC1 stands for the "Joint technical committee of the International Organization for Standardization (ISO)," and IEC stands for the "International Electrotechnical Commission." These international organizations develop, maintain, and promote information technology (IT) and information and communications technology (ICT) standards.

computation complexity of H.264 considers the improved processing capability of CPUs and GPUs on modern devices. H.264 is a family of standards that composes several different video encoding profiles, but because a H.264 decoder installed on a device may not be able to decode all profiles, the decodable profiles need to be informed through exchange of information with the content provider. H.264 compression results in lower bitrates compared to its former standardized video codecs. H.264 lossless encoding is possible but is rarely used. A list of the H.264 video encoding profiles is provided in the following section (`https://doi.org/10.1007/978-3-030-62124-7_12`).

Luma and Chroma

Since we are studying video technologies, it is necessary to understand the terms "luma" and "chroma." In simplest terms, "luma" is used to represent the image's brightness level, and "chroma" is used to represent the image's color, which is combined through red (R), green (G), and blue (B) light sources. This is why luma and chroma are commonly paired together.

The general term "brightness" is commonly used as a perceived concept and is not objectively measurable. This is why "luminance" and "luma" are used in science and engineering. Luminance is defined in a way that is both quantifiable and accurately measurable. In technical terms, "luma" is different from "luminance." Based on the International Commission on Illumination (CIE)[2], application-wise, "luma" is used in video engineering (like the H.264, H.265, H.266 codecs and standards) where "relative luminance" is used in color science.

Luminance represents the level of brightness of a beam of light towards a direction. Luminance is represented by the luminance intensity of a beam of light based on the unit of candela per meter square (cd/m^2),

---

[2] CIE stands for the "Commission internationale de l'éclairage."

which is defined by the International System of Units. The unit *candela* (cd) is the Latin word for "candle," which is the basis of brightness for this unit. One candela (i.e., 1 cd) is the luminous intensity of approximately one (ordinary) wax candle.

In video engineering, "relative luminance" is sometimes used to represent a monitor's brightness. Relative luminance is derived from a weighted sum of linear RGB components. On the other hand, luma uses gamma-compressed RGB components.

The Gamma (γ) encoding applied in the luma computation helps to optimize the bits encoding efficiency of an image. Gamma encoding is based on the gamma correction nonlinear operation used to encode and decode luminance (Y) and luma (Y') values. The basic equation has the form of $Y'=AY^{\gamma}$ (other equations exist), where A=1 is commonly used. If γ<1, the encoding process is called gamma compression. If γ>1, the encoding process is called gamma expansion (e.g., γ=2.2). For the special case of γ=1 and A=1, there is no change, resulting in Y=Y'. The same rule can be applied to RGB as well using $R'=AR^{\gamma}$, $G'=AG^{\gamma}$, and $B'=AB^{\gamma}$ (other equations exist).

Examples of how luma is computed using the weighted sum of gamma-compressed RGB video components are provided (please note that the actual process is more complicated and other equations exist). In the ITU-R Rec. BT.709, relative luminance (Y) is calculated based on a linear combination of R, G, B pure colorimetric values using Y=0.2126R+0.7152G+0.0722B. However, luma (Y') is calculated in the Rec. 709 specs based on the gamma-compressed R, G, B components R', G', B', respectively, using Y'=0.2126R'+0.7152G'+0.0722B'. For luma calculations, the commonly used digital standard CCIR 601 uses Y'=0.299R'+0.587G'+0.114B', and the SMPTE 240M equation Y'=0.212R'+0.701G'+0.087B' is used for transitional 1035i HDTV[3].

---

[3] CCIR stands for the "Comité Consultatif International pour la Radio," and SMPTE stands for the "Society of Motion Picture and Television Engineers."

Chroma is Greek for the word "color" and a shortened version of the word "chrominance." The chroma components notation of $Y'C_bC_r$ is commonly used to represent a family of color spaces, where the luma is Y', the blue-difference is C_b, and red-difference is C_r (https://en.wikipedia.org/wiki/YCbCr).

For example, based on the ITU-R BT.601 conversion 8 bits per sample case, the digital $Y'C_bC_r$ values are derived from analog $R'G'B'$ using the equations $Y'=16+(65.481R'+128.553G'+24.966B')$, $C_b=128+(-37.797R'-74.203G'+112B')$, and $C_r=128+(112R'-93.786G'-18.214B')$.

Human vision is more sensitive to notice changes in brightness than it acknowledges changes in color. This effect is used in "chroma subsampling" technology to reduce the encoded bitrate while maintaining the same perceived quality of an image to the human eyes (which means that there is no difference in the quality of the video to the viewer). Therefore, in chroma subsampling technology, more bits are assigned to the luma (Y') representation, and less bits are assigned to the encoding of the color difference values C_b and C_r (https://en.wikipedia.org/wiki/Chroma_subsampling).

Chroma subsampling schemes are classified using a three number sequence $S_1:S_2:S_3$ or a four number sequence $S_1:S_2:S_3:S_4$. Chroma samples are commonly defined in a matrix format that has two rows of pixels and S_1 columns of pixels (which is commonly 4). S_2 represents the number of chroma samples (C_r, C_b) in the first row of the S_1 pixels. S_3 represents the number of changes of chroma samples (C_r, C_b) between the first and second row of the S_1 pixels. S_4 represents the horizontal factor. Figure 5-1 presents simplified examples of the popular chroma subsampling formats, which include 4:4:4, 4:2:2, 4:2:0, and 4:1:1.

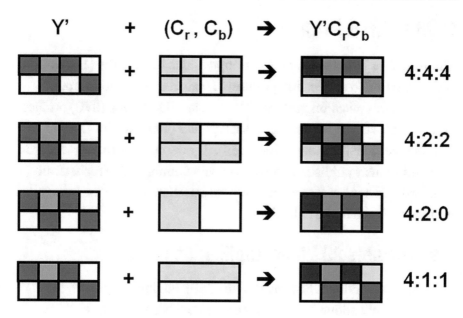

Figure 5-1. *Chroma Subsampling Examples*

The H.264, H.265, and H.266 video codecs can use one or three color plane arrays of the pixel sample value bit depth. The luma color plane is the primary color plane, which is used to represent local brightness information. Chroma planes can be used to represent color hue and saturation. In the 4:4:4 format, all three color planes have the same resolution. In the 4:2:0 format, compared to the luma plane, the chroma planes have half the width and half the height. In the 4:2:2 format, compared to the luma plane, the chroma planes have the same height but half the width. The 4:4:4 format is used by computer desktop sharing and wireless display applications, and the 4:2:0 format is used by many consumer applications (https://ieeexplore.ieee.org/document/9503377).

H.264 Video Profiles

There are four H.264 video profile groups, which include the (1) non-scalable 2D video application profiles; (2) camcorders, editing, and professional application profiles; (3) scalable video coding (SVC) profiles; and (4) multiview video coding (MVC) profiles (`www.itu.int/ITU-T/recommendations/rec.aspx?id=14659`). As new updates to the standards are continuously published, the reader is recommended to recheck all standard updates before making a profile selection, as only the basic profiles are listed in the following.

Non-scalable 2D Video Application Profiles

- Constrained Baseline Profile (CBP): For low-cost applications. Used in videoconferencing and mobile applications

- Baseline Profile (BP): For low-cost applications that require additional data loss robustness. Used in videoconferencing and mobile applications

- Extended Profile (XP): For streaming video. Has a relatively high compression capability with enhanced robustness to support data losses and server stream switching

- Main Profile (MP): For standard-definition digital TV broadcasts using the MPEG-4 DVB Digital Video Broadcasting (DVB) standard. Used for HDTV, but rarely used after high profile (HP)

- High Profile (HP): For DVB HDTV broadcast and disc storage applications. Used as the Blu-ray Disc storage format and DVB HDTV broadcast services

- Progressive High Profile (PHiP): Similar to HP without field coding features

- Constrained High Profile: Similar to PHiP without B (bi-predictive) slices

- High 10 Profile (Hi10P): Builds on HP with added support for up to 10 bits per sample of decoded picture precision

- High 4:2:2 Profile (Hi422P): For professional applications that use interlaced video. Builds on Hi10P with added support for the 4:2:2 chroma subsampling format while using up to 10 bits per sample of decoded picture precision

- High 4:4:4 Predictive Profile (Hi444PP): Builds on top of Hi422P supporting up to 4:4:4 chroma sampling with up to 14 bits per sample. Uses efficient lossless region coding and individual pictures as three separate color planes coding

Camcorders, Editing, and Professional Application Profiles

Four additional Intra-frame-only profiles are used mostly for professional applications involving camera and editing systems:

- High 10 Intra Profile

- High 4:2:2 Intra Profile

- High 4:4:4 Intra Profile

- Context-adaptive variable-length coding (CAVLC) 4:4:4 Intra Profile

Scalable Video Coding (SVC)

- Scalable Constrained Baseline Profile: Primarily for real-time communication applications

- Scalable High Profile: Primarily for broadcast and streaming applications

- Scalable Constrained High Profile: Primarily for real-time communication applications

- Scalable High Intra Profile: Primarily for production applications. Constrained to all-intra use

Multiview Video Coding (MVC)

- Stereo High Profile: Profile for two-view stereoscopic 3D video

- Multiview High Profile: Profile for two or more views using both inter-picture (temporal) and MVC inter-view prediction

- Multiview Depth High Profile: Profile for 3D video content improved compression through depth map and video texture information joint coding

- Enhanced Multiview Depth High Profile: Profile for enhanced combined multiview coding with depth information

H.264 AVC Encoder and Decoder

In this section, more details on the H.264 AVC encoder and decoder are provided (https://doi.org/10.1007/978-3-030-62124-7_12).

H.264 divides an image into a sequential group of macroblocks based on raster scan order, which each group is called a slice. Figure 5-2 presents an example of an image divided into slices.

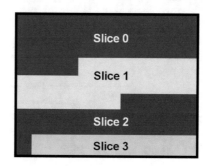

Figure 5-2. *Example of an Image Divided into Slices*

A simplified H.264 AVC encoder is presented in Figure 5-3. The H.264 encoder includes integer transform, variable block-size motion compensation, quarter-pixel accuracy in motion vectors, multiple reference picture motion compensation, intra-frame directional spatial prediction, scaling, quantization, in-loop deblocking filter, context-adaptive variable length coding (CAVLC), context-adaptive binary arithmetic coding (CABAC), entropy coding, etc.

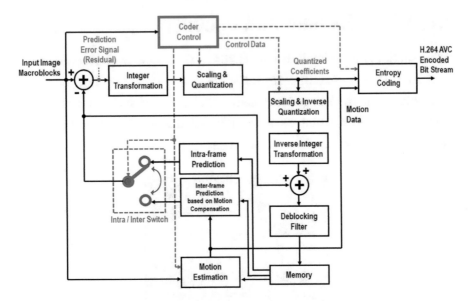

Figure 5-3. *H.264 AVC Encoder Structure*

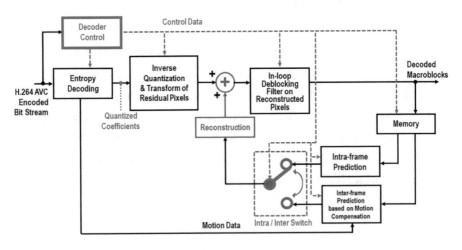

Figure 5-4. *H.264 AVC Decoder Structure*

A simplified H.264 AVC decoder example is presented in Figure 5-4. The decoder operates in the reverse order of the encoder in reconstructing the original image from the compressed encoded bit stream. The decoder uses entropy decoding, inverse quantization, transform of residual pixels, motion compensation, inter-fame prediction, intra-fame prediction, reconstruction, in-loop deblocking filter, etc. in reconstructing the video images.

More details on the H.264 AVC encoder are provided in the following. File size compression is conducted using both intra-frame prediction and inter-frame prediction in H.264. Intra-frame prediction is used to compress the file size of an image using parts mostly within that individual frame. Inter-frame prediction is used to compress the file size of an image using parts mostly from other images (e.g., P and B frames), where more details on I, P, and B frames will be provided later in this chapter. In a video, motion changes take place over multiple images, so motion compensation must use inter-frame prediction algorithms. Since images of a video are interrelated, in-loop processing is used to provide the feedback loop operations needed to compress the video file (in the encoder) and decompress the video file (in the decoder) of the H.264 video codec system.

Integer Transform: After the macroblocks are obtained, integer transform is applied. H.264 uses a simple 4×4 discrete cosine transformation (DCT) with integer-precision. This is based on the fact that the residual pixels have a very low level of spatial correlation in the H.264 I and P frame prediction schemes. Earlier video codec standards used larger and more complex DCTs, which were a burden to the graphics processor and resulted in prediction shift errors due to the rounding errors that occurred in the floating-point calculations that were conducted in the DCT and inverse DCT (IDTC) transformation processes. An inverse integer transform is performed before the deblocking filter and will be used in the feedback loop of the H.264 encoding process.

DCT is a process that converts a time-domain signal into frequency-domain signals, which is a spectral signal decomposition technique. DCT changes a time-domain signal into a sum of multiple frequency domain signals (that are represented with cosine signals) that have different frequencies. Integer transformation is an integer DCT process, which is an integer approximation of the DCT. The integer approximation process enables selectable block sizes to be used, which results in exactly matching integer computations. The integer approximation significantly helps to reduce the computation complexity, which results in low complexity and no drifting. DCT alone (without integer approximation) is known to create undesired prediction shifts due to the rounding errors in the floating-point calculations conducted in the DCT and IDCT processes. Integer transform helps to improve the intra-coding spatial prediction accuracy, which is followed by transform coding.

Scaling and Quantization: After the integer transform, H.264 conducts a combined scaling and quantization process. The integer transform values go through a quantization process using a 4×4 quantization matrix that maps values to quantized levels. Then the scaling process is applied, which is a normalization process of values, where all values are mapped to values within 0 to 1. A scaling and inverse quantization process will be performed before the inverse integer transform is conducted in the feedback loop.

Entropy Coding: Entropy coding is a lossless data compression scheme that has the characteristics to approach the limit of data compression without losing any information or resolution of the image. H.264 uses three entropy coding schemes, which are the Exponential-Golomb (Exp-Golomb) code, context-adaptive variable length coding (CAVLC), and context-adaptive binary arithmetic coding (CABAC). H.264 entropy coding has two modes that are distinguished by the "entropy_coding_mode" parameter settings, which apply different encoding techniques. If the entropy_coding_mode = 0, the header data, motion vectors, and non-residual data are encoded with Exp-Golomb, and the quantized residual coefficients are encoded using CAVLC. Exp-Golomb is a simpler scheme than CAVLC. If the entropy_coding_mode = 1, then CABAC is applied, which is a combination of the binarization, context modeling, and binary arithmetic coding (BAC) processes. BAC is a scheme that results in a high data compression rate. Binarization coverts all nonbinary data into a string of binary bits (bins) for the BAC process. Context modeling has two modes, the regular coding mode and the bypass coding mode. Regular coding mode executes the context model selection and access process, where the statistics of the context are used to derive probability models, which are used to build context models in which the conditional probabilities (for the bins) are stored. Bypass coding mode does not apply context modeling and is used to expedite the coding speed.

CAVLC has a relatively complex process of quantizing the residual coefficients. CABAC is very effective in compressing images that include symbols with a probability greater than 0.5, in which algorithms like CAVLC are inefficient. For example, H.264 main and high profiles use CABAC for compression of selected data parts as well as the quantized residual coefficients. This is why CABAC is continuously applied in H.265 and H.266 entropy coding, but CAVLC is not.

Intra-frame Prediction: H.264 conducts a more sophisticated intra-frame directional spatial prediction process compared to earlier video codec standards (e.g., H.262 and H.263). Neighboring reconstructed pixels from intra-coded or inter-coded reconstructed pixels are used in the prediction process of intra-coded macroblocks. Each intra-coded macroblock can be formed using 16×16 or 4×4 intra prediction block size. Each intra-coded macroblock will be determined through a comparison of different prediction modes applied to the macroblock. The prediction mode that results in the smallest prediction error is applied to the macroblock. The prediction error is the difference (residual value of the subtraction process) between the predicted value and the actual value of the macroblock. The prediction errors go through a 4×4 integer transform coding process. In a macroblock, each 4×4 block can have a different prediction mode applied, which influences the level of the video encoding resolution in H.264.

Deblocking Filter: Due to the macroblock-based encoding mechanism applied, undesirable block structures can become visible. The deblocking filter has two general types (deblocking and smoothing) which are applied to the 4×4 block edges to eliminate the visible undesirable block structures. The deblocking filter's length, strength, and type are adjusted considering the macroblock coding parameters and edge detection based spatial activity. The macroblock coding parameters include the reference frame difference, coded coefficients, as well as the intra-coding or inter-coding method applied.

Variable Block-Size Motion Compensation: In H.264, the default macroblock size is 16×16. Alternatively, dividing the 16×16 macroblock into four 8×8 partitions can be used. Each macroblock or partition can be divided into smaller sub-partitions for more accurate motion estimation. Based on the 16×16 structure, there are four M-type options (sub-partitions) that can be used, which include the 16×16, two 16×8 sub-partitions, two 8×16 sub-partitions, and four 8×8 sub-partitions. Based on the 8×8 partitions, there are also four 8×8-type options (sub-partitions) that can be used, which include the 8×8, two 8×4 sub-partitions, two 4×8 sub-partitions, and four 4×4 sub-partitions. These eight type options are presented in Figure 5-5, which are used as the basic blocks in the H.264 luma image inter-frame motion estimation process. In H.264, the motion compensation accuracy is at a quarter-pixel precision level for luma images. This process is conducted using a six-tap filtering method applied to first obtain the half-pixel position values, and these values were averaged to obtain the quarter-pixel position values.

Using these H.264 video compression techniques, I, P, and B frames are formed. I frames are intra (I) coded independent pictures that serve as keyframes for the following P and B inter-frame prediction processes. P frames are predictive (P) coded pictures obtained from inter-frame prediction of previous I and P frames. B frames are bipredictive (B) coded pictures that are obtained from inter-frame prediction of I, P, and other B frames.

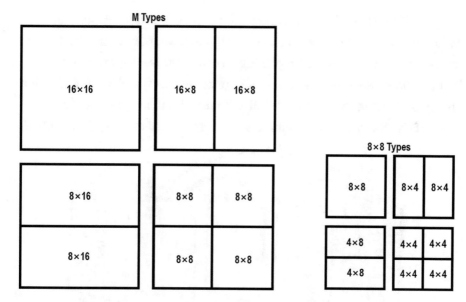

Figure 5-5. *H.264 Macroblock Segmentation-Type Options (M Types and 8×8 Types) for Motion Estimation*

Group of Pictures (GOP): Based on H.264 and related MPEG standards, the first and last frame in a GOP are I frames, and in between these I frames, there are P frames and B frames. The reference frames of a GOP can be an I frame or P frame, and a GOP can have multiple reference frames. Macroblocks in P frames are based on forward prediction of changes in the image. Macroblocks in B frames are predicted using both forward prediction and backward prediction combinations. In Figure 5-6, I_0 is the reference frame for P_1, I_0 and P_1 are the reference frames for P_2, and I_0 and P_2 are the reference frames for P_3. In addition, I_0, P_2, and P_3 are the reference frames for B_1.

H.264 can have a GOP structure that has no B frames, or use multiple reference frames, or apply hierarchical prediction structures.

A H.264 GOP with no B frames would reduce the compression rate, which means that the video file size would be larger. But not using B frames would enable the H.264 video playing device to use less memory (because B frame processing requires more memory to process) and require a lighter image processing load. A H.264 GOP with no B frames is presented in Figure 5-7, where there are four reference frames, which are I_0, P_1, P_2, and P_3.

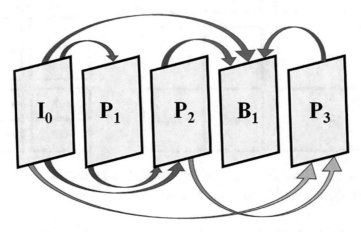

Figure 5-6. *H.264 GOP Formation Example Based on I, P, and B Frames*

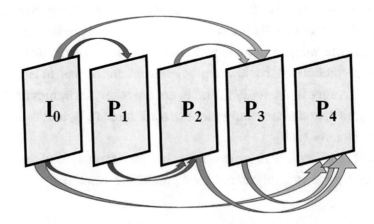

Figure 5-7. *H.264 GOP Formation Process Example with No B Frames*

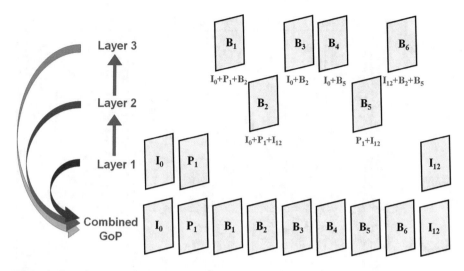

Figure 5-8. *H.264 Hierarchical Prediction Based GOP Formation Example*

Hierarchical Prediction Structure: A H.264 hierarchical prediction example is presented in Figure 5-8, where the GOP starts with I_0 and ends with I_{12}, where I_0 is the reference frame for P_1. Layer 1 is formed with three frames I_0, P_1, and I_{12}. Using layer 1 frames, the layer 2 frames B_2 and B_5 are formed. B_2 is predicted using I_0, P_1, and I_{21}. B_5 is predicted using P_1 and I_{21}. Using the layer 1 and layer 2 frames, the layer 3 frames B_1, B_3, B_4, and B_6 are formed. B_1 is predicted using I_0, P_1, and B_2. B_3 is predicted using I_0 and B_2. B_4 is predicted using I_0 and B_5. B_6 is predicted using I_{12}, B_2, and B_5. For technical accuracy, please note that the "+" sign used in Figure 5-8 indicates a combination of pixel information of image parts used in the inter-prediction process, and not that the actual image pixel values were just all added up. For example, "$I_{12}+B_2+B_5$" means that B_6 was predicted using the frames I_{12}, B_2, and B_5. In addition, in order to control the video compression efficiency, larger quantization parameters can be applied to layers that are formed later down the hierarchy sequence.

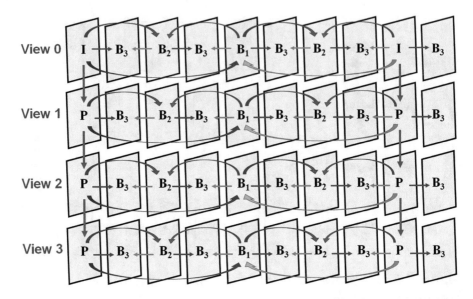

Figure 5-9. *H.264 MVC Process Example*

H.264 supports multiview video coding (MVC), which enables users to select their preferred views (if this option is available). MVC is especially important for new XR systems and advanced multimedia applications. For example, Free Viewpoint Video (FVV) services use MVC. Figure 5-9 shows a H.264 MVC process example based on four views. MVC takes advantage of the hierarchical prediction structure and uses the interview prediction process based on the key pictures. Among the views, View 0 uses I frames as its reference frames, whereas View 1, View 2, and View 3 use P frames which are based on View 0's I frames (and a sequence of P frames), which creates a vertical IPPP frames relation among the different views. Within each view, the same hierarchical prediction structure is applied in the example of Figure 5-9.

H.265/MPEG-5 HEVC Video Technology

In this section, details on the H.265 video codec are provided (https://doi.org/10.1007/978-3-030-62124-7_12). H.265 is also known as MPEG-H Part 2 High Efficiency Video Coding (HEVC), which is a successor of the H.264/MPEG-4 AVC video codec. The H.265 HEVC standards were jointly developed by the Joint Collaborative Team on Video Coding (JCT-VC), which consists of the ISO/IEC MPEG group and the ITU-T VCEG. In April 2013, H.265 standard version 1 was approved. HEVC was also classified in MPEG-H Part 2 by the ISO/IEC which was published in August 2020 in the standard document ISO/IEC 23008-2:2020 titled "Information Technology - High Efficiency Coding and Media Delivery in Heterogeneous Environments - Part 2: High Efficiency Video Coding" (www.iso.org/standard/75484.html).

The two main objectives of H.265 is to improve the compression ratio by 50% compared to H.264 (especially for higher video resolutions like the 7680×4320 for 8K UHDTV) and to reduce the coding and decoding complexity and time (especially by using advanced parallel processing technologies). Several publications claim that H.265 has accomplished a 50% or higher compression ratio compared to H.264 images with the same visual quality.

Extended Macroblock Size (EMS) structures are used in H.265, instead of the macroblocks used in H.264. These are formed using the Coding Tree Block (CTB) structure which has a 64×64 pixel maximum block size, which is much larger than the 16×16 pixel macroblock size used in H.264. These larger block structures are used to form Coding Tree Units (CTUs) to improve the picture sub-partition into a wider range of sized structure blocks.

CTB is the largest block of H.265, where the luma CTB size is N×N and the chroma CTB size is (N/2)×(N/2), where N=16, 32, or 64. CTUs consist of one luma CTB and two chroma CTBs. CTBs consist of coding blocks (CBs) which are square blocks in the quadtree. A luma CB is 8×8 or larger and a chroma CB is 4×4 or larger. A coding unit (CU) has one luma CB and two chroma CBs. To improve the prediction accuracy, a CB can be divided into multiple prediction blocks (PBs). Intra prediction uses the CBs and PBs as processing units. A luma or chroma CB can be divided into one, two, or four PBs that are rectangular but do not have to be a square. Prediction units (PUs) include the prediction syntax and the corresponding luma or chroma PUs. A CB can be divided into multiple transform blocks (TBs) of sizes from 4×4 up to 32×32 to minimize the residual errors of the transform coding process. TBs can span across multiple PB boundaries to increase the compression ratio. A transform unit (TU) contains the luma and chroma of the TBs.

The video image slices are also divided into tiles in H.265, so the video images can be processed parallel using multiple threads. As mentioned above, H.265 was designed to be more efficient in parallel processing systems. The CTU rows can be processed in parallel by assigning them as multiple threads using the wavefront parallel processing (WPP) technology included in H.265.

Figure 5-10 presents an example of the H.265 CTB partitioning, where (a) shows the CTB partitioning in which the CB boundaries are represented with solid lines and the TB boundaries are represented with dotted lines and (b) presents the quadtree of the same CTB.

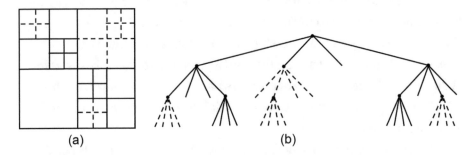

(a)   (b)

Figure 5-10. *H.265 CTB Partitioning Example, Where (a) Shows the CTB Partitioning and (b) Presents the Quadtree of the Same CTB*

Figure 5-11 presents the H.265 HEVC encoder structure and Figure 5-12 presents the H.265 HEVC decoder structure, where parts with major enhancements (compared to H.264) are marked in red. The encoder receives CTUs of the image as inputs to the system and converts the image frames into a compressed encoded bit stream (output). The decoder operates in the reverse order of the encoder to convert the H.265 compressed encoded bit stream back into video image frames.

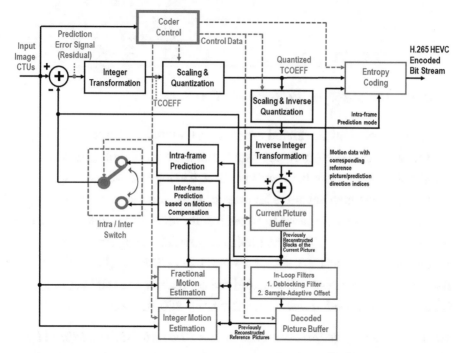

Figure 5-11. *H.265 HEVC Encoder Structure*

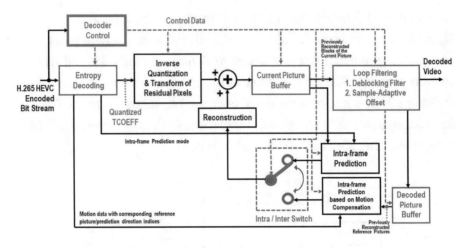

Figure 5-12. *H.265 HEVC Decoder Structure*

H.265 uses many advanced techniques that make its video compression rate extremely high, such that the encoded file size using H.265 will be much smaller than the file size using H.264 encoding. Table 5-2 presents the average bit rate compression rate reduction obtained by H.265 compared to H.264 for the 480p, 720p, 1080p, and 2160p video profiles (https://en.wikipedia.org/wiki/High_Efficiency_Video_Coding). The ITU-T standards for H.265 HEVC can be found at www.itu.int/rec/T-REC-H.265, and the conformance specifications H.265.1 can be found at www.itu.int/rec/T-REC-H.265.1.

Table 5-2. *Average bitrate compression rate reduction obtained by H.265 compared to H.264*

Video profiles	480p	720p	1080p	2160p
H.265	52%	56%	62%	64%

This benefit of resulting in a smaller file size is very beneficial for saving and sending video files over the Internet, as a smaller file can be delivered quicker while using less network bandwidth. In addition, H.265

profiles include improved video quality (e.g., reduced blocking artifacts and distortion, improved color and resolution) and support of videos for wider and diverse screen types. H.265 requires much more processing compared to H.624, which is why many multimedia services still use H.264. There are many advanced technologies applied to H.265, where a few features are described in the following.

Large Transform Size (LTS): H.265 uses discrete cosine transform (DCT) and discrete sine transform (DST) with block sizes from 4×4 up to 32×32. This is much larger than the DCT block sizes of 4×4 and 8×8 used in H.264.

Internal Bit Depth Increase (IBDI): For each pixel of an image, the number of bits used to define its color is called the bit depth, color depth, or colour depth. H.265 uses IBDI to increase the bit depth so the rounding errors that occur in internal calculations can be reduced. IBDI is beneficial to the color quality representation and compression rate as well as helps to determine the output bit depth.

Sample Adaptive Offset (SAO): In-loop filtering is used to eliminate the blocking artifacts of the recon picture. In H.264, only the deblocking filter (DF) was used in a passive way. In H.265, in addition to using a DF, SAO is also applied in low complexity (LC) conditions. For H.265 high efficiency (HE) conditions, in addition to using DF and SAO, an adaptive loop filter (ALF) is also applied. For neighboring pixels near block edges that have large levels of distortion, a compensation offset is adaptively applied using the SAO filter. ALFs have been used in many video codecs where the optimal coefficients are derived to minimize the difference between the original image and the decoded image from the compressed video file.

CABAC: CABAC is an entropy coding engine used in H.264 that had some throughput bottleneck issues that were improved in H.265. Entropy coding is used in H.264 and H.265 to compress syntax elements during the video encoding process final steps. The encoded and compressed syntax elements include motion vectors, prediction modes, and coefficients.

Since entropy coding is used in the final steps of the encoding process, entropy decoding is used in the first step of the video decoding process. Many improvements in H.265 were made to CABAC, which include reduction in context coded bins, reduction in total bins, and grouping of bypass bins (www.researchgate.net/publication/261416853_A_comparison_of_CABAC_throughput_for_HEVCH265_vs_AVCH264).

H.265 profile version 1 was released in 2013, version 2 was released in 2014, version 3 was released in 2015, and version 4 was released in 2016. As new updates to the standards are continuously published, the reader is recommended to recheck all standard updates before making a profile selection, as only the basic profiles are listed in the following:

- Version 1 (2013)

    - Main: For 8-bit colors per sample with 4:2:0 chroma sampling

    - Main 10: For 10-bit colors per sample

    - Main Still Picture: Allows for a single still picture to be encoded

- Version 2 (2014)

    - Main 12: For 8 bits to 12 bits per sample with 4:0:0 and 4:2:0 chroma sampling

    - Main 4:4:4 Intra: Supports 4:0:0, 4:2:2, 4:4:4 chroma sampling. To be used by intra (I) frames only

    - High Throughput 4:4:4 16 Intra: For 8 bits to 16 bits per sample with 4:0:0, 4:2:0, 4:2:2, and 4:4:4 chroma sampling. To be used for high end professional content creation

    - Scalable Main: Appropriate for Internet streaming and broadcasting

- Monochrome: For black and white video with 4:0:0 chroma sampling

- Multiview (MV) Profile: For multiview video image synthesizing taken from multiple cameras based on various viewpoints

- Version 3 (2015)

  - High Throughput 4:4:4: For 8 bits to 10 bits per sample. Provides a maximum bit rate six times higher than the Main 4:4:4 profile

  - 3D Main: For three-dimensional video

  - Screen-Extended Main: Suitable for graphic and animation video

  - Screen-Extended High Throughput 4:4:4: Combines the characteristics of screen-extended main profile and high throughput profile

  - Scalable Monochrome: Combines monochrome profile for black and white video and scalable profile for streaming

- Version 4 (2016)

  - Screen Content Coding (SCC) Extensions: For screen content video which contains text and graphics, adaptive color transform, and adaptive motion vector transform

  - Scalable Range Extensions: Scalable Monochrome profiles, Scalable Main 4:4:4

H.266 VCC Video Technology

This section describes the H.266 video codec key parts (`https://doi.org/10.1007/978-3-030-62124-7_12`). H.266 Versatile Video Coding (VVC) is the successor of the H.265 HEVC. VVC was created by the Joint Video Exploration Team (JVET), composed of MPEG and VCEG. H.266 provides support for diverse video resolutions from SD, HD, 4K, 8K, 16K, and High Dynamic Range Rendering (HDRR) video. H.266 is extremely effective in video compression while preserving the video's original quality. In comparison with H.265, the encoding complexity of H.266 is expected to be about ten times higher, and the decoding complexity is expected to be about two times higher. The ITU-T standards for H.266 VVC can be found at `www.itu.int/rec/T-REC-H.266-202204-I/en`.

The core structure of the H.266 VVC system uses the block-based hybrid video coding process, transport interface, parameter sets, and network abstraction layer (NAL) units based bitstream structure that are similar to H.264 AVC and H.265 HEVC. Among the many enhancements included in H.266 VVC (compared to H.264 AVC and H.265 HEVC), the essential ones are summarized in the following and marked red in Figure 5-13, which present the H.266 VVC encoder block diagram. Some of the H.266 VVC encoder differences compared to the H.265 HEVC encoder include improved luma mapping with chroma scaling, a combined inter-prediction and intra-picture prediction option, and advanced in-loop filters (`https://ieeexplore.ieee.org/document/9503377`). The corresponding new parts in the H.266 decoder are marked red in Figure 5-14.

The main H.266 codec functions include block partitioning, intra-picture prediction, inter-picture prediction, transforms and quantization, entropy coding, in-loop filters, and screen content coding tools. These seven enhancement parts of H.266 are summarized in the following, which include the three major encoder improvement (i.e., luma mapping with chroma scaling, combined inter-prediction and intra-picture prediction option, and advanced in-loop filters) technologies.

Block Partitioning: H.266 can conduct more flexible partitioning while supporting larger block sizes than in H.265 because the H.266 CTU quadtree partitioning has been extended. As a result, H.266 supports recursive non-square splits and separate partitioning for luma and chroma for video encoding enhancements. H.266 block partitioning technology includes use of Quadtree Plus Multi-Type Tree (QT+MTT), Chroma Separate Tree (CST), and Virtual Pipeline Data Units (VPDUs).

Intra-picture Prediction: H.266 uses advanced intra-picture prediction techniques based on DC mode and planar modes by using 93 angles in angular prediction (H.265 uses 33 angles). In addition, H.266 uses more advanced luma matrix-based prediction modes and chroma cross-component prediction modes. H.266 intra-picture prediction technology includes use of finer-granularity angular prediction, wide-angle intra prediction (WAIP), four-tap fractional sample interpolation filters, position-dependent prediction combination (PDPC), multiple reference lines (MRL), matrix-based intra-picture prediction (MIP), intra sub-partition (ISP) mode, cross-component linear model (CCLM), and extended most probable mode (MPM) signaling.

Inter-picture Prediction: H.266 inter-picture prediction is improved by the following four factors. First, H.266 includes many new coding tools to improve the representation efficiency, provide more accurate prediction and coding of motion compensation control information, and enhance the motion compensation process. H.266 inter-picture prediction is improved due to more advanced coding motion information by using history-based MV prediction (HMVP), symmetric MVD (SMVD), adaptive MV resolution (AMVR), pairwise average MV merge candidate, and merge with MVD (MMVD) technologies. Second, the CU level motion compensation is enhanced in H.266 by using more flexible weights on prediction signals and by including a combination of inter-picture prediction and intra-picture prediction with signaling of biprediction weights at the CU level. By adding the ability to predict non-rectangular partitions inside a CU by applying weighting matrices on prediction signals, the motion compensation performance is enhanced. CU level motion compensation technologies include geometric partitioning mode (GPM), combined intra-/inter-picture prediction (CIIP), and biprediction with CU-level weights (BCW). Third, H.266 uses refined subblock-based motion compensation which helps in motion representation with higher accuracy. The essential techniques include subblock-based temporal MV prediction (SBTMVP), prediction refinement with optical flow (PROF), decoder MV refinement (DMVR), bidirectional optical flow (BDOF), and affine motion which can help to reduce high-order deformation due to non-translational motion (e.g., zooming and rotation) as well as improve representation of translational motion between the reference picture and other pictures. Fourth, H.266 uses horizontal wraparound motion compensation to provide improved support for specific immersive video projection formats.

Integer Transform: H.266 applies integer transform to the prediction residual and then conducts quantization of the transform coefficients using the following functions: larger and non-square transforms, multiple transform selection (MTS), low frequency non-separable transform (LFNST), subblock transform (SBT) mode, extended quantization control, adaptive chroma QP offset, dependent quantization (DQ), and joint coding of chroma residuals (JCCR).

Entropy Coding: The entropy coding used in H.266 is CABAC with improved coefficient coding and high-accuracy multi-hypothesis probability estimation technology.

In-Loop Filters: The in-loop filters in H.266 that are applied to the reconstructed video signal include luma mapping with chroma scaling (LMCS), long deblocking filters, luma-adaptive deblocking, adaptive loop filter (ALF), and cross-component ALF (CC-ALF).

Screen Content Coding Tools: H.266 includes screen content coding tools to increase the coding efficiency for diverse camera-captured content, which include screen sharing apps and gaming apps. Applied technologies include palette mode, adaptive color transform (ACT), intra-picture block copy (IBC), block-based differential pulse-code modulation (BDPCM), and transform skip residual coding (TSRC).

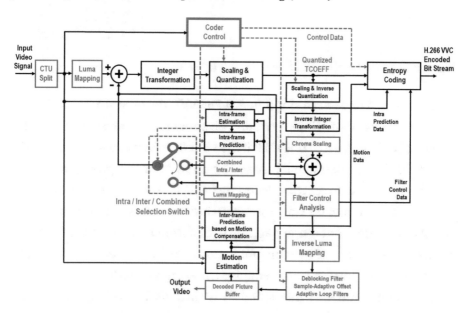

Figure 5-13. *H.266 VVC Encoder Structure*

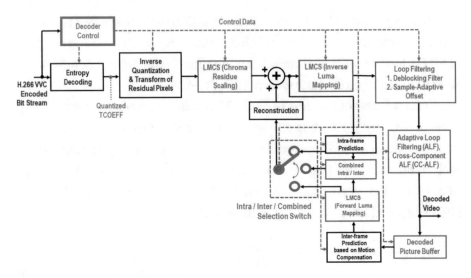

Figure 5-14. *H.266 VVC Decoder Structure*

Figure 5-14 presents a simplified H.266 VVC decoder structure. The decoder processes the H.266 encoded bit stream in the reverse order of the encoder. CTUs consist of one CTB if the video signal is monochrome and three CTBs if the video signal is based on three color components. H.266 decoding begins with entropy decoding using CABAC. Next the inverse quantization and inverse transformation are conducted outputting the decoded residue. After luma mapping with chroma scaling (LMCS), the residuals are combined with the prediction signals. The prediction signals are based on the intra-frame prediction, inter-frame prediction, and the combined inter and intra prediction (CIIP) signals. LMCS helps to increase the coding efficiency by remapping the luma and rescaling the chroma such that the signal range is more effectively used. In the decoder, LMCS based inverse luma mapping is conducted because the deblocking filter was designed to be processed on the subjective criteria of the original sample domain values. The blocking artifacts are minimized through the deblocking filter. The ringing artifacts are minimized, and corrections in the local average intensity variations are made by the sample adaptive offset process. Next, adaptive loop filtering (ALF) and cross-component ALF (CC-ALF) are conducted to correct the signal based on linear filtering and adaptive filtering. Compared to H.265, H.266 applies additional ALF, CC-ALF, and LMCS processes, which are the new in-loop filtering technologies (https://ieeexplore.ieee.org/document/9399506).

Holography Technology

Holographic displays control light diffraction to create a virtual 3D object using a special display system (e.g., special glass display, 3D monitor, particle chamber, project devices, etc.), where the generated 3D object is called a holograph. Due to this characteristic, holographic displays are different from 3D displays (https://en.wikipedia.org/wiki/Holographic_display). There are many methods to generate a holograph, and currently there are few commercial products that can be used for video services.

There are AR systems that can display holographic images, but technical development and standardization of holographic display technology is needed for it to be incorporated into successful consumer electronics (CE) products.

Hologram Generation Technologies

Holography generation methods include laser transmission, electroholographic displays, parallax techniques, and microelectromechanical system (MEMS) methods, which are described in the following.

Laser Transmission Holograms

Lasers are commonly used as the coherent light source of the hologram. For hologram generation, two laser beams are commonly used. A holograph is formed of numerous points located in a 3D domain that have different illumination colors and brightness levels. Each of these 3D points has two laser beams intersecting to generate the modeled interference pattern, which becomes the holographic 3D image. As presented in Figure 5-15, the laser beam is divided into an object beam and a reference beam (using mirrors and lenses), where the object beam expands through lens and is used to illuminate the modeled 3D object. By illuminating the hologram plate with the same reference beam, the modeled object's wavefront is generated. Diffraction of the laser beams at the modeled object's 3D formation points contained in the interference pattern is how the holograph is reconstructed (`www.researchgate.net/figure/How-reflection-hologram-works-B-Transmission-holograms-Transmission-holograms-Fig-2_fig1_336071507`).

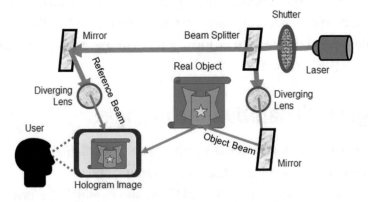

Figure 5-15. Laser Transmission Hologram Generation Example

Electroholography Holograms

Electroholographic displays use electromagnetic resonators to create the holographic image on a red-green-blue (RGB) color laser monitor. The digital holograph image file is sent to the electromagnetic resonator which generates a signal that enters the acoustic-optic modulator to be converted into a signal that can be displayed on the color laser monitor. Please note that the actual system operations of electroholographic displays are much more complex, and this is only an abstract description. Electroholographic technology is known to have higher picture accuracy and a wider range of color display.

Parallax Holograms

Many holographic displays work well when the users are within a certain viewing angle but may show a distorted form when viewed from other angles. Full parallax holography has the benefit of generating a holographic image that has the same perspective of a scene from any angle of view. Full parallax holography systems achieve this by supporting optical information display in both the X and Y directions. The resulting image will therefore provide the same perspective of a scene to all viewers regardless of the viewing angle. Full parallax systems require significant processing and are very complex and expensive, so reduced versions have been proposed, which are the horizontal parallax only (HPO) and vertical parallax only (VPO) displays. HPO and VPO are 2D optical information based holographic systems that perform well for a user within the proper angle of view but will show distortion beyond this range. Considering that human eyes are positioned side by side, the horizontal mode HPO displays are commonly used. HPO and VPO systems require much less processing and can be implemented with much less complexity and may result in less expensive CE products compared to full parallax systems.

MEMS Holograms

MEMS is a micrometer (10^{-6} m = µm = micron) level miniature integrated system consisting of electronics and mechanical components. It is worthy to note that the smallest object recognizable to the human naked eye is in the range of 55~75 microns and a human head's single hair has an average diameter of 20~40 microns (https://en.wikipedia.org/wiki/Naked_eye). It is easy to see how MEMS devices with mechanically controllable reflectors/mirrors can be used to create a holographic image. For example, the piston holographic display uses MEMS based micropistons with reflectors/mirrors attached at pixel positions in the display, so a sharp 3D holographic image can be generated.

The first MEMS based micromagnetic piston display was invented in 2011 by IMEC in Belgium, and a successful commercial product release is expected in the future. The MEMS microscopic pistons located at each pixel position are controlled to change the light/laser reflection to form the hologram image's shape, color, brightness, and texture. Possible limitations of micromagnetic piston displays include high complexity and cost as each pixel needs to be a controllable MEMS device. This may also create challenges in system repair when needed.

Laser Plasma Holograms

Laser plasma displays can generate a hologram image in thin air, without using a screen or refraction media display, but the resolution and picture quality of the hologram are relatively low. Laser plasma technology was invented in 2005 at the University of Texas using multiple focused lasers that are powerful enough to create plasmatic excitation of oxygen and nitrogen molecules in the air at the modeled locations. Laser plasma-based holograms are very bright and visible, but details of the generated object may be difficult to express due to the low resolution.

Holographic Television

Although the technical implementation details are somewhat different, a holographic television can display a combination of a full parallax hologram and a laser transmission hologram in a unique advanced way. The first holographic television display was invented in 2013 at MIT by Michael Bove. In this system, a Microsoft Kinect camera was used to detect the 3D environment and objects. Using multiple laser diodes, a 3D 360 degree viewable hologram was generated. There are expectations for holographic television display CE products to be released in the future.

Touchable Holograms

Touchable holograms add on user touch sensors and response technology such that acts of touching will result in a response in the displayed hologram. In addition, some systems use ultrasonic air blasts to give the user's hand a haptic response feeling of its interaction with the hologram. Touchable holograms first originated in Japan and were further improved by Intel in the United States. Using a touchable hologram, keyboards and buttons can be implemented as virtual holograms without any physical interface hardware. Especially in times like the COVID-19 pandemic, hologram keyboards can help prevent disease spreading as there is no physical interaction between users. Expectations of future touchable holograms are significant as many examples have been demonstrated in sci-fi movies including Star Wars and Star Trek.

Summary

This chapter provided details of the video technologies used in metaverse XR devices (e.g., Meta Quest 2 and Microsoft HoloLens 2) and popular OTT multimedia services (e.g., Netflix, Disney+, and YouTube), which include the H.264 Advanced Video Coding (AVC), H.265 High Efficiency Video

Coding (HEVC), and H.266 Versatile Video Coding (VVC) standards. In addition, holography technologies are also described. H.264, H.265, and H.266 are used in recording, compression, and distribution of a diverse range of video profiles. The high compression rate of H.264, H.265, and H.266 makes video files very small in size for efficient storage and network transfer. In the following Chapter 6, an introduction to the Moving Picture Experts Group – Dynamic Adaptive Streaming over HTTP (MPEG-DASH) technology as well as its Multimedia Presentation Description (MPD) and Group of Pictures (GOP) is provided. In addition, a YouTube MPEG-DASH operation example and the MPEG-DASH features are described.

CHAPTER 6

Multimedia Streaming with MPEG-DASH

This chapter focuses on advanced video streaming techniques and details on MPEG-DASH, which stands for "Moving Picture Experts Group – Dynamic Adaptive Streaming over HTTP." First, the differences of push- vs. pull-based media streaming are described, in which the advantages of pull-based media streaming become evident. Second, the most popular pull-based media streaming protocol Hypertext Transfer Protocol (HTTP) is introduced, and the various types of streaming are described, which include regular HTTP streaming, progressive download, and adaptive streaming over HTTP. Third, details of MPEG-DASH are introduced. In addition, details on the MPEG-DASH Multimedia Presentation Description (MPD) are introduced. Next, the video frames (I, P, B frames) and Group of Pictures (GOP) descriptions are provided followed by a YouTube MPEG-DASH operation example and a list of MPEG-DASH features. The major sections of this chapter are listed in the following:

- Push vs. Pull Media Streaming
- HTTP Streaming
- MPEG-DASH

Push vs. Pull Media Streaming

MPEG-DASH multimedia streaming is used by all MMOGs, metaverse applications, content delivery networks (CDNs), and video streaming services (including Netflix, Disney+, YouTube, etc.), which is why the details of its technical operation are important.

In multimedia streaming, there are two general types of methods that can be used. One is **push**-based media streaming and the other is **pull**-based media streaming. Among the two, push-based media streaming was implemented first, but currently, pull-based media streaming is the dominant method that is used and implemented in MPEG-DASH technology (`https://ur.art1lib.com/book/35827014/93a35c`). But before explaining MPEG-DASH pull-based media streaming technology, the former push-based media streaming technology is described along with its issues (`https://ieeexplore.ieee.org/document/5677508`).

Push-Based Media Streaming

In push-based media streaming, the content Server streams packets to the Client until the Client stops or interrupts the session. The Client would be an application (app) or web browser running on a computer, IPTV, smartphone, personal computer (PC), etc. The Server maintains a session state with the Client and listens for commands from the Client regarding session-state changes. The data streaming process is controlled by the Server using the Real-time Streaming Protocol (RTSP), which is an Internet Engineering Task Force (IETF) standard (RFC 2326). Session control signals are commonly exchanged using the Session Control Protocol (SCP), and IP data packets are transmitted using the Real-time Transport Protocol (RTP) with the User Datagram Protocol (UDP). RTP is defined by the IETF as a standard in RFC 3550. RTP on UDP lets the Server push packets to the Client at a Server bitrate that is determined by the application's QoS requirements and Client and Server characteristics.

There are several problems with push-based media streaming. First, the Server has too much to do and becomes overburdened when it is serving multiple media streaming sessions simultaneously. Second, the media playing device's status is hard to track as it is far away from the Server, and from the time media playing Client device's status is measured to the time the measurement information is received at the Server, the status of the media playing Client device could have changed. Third, many firewalls will block RTP packets, because the firewalls see these streaming packets enter the subnet which may be virus contaminated or an ongoing cyberattack or a Denial of Service (DoS) attack in progress. In either case, the Server cannot confirm if the RTP packets are sent due to a valid media streaming session, and therefore, the firewall will block the session. Fourth, many Internet service networks and all global video/multimedia streaming services use CDNs, which do not support RTP. More details on video/multimedia streaming CDNs are provided in the following Chapter 7.

Pull-Based Adaptive Media Streaming

Pull-based adaptive media streaming is the most common streaming method used in all IPTV and OTT services. In pull-based adaptive media streaming, the media Client sends a HTTP request to the Server to quickly receive (pulling) content packets in burst mode. After the minimum required buffer level is filled in the Client device, the Client will begin to play the media. The Server transmits at the media encoding bitrate that matches the media consumption rate. If the Client buffer level remains stable, then the network resources will be efficiently used. If network packet loss or transmission delay occurs, buffer underflow (emptying) will occur, and playback will be interrupted. To reduce packet loss and delays, the Server may have to dynamically switch to a lower bitrate stream (in which control status communication with the Client will be maintained).

To avoid noticeable visual quality degradation, gradual bitrate stream reductions will be used. If network conditions improve, the Server will switch to a higher bitrate until the media encoding bitrate is recovered.

HTTP Streaming

HTTP progressive download is the most widely used pull-based media streaming method. It is used in almost all applications and web services over the Internet (https://en.wikipedia.org/wiki/Hypertext_Transfer_Protocol).

For example, YouTube uses HTTP over Transmission Control Protocol (TCP), where TCP supports reordering of data segments. Erroneous and lost packets are recovered by TCP's error and flow control of data segments. YouTube needs adaptive transmission control support to avoid video stalling, which is provided by MPEG-DASH.

HTTP is an application protocol that enables data communication for the World Wide Web (WWW). HTTP supports distributed, collaborative, hypermedia information systems. HTTP is the protocol used to exchange or transfer hypertext. Hypertext is structured text (i.e., text with a special format) that uses hyperlinks (e.g., website address) between PCs, smartphones, and servers. HTTP was created in 1989 by Sir Tim Berners-Lee from the European Organization for Nuclear Research, CERN[1]. It was standardized by the IETF and the World Wide Web Consortium (W3C). HTTP/1.0 is the original HTTP, which was standardized as RFC 2068 in 1997. HTTP/1.0 makes a separate connection to the same Server for every resource request received and can reuse a connection multiple times for downloading video, audio, data, etc. HTTP/1.1 was revised and RFC 2068 was obsoleted (replaced) by RFC 2616 in 1999. HTTP/1.1 is a widely used HTTP version on the Internet. HTTP/2 was standardized in 2015, which is now supported by major web servers.

---

[1] CERN stands for "Conseil Européen pour la Recherche Nucléaire."

HTTP functions as a request-response protocol in the Client-Server computing model. For example, assume that a smartphone's web browser is the Client, and the Server is on a cloud network hosting all of the website's information. As the Client sends a HTTP request message to the Server, then the Server provides resources (e.g., HTML files, website, and video content) or functions to the Client. The Server's response message includes status information of the request processed. HTTP permits intermediate network elements to improve or enable communications between the Client and Server. HTTP is an application layer protocol that needs a reliable transport layer protocol like TCP. HTTP can also use unreliable protocols like UDP as in HTTPU and Simple Service Discovery Protocol (SSDP). A HTTP resource is identified in the Internet using a Uniform Resource Locator (URL). URLs use the Uniform Resource Identifier (URI) of HTTP and the HTTP Secure (HTTPS) protocol. URIs and hyperlinks in Hypertext Markup Language (HTML) documents form interlinked hypertext documents.

HTTP provides many benefits. First, HTTP is security friendly, which is why HTTP is commonly supported by firewalls, so connection blocking due to security issues rarely occurs. Second, because the Client (e.g., smartphone, PC, etc.) device controls the streaming, the Server does not need to maintain session-state information of the Client device. This is a big relief on the Server's load, especially when there are many streaming Clients (e.g., YouTube, Netflix, Facebook, and Disney+ servers). Third, HTTP/1.1 can reuse a connection multiple times for downloading video, audio, data, etc. Fourth, popular websites can benefit from web cache servers and can send previously stored content on behalf of an upstream Server to reduce the response time. Fifth, HTTP proxy servers at private network boundaries can facilitate communication for Clients without a globally routable address, which is enabled by relaying messages with external servers.

MPEG-DASH is a representative form of adaptive HTTP streaming, which is a combination of adaptive video rate control and progressive downloading. There are several adaptive HTTP streaming–based proprietary services which include Microsoft Smooth Streaming, Adobe HTTP Dynamic Streaming, and Apple HTTP Live Streaming. In adaptive HTTP streaming, several representations with different quality (resolution and bitrate levels) of the same video are stored in the Server. Videos are commonly divided into fragments of 2~10 s in length. The Client device periodically checks the network's conditions every 2~10 s and may make changes. The Client device tries to avoid video stalling due to an empty buffer (buffer starvation). Client devices commonly select a video player quality level that requires a slightly lower bitrate than the bitrate limit supported by the network, which has the effect of saving network bandwidth (which helps to avoid network congestion) and enables more reliable packet reception.

There are three types of HTTP video streaming methods:

- Regular HTTP Streaming: Completely downloads the video to the Client device.

- Progressive Download: Progressive downloading of the video at a fixed quality.

- Adaptive Streaming over HTTP: Combination of adaptive video quality (bitrate) control and progressive downloading. MPEG-DASH is the representative adaptive streaming over HTTP protocol.

Progressive downloading has the following three advantages. First, the mobile smart device (e.g., smartphone) may not be able to store the entire video due to limited memory space. Second, progressive downloading provides savings in both personal data usages and Internet bandwidth. Third, many users do not watch the entire video. In reality, many users watch less than 20% of the entire video, so progressive downloading provides a significant savings of resources.

MPEG-DASH uses two adaptive HTTP streaming phases. Phase 1 is the Burst Downloading Phase, where the Client buffer fills up quickly. This is used for quick video playback. Phase 2 is the Throttle Downloading Phase, where the objective is to maintain the buffer fill-up level to avoid any possible video stalling (https://en.wikipedia.org/wiki/Dynamic_Adaptive_Streaming_over_HTTP).

Figure 6-1 shows an example of pull-based adaptive streaming bitrate adaptation under varying network conditions (https://ieeexplore.ieee.org/document/5677508). The session starts with the Client IPTV sending a Request manifest for movie X, where the video content provider Server replies with a Manifest acknowledgment. On receiving this Manifest acknowledgment from the Server, the IPTV sends a Request Movie X to the Server to initiate the receiving session of video packets at a bitrate of 100 kbps (bps = bits/s) at time t=0. The Server starts to send the streaming video data packets at 100 kbps to the IPTV. The IPTV decides to receive the streaming video at a higher bitrate and sends a Request Movie A to the Server to increase the bitrate to 500 kbps at time t=3. On receiving this, the Server changes the streaming video bitrate to 500 kbps. Then the IPTV decides to receive the streaming video at an even higher bitrate and sends a Request Movie X to the Server to increase the bitrate to 1 Mbps at time t=5. On receiving this, the Server changes the streaming video bitrate to 1 Mbps. Due to the higher bitrate and influence of other traffic flows, the IPTV detects packet loss and congestion in the network and, therefore, decides to reduce the receiving bitrate of the video streaming session. So, the IPTV sends a Request Movie X to the Server to reduce the streaming bitrate to 800 kbps at time t=7. On receiving this, the Server reduces the speed of the streaming video bitrate to 800 kbps. As network conditions recover, the IPTV decides to receive the streaming video at a higher bitrate and sends a Request Movie X the Server to increase the bitrate to 1 Mbps at time t=10. On receiving this, the Server increases the streaming video data rate to 1 Mbps.

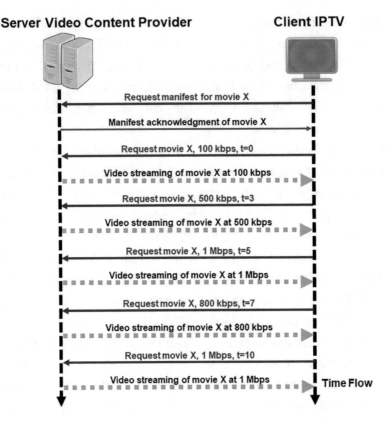

Figure 6-1. *Pull-Based Adaptive Streaming Bitrate Adaptation Example Under Varying Network Conditions*

Pull-based adaptive media streaming uses fragmented MP4 files to exchange control information of the streaming media flow, as presented in Figure 6-2. Video and audio data are included in the mdat boxes, where the mdat boxes and metadata form a fragment. These information fragments are retrieved using HTTP GET request messages (`https://ieeexplore.ieee.org/document/5677508`).

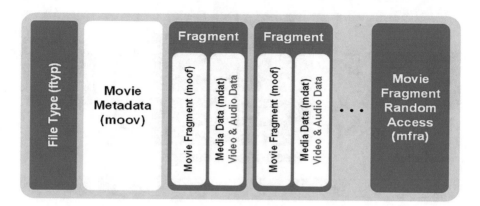

Figure 6-2. *A Fragmented MP4 File Used in Pull-Based Adaptive Media Streaming Control*

Figure 6-3 presents a Request and Response message exchange example between a HTTP Client and Server and an example HTTP GET request message, where the video mode (e.g., 1080p) is indicated followed by the quality level (e.g., 1500000) and fragment number (e.g., 122200778) of the video data and the HTTP version (e.g., version 1.1) used (`https://en.wikipedia.org/wiki/Hypertext_Transfer_Protocol`). Each fragment is downloaded based on a unique HTTP request-response pair. The HTTP request message header contains two pieces of information, the Bitrate and Time Offset of the requested fragment.

Figure 6-3. *Request and Response Message Exchange Example Between a HTTP Client and Server and an Example HTTP Request Message*

In pull-based adaptive streaming, the Client manages the manifest(s), HTTP transport, and TCP connection(s). In addition, the Client monitors the playout buffer, download times and throughput, local resources (CPU, GPU, memory, etc.), and dropped frames. Using this information, the Client decides how to make adaptations and includes the adaptation result in the Get request message sent to the Server.

The Client acquires media from fragments of a file over one or more connections according to the playout buffer state and other conditions. At minimum, the Server provides standard responses to the HTTP GET request. The Client gets a manifest file that identifies files containing media presentations at alternative bitrates. The Client needs a Client-side Manifest or Playlist file to map fragment requests to specific files or to map byte ranges or time offsets to files. In some adaptive streaming schemes, a similar file on the Server translates Client requests. The playout buffer management selects fragments from a file at a particular bitrate in response to the buffer state and other variables. The adaptive streaming Client keeps a playout buffer of several seconds (between 5 and 30 s) (http://inase.org/library/2015/zakynthos/bypaper/COMMUN/COMMUN-07.pdf).

MPEG-DASH

MPEG-DASH specifications are defined in the ISO/IEC 23009-1 documents (www.iso.org/standard/75485.html). The MPEG-DASH standard defines the Multimedia Presentation Description (MPD) and the segment formats. The MPD delivery, format of media encoding that includes the video segments, adaptive downloading, and video playing control are all determined by the application on the Client device. The HTTP Server controls the MPD setup as well as the video and audio data segments which are sent to the Client device through IP packets.

The following eight steps explain the operations involved in how a video is played on a DASH Client:

1. DASH Client requests for MPD from the Server.

2. MPD is delivered to the Client using HTTP.

3. Client parses the MPD.

4. Client's MPEG-DASH application reads the MPD information, which includes program timing, media content availability, media types, resolutions, minimum and maximum bandwidths, available multimedia resolution types, etc.

5. Client selects the appropriate encoded alternative and starts streaming the content by fetching the segments using HTTP GET requests.

6. Appropriate buffering is used to compensate for network throughput variations.

7. Client continues to fetch subsequent segments and monitors the network bandwidth fluctuations.

8. Client adapts to the available bandwidth by fetching segments with lower or higher bitrates to maintain an adequate buffer.

Figure 6-4 presents the HTTP Server and DASH Client internal functions used in MPEG-DASH operations on the DASH Client side, which include the HTTP Client, MPD and segment parser, media player, and the control heuristics device (https://ieeexplore.ieee.org/document/6077864).

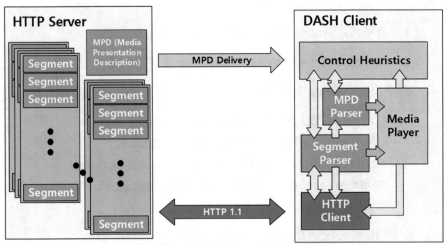

MPEG-DASH system blocks and functionalities

Figure 6-4. *HTTP Server and DASH Client Internal Functions Used in MPEG-DASH Operations*

Video Frame Types

There are three basic types of video frames (I frame, P frame, and B frame) used in MPEG-DASH video streaming technology, which are commonly H.264, H.265, H.266 frames or could be some other video codec scheme. As described in Chapter 5, I frames (Intra-coded frames) are independently encoded pictures that contain full picture information. P frames (Predicted frames) are frames that depend on previous I or P frames. B frames (Bi-predictive frames) depend on multiple previously decoded frames (e.g., multiple I or P frames). P and B frames have high compression rates since they encode the motion-compensated differences (relative information) of other frames. Video fragments are made of one or multiple Group of Pictures (GOPs). Each GOP begins with an I frame followed by P or B frames. This results in a much smaller video file size compared to using all I frames. Very high data compression rates are achieved due to the P and B frames in the GOP. There are two GOP types, closed and open. In closed GOPs, P and B frame decoding depends only on frames within its GOP. In an open GOP, P and B frame decoding may depend on frames in other neighboring GOPs.

MPD Decoding and Playing Method

Figure 6-5 shows the internal structure and media segments included in the MPD to support video streaming using MPEG-DASH. An MPD contains multiple Periods, where each Period contains multiple Adaptation Sets. Period is a program time interval which includes information on starting time and duration. An Adaptation Set contains multiple Representations. Each Representation has a different bitrate encoding of video or audio of the same multimedia content. The bitrate is based on the video's resolution, number of channels, etc. A Representation for Trick Mode can be included (`https://ieeexplore.ieee.org/document/6077864`).

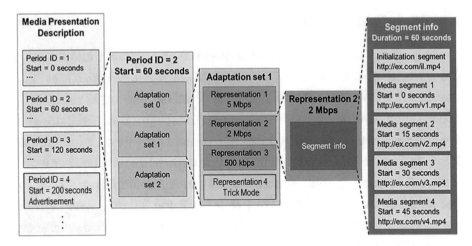

Figure 6-5. *Internal Structure and Media Segments Included in the MPD to Support Video Streaming Using MPEG-DASH*

A Trick Mode example is shown in Figure 6-6, in which the scroll bar can be used to move to a specific point in the video. In some cases, small images (commonly I frames are used since they are complete images) will be presented near the scroll bar to help find the appropriate place to return to viewing the video. Representations consist of multiple media Segments information. Segments are chunks of the media stream in a time order sequence, where each segment has a URI. The URI is used as the Server's address location from where the multimedia content can be downloaded from. For downloading, the HTTP GET (may include byte ranges) message is used. Segment information includes its initialization segment and information of multiple media segments (www.coursera.org/instructor/jmcyonsei).

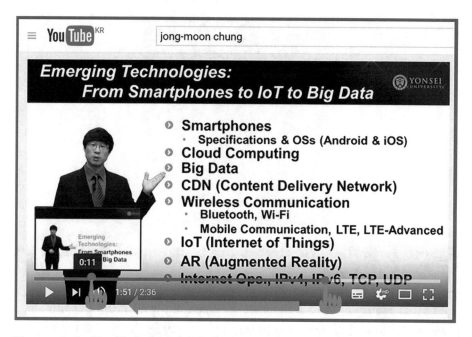

Figure 6-6. *YouTube Trick Mode Example*

YouTube MPEG-DASH Operation Example

In this example, a smartphone is playing a movie on YouTube in which
MPEG-DASH is used to conduct adaptive streaming over HTTP. Figure 6-7
presents the multiple resolutions of the same movie that YouTube uses
in this MPEG-DASH video streaming example. Figure 6-8 illustrates an
example of YouTube MPEG-DASH adaptation operations. In this example,
YouTube uses adaptive HTTP streaming using eight video resolution files
of the same movie in the Server (https://dl.acm.org/doi/10.1007/
s11042-017-4695-9).

Resolution	Pixels (width x height)
144p	256 x 144
240p	426 x 240
360p	640 x 360
480p	854 x 480
720p	1280 x 720
1080p	1920 x 1080
1440p	2560 x 1440
2160p	3840 x 2160

Figure 6-7. *YouTube Video Streaming Using Multiple Resolutions in MPEG-DASH Example*

In this example, 144p is the lowest video quality and 2160p is the highest video quality, and in between there are 240p, 360p, 480p, 720p, 1080p, and 1440p, where the higher pixel resolution movie files require a higher data rate network transfer as well as a larger memory allocation, higher CPU/GPU processing speeds, and more energy consumption of the smartphone (https://ieeexplore.ieee.org/document/6077864).

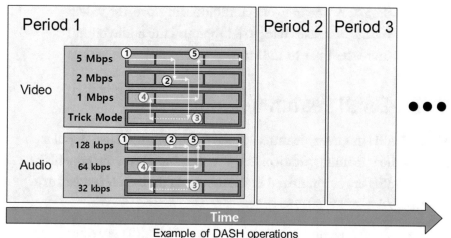

Example of DASH operations

Numbered circles represent the action points controlled by the Client device

Figure 6-8. *YouTube MPEG-DASH Adaptation Operation Example*

In the example presented in Figure 6-8, the circled numbers in Period 1 represent the action points controlled in the YouTube video and audio by the Client smartphone device.

- Step ①: In this example, the initial video bitrate is 5 Mbps and the audio bitrate is 128 kbps. This continues until the network conditions deteriorate.

- Step ②: Due to the worsening network conditions, the video bitrate decreases to 2 Mbps, yet the audio bitrate is maintained at 128 kbps.

- Step ③: Due to use of Trick Mode the video goes into Trick Mode while the audio bitrate decreases to 32 kbps.

- Step ④: After the Trick Mode adjustments are made, the video bitrate is adjusted to 1 Mbps and the audio bitrate is adjusted to 64 kbps.

- Step ⑤: As the network conditions improve, the video bitrate increases back to 5 Mbps and the audio bitrate increases back to 128 kbps.

MPEG-DASH Features

MPEG-DASH has many features, which is why it is the most popular multimedia streaming protocol in the world. Details on the benefits of MPEG-DASH are summarized in the following (https://ieeexplore. ieee.org/document/6077864):

- Switching and Selectable Streams: The MPD provides adequate information to the Client for selecting and switching between streams. This option includes selecting one audio stream from different languages, selecting video between different camera angles, selecting the subtitles from provided languages, and dynamically switching between different bitrates of the same video camera. An example is shown in Figure 6-9.

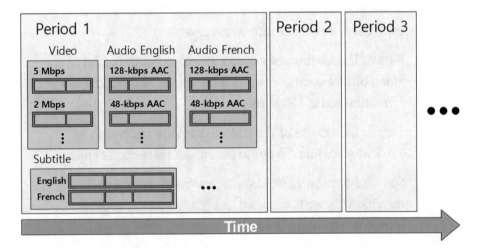

Figure 6-9. *Example of Multiple Language and Data Rate Video, Audio, and Subtitle Files Used in MPEG-DASH*

- Advertisements Insertion: Advertisements can be inserted as a period between periods or segments in both on-demand and live cases. An example of an advertisement included in the MPD is shown in Figure 6-5.

- Compact Manifest: Segments' address URLs can be signaled using a template scheme, which results in a more compact MPD.

- Fragmented Manifest: MPD can be divided into multiple parts, or some of its elements can be externally referenced.

- Segments with Variable Durations: Duration of segments can be varied. In live video streaming, the duration of the next segment can be provided in advance along with the delivery of the current segment. This enables downloading of a MPD in multiple steps. An example is shown in Figure 6-10.

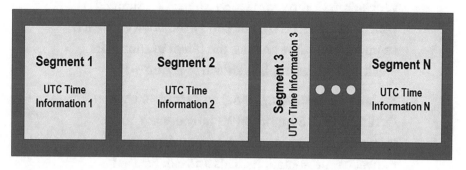

Figure 6-10. *Example of Segments with Different Lengths and UTC Time Information in MPEG-DASH*

- Multiple Base URLs: Since the same content can be available at multiple URLs, this feature gives the options for the Client to stream from any URL. An example is shown in Figure 6-11.

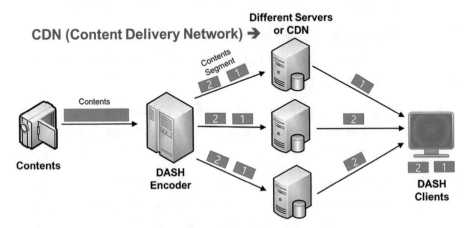

Figure 6-11. *Example of Using Multiple Base URLs to Receive Video Streams When Using MPEG-DASH*

- Clock-Drift Control for Live Sessions: Coordinated Universal Time (UTC) time can be included with each segment. UTC time enables the Client to control its clock drift. An example is shown in Figure 6-10.

- Scalable Video Coding (SVC) and Multiview Video Coding (MVC) Support: MPD provides adequate information regarding the decoding dependencies between representations. This info can be used for streaming any (e.g., SVC, MVC) multilayer coded stream.

- Flexible Set of Descriptors: A variety of descriptors can be used to describe the content rating, components' roles, accessibility features, camera views, frame packing, audio channels' configuration, etc.

- Subsetting Adaptation Sets into Groups: Grouping occurs according to the content author's guidance.

- Quality Metrics for Reporting the Session Experience: MPEG-DASH standards have a set of quality metrics, which are used by the Client to measure and report back to a Server.

Most of these features are provided in flexible and extensible ways, which enables MPEG-DASH to be used in flexible ways in various future applications.

Summary

This chapter provided details of MPEG-DASH along with the technical aspects of its MPD and GOP. In addition, a YouTube MPEG-DASH operation example and a list of MPEG-DASH features are described. Because all metaverse and multimedia services use MPEG-DASH, understanding the features and advantages of it is important as it is used in device design, server control, and network management. In the following Chapter 7, an introduction to content delivery network (CDN) and its technical features are described, which include details of CDN multimedia streaming operations, CDN caching services, and mobile CDN services.

CHAPTER 7

Content Delivery Network (CDN) Technology

This chapter focuses on the benefits and operations of advanced content delivery network (CDN) technologies used in OTT and metaverse services. First, an introduction to how Netflix, Disney+, and Facebook use CDNs is described. Second, the CDN structure and operations of CDN content delivery are introduced, which include details on CDN hierarchical content delivery. Third, CDN caching services and content updating operations along with CDN popularity prediction and content update techniques (with operational examples of the Least Recently Used (LRU) and Least Frequently Used (LFU) strategies) are introduced. Fourth, the characteristics of mobile CDN services are described.

- Metaverse and Multimedia Streaming CDN
- CDN Multimedia Streaming Technology
- CDN Caching Services
- Mobile CDN Services

© Jong-Moon Chung 2023
J.-M. Chung, *Emerging Metaverse XR and Video Multimedia Technologies*,
https://doi.org/10.1007/978-1-4842-8928-0_7

Metaverse and Multimedia Streaming CDN

Evidently MMOG, metaverse, and multimedia streaming companies all use CDN services. This is because CDNs play a critical role in enabling faster and more reliable customer services (www.marketsandmarkets. com/Market-Reports/content-delivery-networks-cdn-market-657. html#utm_source=PRNewswires&utm_medium=Referral&utm_ campaign=PRNewswires). In addition, because a CDN can serve an entire region of customers, CDNs significantly reduce the amount of traffic used on the network while better serving the customers of the company. Larger companies with longer history have a tendency to build their own CDN (e.g., Netflix and Facebook), and companies with shorter history or smaller companies have a tendency to use the CDN services of other companies. Disney+ (which was launched in November 2019) uses multiple CDN providers, which include Akamai, Lumen, Limelight, Edgecast, CloudFront, and Fastly, for its worldwide video content distribution (https://medium. com/predict/content-delivery-network-is-the-magic-inside-disneys-streaming-services-8699e8f441e). When a MMOG, metaverse, or multimedia streaming company becomes a certain size in business, having a CDN owned by the company can be more profitable, and customized service features can be added on more easily. CDN services used by Facebook and Netflix are introduced in the following sections.

Facebook CDN

Facebook has its own global CDN named Facebook CDN (fbcdn.net) to support its global social networking and metaverse services but also supports other industrial customer businesses (https://enlyft.com/ tech/products/facebook-cdn). Facebook CDN is used by approximately 363,382 companies worldwide, where most of these companies are located in the United States. Among the industries that use Facebook CDN, the most are in retail, at approximately 7% of Facebook CDN users, where a majority of these companies are companies with 10 to 50 employees that have a revenue in the range of $1 million to $10 million. For example, the organizations Regal Entertainment Group (regmovies.com), George Mason University (gmu.edu), University of California-Los Angeles (ucla.edu), and Confidential Records, Inc. (confidentialrecordsinc.com) use Facebook CDN. Because Facebook is used worldwide, Facebook CDN enables a global platform of CDN services for these companies. In descending order of highest usage of Facebook CDN based on industry types, the order is as follows: retail, hospitals and healthcare, construction, restaurants, financial services, automotive, education management, real estate, recreational facilities and services, nonprofit organization management, etc. Overall, Facebook CDN occupies approximately 13.9% of the CDN market share.

Netflix Open Connect CDN

Netflix used to use CDN services from other companies, but now it has its own "Open Connect" CDN. Netflix's Open Connect CDN uses multiple local servers that are called Open Connect Appliances (OCAs) and a backbone CDN, which is a hierarchical CDN infrastructure. Technical details on hierarchical CDNs will be described in a later section of this chapter. The Open Connect CDN was launched by Netflix in 2011. Netflix has invested over $1 billion in developing and deploying its Open Connect CDN which now has over 14,000 OCAs located throughout 142 countries worldwide. Netflix's OCAs update content every night. The OCAs can be located in Internet exchange points (IXPs) or within the Internet service provider (ISP) network. For security purposes, the locations of the OCAs are kept a secret. IXPs are the physical networking facilities that a CDN connects with the local ISP, which are typically located at the edge of the ISP network. Based on the 2021 Netflix briefing paper titled "A Cooperative Approach to Content Delivery" (https://openconnect.netflix.com/ Open-Connect-Overview.pdf), Netflix has provided an estimated $1.2 billion cost saving for their ISP partners in 2020 through the Netflix

Open Connect CDN services and improved multimedia encoding and compression techniques by using H.264 and H.265 and other multimedia protocols (technical details on multimedia encoding and compression techniques are described in Chapter 5 of this book).

CDN Multimedia Streaming Technology

CDN is a network constructed from a group of strategically placed and geographically distributed Caching Servers that are designed to efficiently and reliably deliver multimedia content, as illustrated in Figure 7-1 (www.itu.int/rec/T-REC-Y.2019). Using a CDN is the most efficient solution for content providers (CPs) that are serving a large number of user devices while reducing the content download time and network traffic. This is why CDNs are used by all major metaverse companies, MMOGs, and video streaming companies that provide global services (www.cisco. com/c/en/us/solutions/collateral/executive-perspectives/annual-internet-report/white-paper-c11-741490.html).

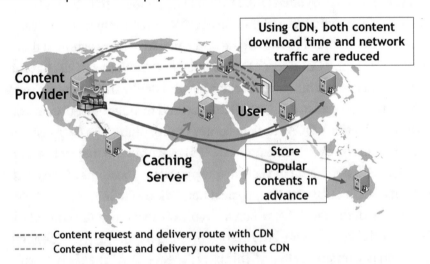

Figure 7-1. A CDN Global Service Delivery Example Showing Interaction Between the CP and Caching Servers

CDNs commonly consist of a CP and Caching Servers, as presented in Figure 7-2. The CP possesses all contents to serve. The Caching Servers are distributed throughout the network containing selected contents that the CP stores. The Caching Servers have only selected contents because their cache memory size is much smaller than the CP. Therefore, the Caching Servers have to determine the best content files to keep in their cache. The selected content files of the CP that are downloaded in advance by the Caching Servers are chosen based on popularity or usage algorithms that are introduced later in this chapter. When a user requests for a content to be delivered to its nearest Caching Server, the server can deliver the content if the requested content is in its cache. Otherwise, the Caching Server redirects the user's request to the remotely located CP (https:// en.wikipedia.org/wiki/Content_delivery_network).

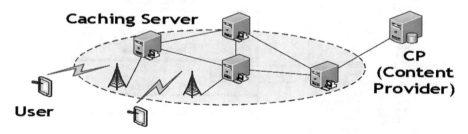

Figure 7-2. *A CDN Example Consisting of a CP and Multiple Caching Servers*

CDN Operations

When a user sends a request for content delivery to its nearest Caching Server, the local Caching Server can deliver the content if the requested content is in its cache. As illustrated in Figure 7-3, these procedures are initiated by the user device sending a Session Request message to the Local Caching Server (LCS), where in this message the requested content details

are included (www.researchgate.net/publication/285100522_Content_
Delivery_Networks_Technology_Survey_and_Research_Challenges). If
the LCS has the content, then a Session Response message is retuned back
to the user device with information on the content that will be streamed
to the user device. The user device will conduct resource allocation (e.g.,
using the memory allocation function malloc( ) in C programming)
to prepare to receive this content file. Once the user device is ready, a
Content Request message is sent to the LCS, and the LCS starts to stream
the content file to the user device (www.itu.int/rec/T-REC-Y.2019).
Figure 7-3 also presents the user device internal CDN functions.

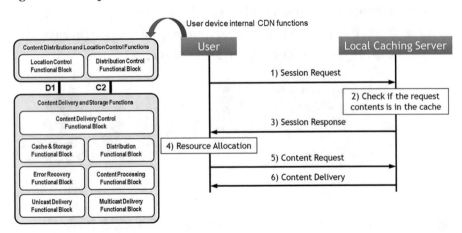

Figure 7-3. *CDN Operation Procedures of a User Device Receiving
the Requested Content from Its Local Caching Server and Internal
CDN Functions*

If the requested content is not in the LCS, the content request is
redirected to the remotely located CP server, based on the procedures
illustrated in Figure 7-4. The sequence of operations begins with the
user device making a request of content delivery using a Session Request
message sent to the LCS. The LCS checks if the content is in its cache, and
because the requested content is not available in this example, the LCS
prepares resource allocation and sends the CP a Content Request message.

The CP sends the requested content to the LCS. As the LCS now possess the requested content, the LCS sends a Session Response message to the user device. The user device prepares resource allocation and sends a Content Request message to the LCS. In response, the LCS sends the content file to the user device. Figure 7-4 also presents the Local Caching Server's internal CDN functions (www.itu.int/rec/T-REC-Y.2019).

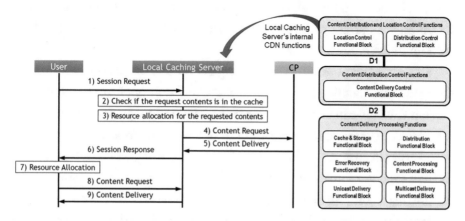

Figure 7-4. *CDN Operation Procedures of a User Device Receiving the Requested Content from the CP Because the LCS Does Not Have the Content in Its Cache*

The content aging process used by the LCS is focused on delivering the most popular contents to users in the most effective way. The content aging process depends on the factors of location of the caching server, number of caching servers in the region, and limited memory size of the caching server. Content aging determines the content files to delete or keep in its cache and what content files to download in advance from the CP. Each content in the LCS has a content update period, which is the time duration that a content file will be kept in the LCS's memory. The content update period is only a few seconds for online trading data, a few seconds for auction information, and 24 hours or more for movies. An example of two algorithms used in content update period extension or expiration is provided in the following section of this chapter.

CDN Hierarchical Content Delivery

Hierarchical content delivery is used in CDNs to enhance the content delivery and management efficiency. This is needed, because having one CP severing all LCSs of a global CDN will create an extreme overload on the CP and the remote distance of the CP will create very long time delays. In addition, for a global CDN, content popularity is very different for different regions and countries. This is why CDNs use a hierarchical content delivery network structure.

Since it is not possible for a Caching Server to save all contents that the CP serves, Caching Servers need to retrieve content from the remotely located CP. This can cause long content downloading durations which is bad for the users, and a large amount of traffic will be generated by each server in support of the content's packet routing, which is bad for the network. For the given cache size of each server, it is important to maximize the hit rate of the local caching server such that the requested contents do not have to be retrieved from the CP. Hierarchical CDN accomplishes this objective in the Internet in a scalable way.

Hierarchical cooperative content delivery techniques are used in providing content delivery to local caching servers using the following structure. The Content Distribution & Location Control Functions (CD & LCF) controls the overall content delivery process and has all content identity documents (IDs) of the CDN. The Cluster Control Function (CCF) controls multiple Content Delivery Processing Functions (CDPFs) and saves content IDs of the cluster. The CDPF stores and delivers the contents to the users. An example hierarchical CDN structure is presented in Figure 7-5.

In Figure 7-5, reference point D1 connects the CD & LCF and CCF, which is used by the CD & LCF to obtain the CCF's status information, which includes the load status of the content delivery functions. Reference point D2 connects the CCF and CDPF to enable the CD & LCF to obtain the CDPF's status information, which includes the CCF controller load status. The functionality of the reference points D3, D4, and D5 is described in the following, in which these reference points enhance functionality but are optional. Reference point D3 enables selection of optimal CD & LCF instances by supporting interconnection between different CD & LCF instances. Reference point D4 enables content distribution control and content location control signaling transfer by supporting interconnection between different CCF instances. Reference point D5 enables content distribution by supporting interconnection between different CDPF instances (www.itu.int/rec/T-REC-Y.2019).

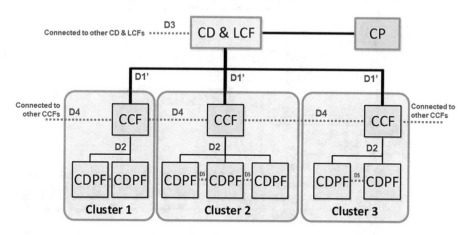

Figure 7-5. *An Example Hierarchical CDN Structure*

The content delivery procedures of a hierarchical CDN are described based on three case examples, which are described in the following (www.researchgate.net/publication/285100522_Content_Delivery_Networks_Technology_Survey_and_Research_Challenges).

In the Case 1 example, the requested content is in the local cluster. Figure 7-6 illustrates the hierarchical content delivery procedures for the Case 1 example. The user device's content request message is delivered to the CCF through a Session Request message. The CCF checks if the requested content is in the local cluster. Because the local cluster has the requested content, the CCF commands the Target CDPF to set up a session, and the CCF sends a Session Response to the user device to prepare for content reception. The user device conducts resource allocation and sends a Content Request to the CCF which is forwarded to the Target CDPF. This Content Request includes the user device's IP address and user information. The Target CDPF directly sends the content to the user device (www.itu.int/rec/T-REC-Y.2019).

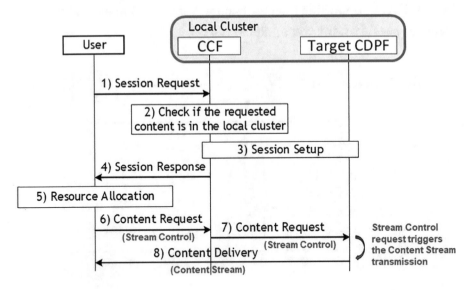

Figure 7-6. *Hierarchical Content Delivery Procedures for the Case 1 Example*

In the Case 2 example, the requested content is not in the local cluster, but in a neighboring target cluster. Figure 7-7 illustrates the hierarchical content delivery procedures for the Case 2 example. The procedures are different in Case 2, whereas the CCF of the local cluster searches for the content within the cluster and identifies that the cluster does not have the requested content. The CCF of the local cluster sends a Redirect Request message to the CD & LCF to find the content. The CD & LCF finds the content in a neighboring cluster and checks if that cluster can directly send the content to the user device or if the content delivery has to go through the local cluster. In this example, the CD & LCF confirms that the content in a neighboring cluster can be directly sent to the user device, so the CD & LCF informs the local cluster's CCF of the content delivery procedures through a Response message. The local cluster's CCF sends a Session Request message to the CCF of the target cluster. The CCF of the target cluster set ups a session with its CDPF and sends a Session Response message to the CCF of the local cluster, which is forwarded to the user device. The user device will conduct resource allocation and send a Content Request message to the CCF of the target cluster, which is forwarded to the CDPF in the target cluster. Then the CDPF of the target cluster will conduct content delivery to the user device.

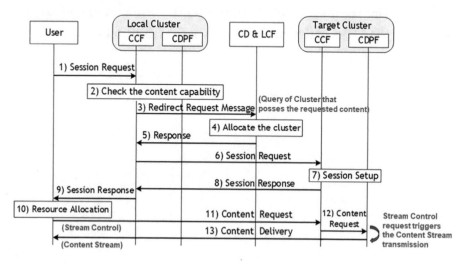

Figure 7-7. *Hierarchical Content Delivery Procedures for the Case 2 Example*

In the Case 3 example, the requested content is not in any other cluster of the CDN. Figure 7-8 illustrates the hierarchical content delivery procedures for the Case 3 example. The procedures are different in Case 3, as the CCF of the local cluster searches for the content within the cluster and identifies that it does not have the requested content. The CCF of the local cluster sends a Redirect Request message to the CD & LCF to find the content. The CD & LCF realizes that no cluster in the CDN has the requested content, so it contacts the CP using a Content Injection Request message. The CP sends back a Content Injection Response message to the CD & LCF which is forwarded to the CCF of the local cluster. The local cluster's CCF forwards the Content Injection Response message to its CDPF. The CDPF sends a Content Download Request message to the CCF, which is forwarded to the CD & LCF, which forwards this message to the CP. The CP directly sends the content file to the CDPF of the local cluster. The CDPF of the local cluster sends a Response message to the CCF informing the CCF that it has received the content from the CP. The local cluster's CCF sends a Session Response message to the user device. The user device conducts resource allocation and sends a Content Request message to the CDPF of the local cluster, and the CDPF delivers the content to the user device.

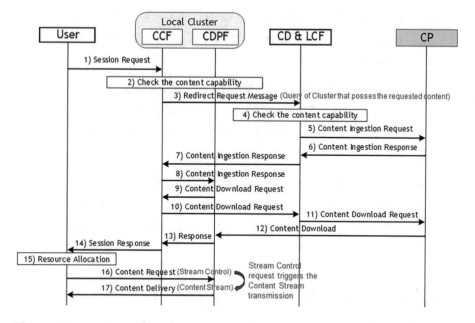

Figure 7-8. *Hierarchical Content Delivery Procedures for the Case 3 Example*

CDN Caching Schemes

CDNs use cooperative caching and content routing schemes to make their performance more efficient and reliable. The representative schemes are introduced in the following (https://ieeexplore.ieee.org/document/1204454):

- Query-Based Scheme: A CDN server broadcasts a query for the requested content to other CDN servers inside the same cluster if it does not have the content.

- Digest-Based Scheme: Each CDN server maintains a content digest which includes the information of other CDN servers of the same cluster.

- Directory-Based Scheme: A directory server maintains the content information of the CDN servers in the same cluster.

- Hashing-Based Scheme: The CDN servers maintain the same hashing function. The contents are allocated by the content's URL, unique IDs of the CDN servers, and the hashing functions.

- Semi-hashing-Based Scheme: A CDN server allocates a certain portion of its storage to cache the most popular contents and the rest to share with other servers using hashing functions.

CDN Content Popularity Prediction

CDN content popularity predictions commonly use the Zipf distribution function which is explained in the following. The Zipf distribution is a verified statistical model of content distribution in the real world, where the popularity of the ith popular content (p_i) is described as

$$p_i = \frac{\Omega}{i^\alpha} \text{ in which } \Omega = 1 / \sum_{i=1}^{N} \left(\frac{1}{i^\alpha} \right)$$

where there are N total number of contents and α is the Zipf parameter which determines the skewness of a content's popularity. An example is provided in Figure 7-9 based on the setting of $\alpha = 1$ and $N = 10$ for the Zipf function (https://en.wikipedia.org/wiki/Zipf%27s_law).

i	p_i	Value (Popularity)
1	Ω	0.3414
2	$\Omega/2$	0.3414/2=0.1707
3	$\Omega/3$	0.3414/3=0.1138
...	...	...
9	$\Omega/9$	0.3414/9=0.0379
10	$\Omega/10$	0.3414/10=0.0341

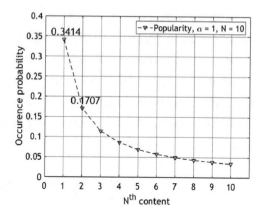

Figure 7-9. *Example of CDN Content Popularity Prediction Using the Zipf Distribution Function*

Among many CDN content update strategies that exist, the following two strategies are used in CDN content popularity predictions to assist content keeping and discarding selections in local content servers (https://ieeexplore.ieee.org/stamp/stamp.jsp?tp=&arnumber=7343641)

(https://www.researchgate.net/publication/3864098_Effective_caching_of_Web_objects_using_Zipf's_law).

Least Recently Used (LRU) Strategy

The LRU strategy replaces the least recently used contents in the CDN cache. This is because the recently used contents and more frequently used contents are more likely to be requested for use in the near future. Therefore, the algorithm gives a higher priority to the contents that have been recently used. The LRU strategy predicts the popularity of contents according to observation of the requests based on a time duration. This strategy makes an evaluation one step ahead and then executes in the following step. Thus, the evaluation is made at time instant $t-1$ and then executed at time instant t in the algorithm (https://en.wikipedia.org/wiki/Cache_replacement_policies).

The following example of procedures of the LRU strategy is illustrated step-by-step in Figure 7-10 through Figure 7-18. In this example, the server is assumed to have a small cache capacity that can contain only three content files. Figure 7-10 shows the initial state where the server's cache is empty, and content requests will occur in the order of 2, 3, 1, 2, 1, 4, 4, 3. The procedures of how the server will operate at every time instant of 1, 2, 3, 4, 5, 6, 7, 8 will be illustrated.

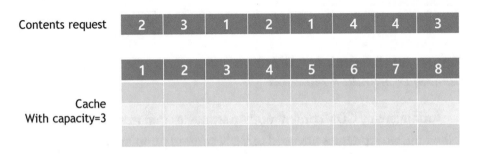

Figure 7-10. *LRU Example of the Server's Cache at Time Instant 0*

Figure 7-11 presents the LRU strategy example of the server's cache at time instant 1, where a request for content 2 is received, so the server caches content 2. At time instant 2, a request for content 3 is received, so the server caches content 3 as shown in Figure 7-12. At time instant 3, a request for content 1 is received, so the server caches content 1 as shown in Figure 7-13.

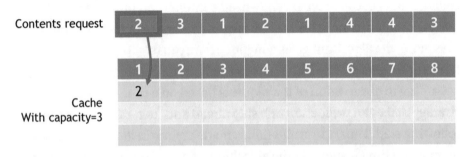

Figure 7-11. *LRU Example of the Server's Cache at Time Instant 1*

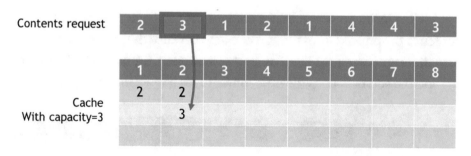

Figure 7-12. *LRU Example of the Server's Cache at Time Instant 2*

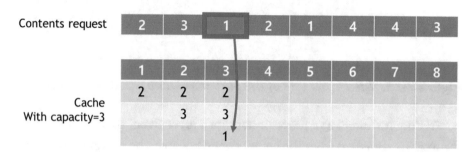

Figure 7-13. *LRU Example of the Server's Cache at Time Instant 3*

At time instant 4, a request for content 2 is received, so the older content 2 is removed from the server cache because the server's capacity is only three and content 2 has been requested again. So, contents 3 and 1 are shifted up and the server caches the new content 2, as shown in Figure 7-14.

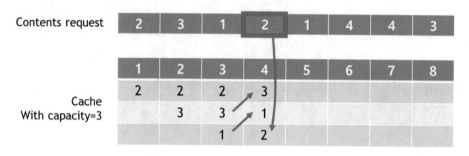

Figure 7-14. *LRU Example of the Server's Cache at Time Instant 4*

At time instant 5, a request for content 1 is received, so the older content 1 is removed from the server cache because the server's capacity is only three and content 1 has been requested again. So, content 2 is shifted up, and the server caches the new content 1, as shown in Figure 7-15.

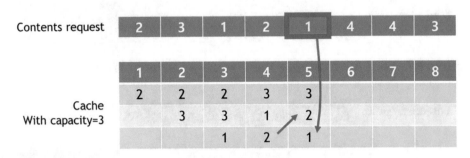

Contents request	2	3	1	2	1	4	4	3

	1	2	3	4	5	6	7	8
Cache With capacity=3	2	2	2	3	3			
		3	3	1	2			
			1	2	1			

Figure 7-15. *LRU Example of the Server's Cache at Time Instant 5*

At time instant 6, a request for content 4 is received, so the older content 3 is removed from the server cache because the server's capacity is only three and content 3 has been requested only once and not most recently. So, contents 2 and 1 are shifted up, and the server caches the new content 4, as shown in Figure 7-16.

Contents request	2	3	1	2	1	4	4	3

	1	2	3	4	5	6	7	8
Cache With capacity=3	2	2	2	3	3	2		
		3	3	1	2	1		
			1	2	1	4		

Figure 7-16. *LRU Example of the Server's Cache at Time Instant 6*

At time instant 7, a request for content 4 is received again, but the server does not erase content 2 or 1 because the server's capacity is three and contents 2 and 1 have been each requested twice and recently. So, the server caches the new content 4, as shown in Figure 7-17.

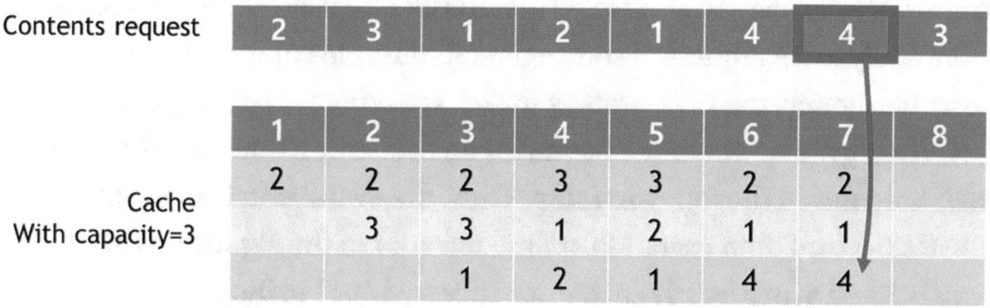

Contents request	2	3	1	2	1	4	4	3

	1	2	3	4	5	6	7	8
Cache	2	2	2	3	3	2	2	
With capacity=3		3	3	1	2	1	1	
			1	2	1	4	4	

Figure 7-17. *LRU Example of the Server's Cache at Time Instant 7*

At time instant 8, a request for content 3 is received, so the older content 2 is removed from the server cache because the server's capacity is only three, and even though content 2 has been requested twice, contents 1 and 4 have also been requested twice and more recently than content 2. So, contents 1 and 4 are shifted up, and the server caches the new content 3, as shown in Figure 7-18.

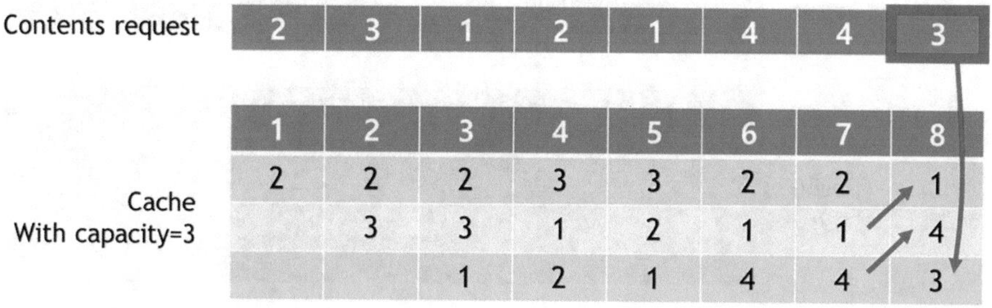

Contents request	2	3	1	2	1	4	4	3

	1	2	3	4	5	6	7	8
Cache	2	2	2	3	3	2	2	1
With capacity=3		3	3	1	2	1	1	4
			1	2	1	4	4	3

Figure 7-18. *LRU Example of the Server's Cache at Time Instant 8*

Least Frequently Used (LFU) Strategy

The LFU strategy keeps contents that have the highest request frequency within a specific time duration in the server's cache. The algorithm keeps track of the frequency of content requests to evaluate its popularity. The strategy is based on the logic that frequently used contents will be more likely to be requested soon again. If multiple contents have the same frequency, the LFU strategy makes selections according to the LRU strategy. This strategy also makes an evaluation one step ahead and then executes in the following step. Thus, the evaluation is made at time instant $t-1$ and then executed at time instant t in the algorithm (https://en.wikipedia.org/wiki/Cache_replacement_policies).

The following examples of procedures of the LFU strategy are illustrated step-by-step in Figure 7-19 through Figure 7-27. In this example, the server is assumed to have a small cache capacity that can contain only three content files. Figure 7-19 shows the initial state where the server's cache is empty, and content requests will occur in the order of 2, 3, 1, 2, 1, 4, 4, 3. The procedures of how the server will operate at every time instant of 1, 2, 3, 4, 5, 6, 7, 8 will be illustrated. This is the same scenario as in the preceding the LRU example.

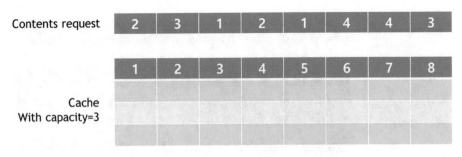

Figure 7-19. *LFU Example of the Server's Cache at Time Instant 0*

Figure 7-20 presents the LFU strategy example of the server's cache at time instant 1, where a request for content 2 is received, so the server caches content 2. At time instant 2, a request for content 3 is received, so the server caches content 3 as shown in Figure 7-21. At time instant 3, a request for content 1 is received, so the server caches content 1 as shown in Figure 7-22. So far, the LFU and LRU have performed the same.

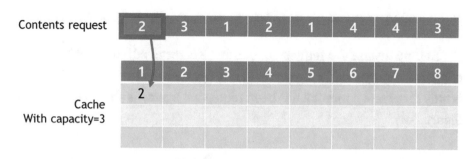

Figure 7-20. *LFU Example of the Server's Cache at Time Instant 1*

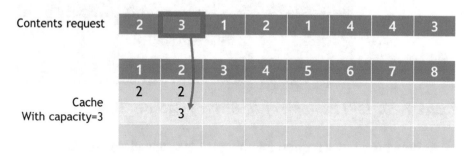

Figure 7-21. *LFU Example of the Server's Cache at Time Instant 2*

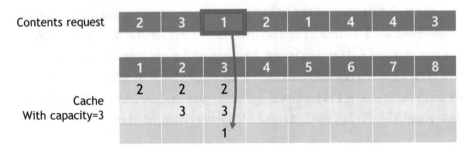

Figure 7-22. *LFU Example of the Server's Cache at Time Instant 3*

At time instant 4, a request for content 2 is received, so the older content 2 is refreshed in the server cache because the server's capacity is only three and content 2 has been requested again, as shown in Figure 7-23.

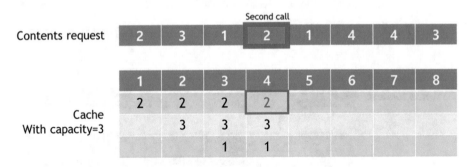

Figure 7-23. *LFU Example of the Server's Cache at Time Instant 4*

At time instant 5, a request for content 1 is received, so the older content 1 is refreshed in the server cache because the server's capacity is only three and content 1 has been requested again, as shown in Figure 7-24.

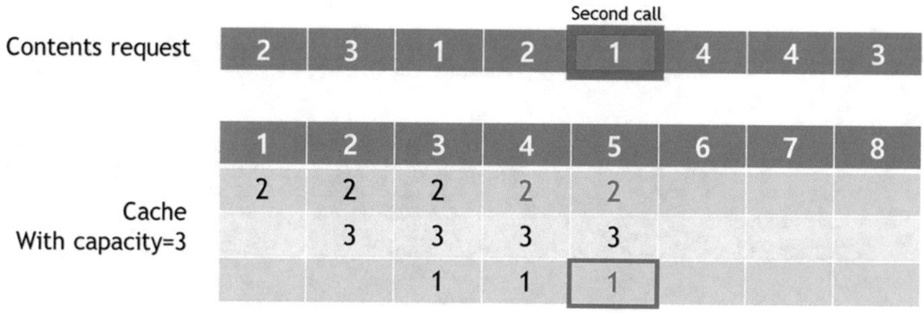

Figure 7-24. *LFU Example of the Server's Cache at Time Instant 5*

At time instant 6, a request for content 4 is received, so the older content 3 is replaced with content 4 because the server's capacity is only three and content 3 has been requested only once and not most recently, as shown in Figure 7-25.

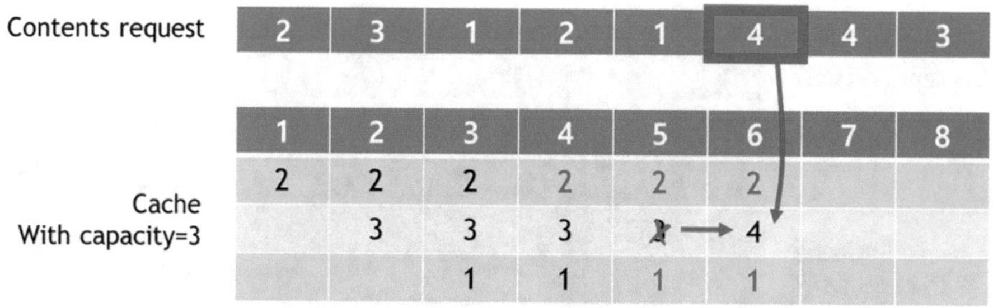

Figure 7-25. *LFU Example of the Server's Cache at Time Instant 6*

At time instant 7, a request for content 4 is received again, so the older content 4 is refreshed in the server cache because the server's capacity is only three and content 4 has been requested again, as shown in Figure 7-26.

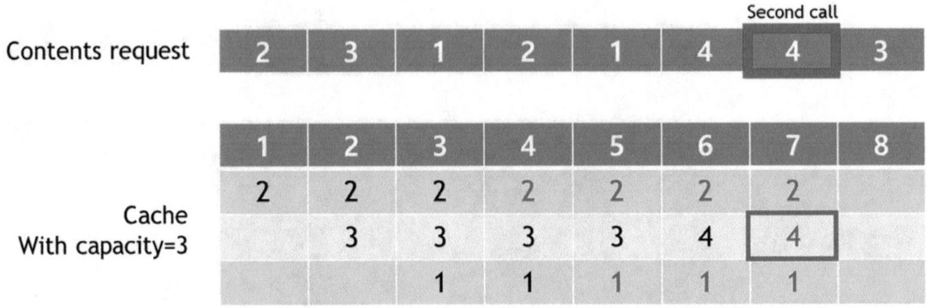

Second call

Contents request	2	3	1	2	1	4	4	3

	1	2	3	4	5	6	7	8
	2	2	2	2	2	2	2	
Cache With capacity=3		3	3	3	3	4	4	
			1	1	1	1	1	

Figure 7-26. *LFU Example of the Server's Cache at Time Instant 7*

At time instant 8, a request for content 3 is received, so the older content 2 is replaced with content 3 because the server's capacity is only 3, and even though content 2 has been requested twice, both requests were made much earlier than the other contents in the cache currently, as shown in Figure 7-27.

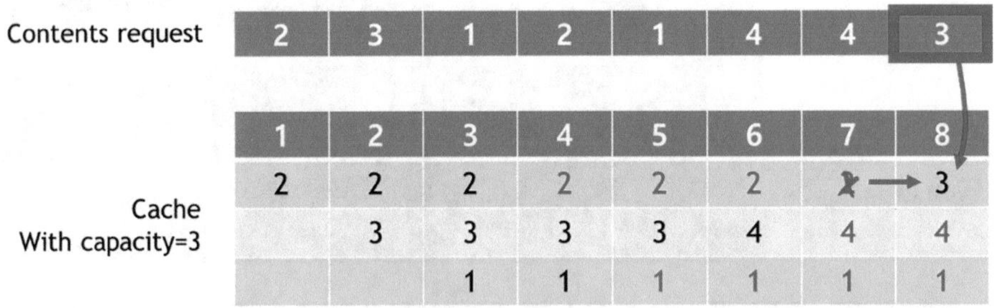

Contents request	2	3	1	2	1	4	4	3

	1	2	3	4	5	6	7	8
	2	2	2	2	2	2	✗ → 3	3
Cache With capacity=3		3	3	3	3	4	4	4
			1	1	1	1	1	1

Figure 7-27. *LFU Example of the Server's Cache at Time Instant 8*

Although LFU and LRU seem similar in these simple examples, in a server with a larger cache capacity and much more content requests being made by multiple user devices, a more significant difference of the two schemes can be observed easily.

Mobile CDN Services

CDNs are even more important in mobile networks because mobile communication networks have a stronger need for both reduced traffic load and shorter content delivery time. This is why international and intercontinental mobile networks have a critical need for CDN support.

It is necessary to note that the Internet is divided into multiple autonomous systems (ASs), where each AS is assigned Internet Protocol (IP) addresses (e.g., IPv4 and IPv6 addresses) with the same prefix. Based on having the same IP address prefix, the computers and devices within the AS can be controlled together by the same network operator(s). The Internet Assigned Numbers Authority (IANA) provides the Regional Internet Registries (RIRs) a group of autonomous system numbers (ASNs) to be assigned (which is why computers and devices within an AS have the same IP address prefixes), where each AS is assigned an ASN. ASNs are used for Border Gateway Protocol (BGP) routing as well as IP address assignments which are used for Interior Gateway Protocol (IGP) routing.

Border Gateway Protocol ver. 4 (BGP4) is used between AS networks. Network traffic that is accessed by mobile users (e.g., smartphones, laptops, tablets/pads) is continuously increasing. The quality of mobile services is highly dependent on the content download time of multimedia data and applications. Several mobile network operators have suffered from service outage or performance deterioration due to the significant increase in multimedia access from mobile devices, which is why CDN support is essential.

Mobile CDNs are needed for transportation systems and various mobile user streaming services via OTT, which are becoming more popular every day. In addition to mobile OTT services, mobile systems need to access GPS navigation information, Intelligent Transportation System (ITS) information, and Location-Based Services (LBSs), which are commonly supported by CDNs. CDN-based LBS can provide location oriented real-time services to mobile users. Efficient content provisioning is required to provide scalable control over wide coverage areas while providing high levels of QoS with limited content resources.

CDNs and mobile CDNs support mostly the same content types; however, the user and surrogate locations need to be updated to consider the mobility of users in mobile CDNs. The surrogate topology for CDNs by the Internet service providers (ISPs) is focused on local service area support. The surrogate topology for mobile CDNs needs to additionally include the base stations (BSs), access points (APs), radio access network (RAN), as well as the mobile devices. Due to the frequently updating requirements of mobile CDNs, the maintenance complexity of a mobile CDN is higher compared to a CDN. The services provided by a CDN are mostly multimedia and data services. In addition to this, mobile CDNs also have to support mobile apps, LBS, cloud and edge computing, and mobile cloud services (`www.researchgate.net/publication/285100522_ Content_Delivery_Networks_Technology_Survey_and_Research_ Challenges`).

Mobile wireless networks have additional challenges in supporting CDN services compared to CDNs on wired networks. Mobile system constraints (e.g., limited storage, processing power, and input capability) are stricter due to the portable size of mobile devices. In addition, in mobile networks, wireless network disconnections occur with much higher probability due to user mobility.

Summary

This chapter introduced the essential CDN technologies, which include details of multimedia streaming operations, caching services, and mobile CDN services. Because all global metaverse and multimedia services use CDNs, understanding the features and advantages can significantly help in performance analysis, service management, deployment planning, as well as Internet service provider (ISP) contracting. In the following Chapter 8, an introduction to cloud computing and edge cloud technologies is provided. An explanation of how cloud services are used by Netflix and Disney+ and details of cloud computing service models and edge computing are provided.

CHAPTER 8

Cloud Computing and Edge Cloud Technologies

This chapter covers the details of cloud computing and edge cloud technologies. First, an introduction of how Amazon Web Service (AWS) cloud services are used to support Netflix and Disney+ is provided. Second, the cloud computing service models are introduced. These models include Software as a Service (SaaS), Platform as a Service (PaaS), and Infrastructure as a Service (IaaS). Third, the newer containers, Dockers, and Kubernetes technologies are introduced. Fourth, the technical details of edge computing and multiple-access edge computing (MEC) technology is introduced. Finally, details of the two most popular edge services, which are the AWS edge cloud services and the Microsoft Azure edge cloud services, are introduced. The sections of this chapter are listed in the following:

- AWS Cloud Support for Netflix and Disney+

- Cloud Service Models (IaaS, PaaS, SaaS)

- Containers, Dockers, and Kubernetes

- Edge Computing and MEC

- Amazon AWS and Microsoft Azure Edge Cloud Services

© Jong-Moon Chung 2023
J.-M. Chung, *Emerging Metaverse XR and Video Multimedia Technologies*,
https://doi.org/10.1007/978-1-4842-8928-0_8

AWS Cloud Support for Netflix and Disney+

Amazon started its e-commerce-as-a-service platform in 2000 to enable web-store services for third-party retailers. This is the beginning of Amazon's cloud computing services, which has now become AWS. AWS has been the global dominant leader in cloud services for many years. In March 2006, Amazon Simple Storage Service (S3) cloud storage was launched, and in August 2006, Amazon Elastic Compute Cloud (EC2) was launched (`https://en.wikipedia.org/wiki/Amazon_Web_Services`).

From the beginning of Netflix's video streaming services in 2007, Netflix has been consistently using Amazon's cloud computing services, which is now AWS. Because the Amazon S3 and EC2 were in early stages, Netflix contributed to many innovative technologies in cloud service control and management and multimedia streaming services. Many cloud service innovations made by Netflix were made open source to enable other companies and academia to use, study, and contribute to the software development, which became the Netflix Open Source Software (OSS). However, Netflix does keep the core software for its multimedia streaming services a secret (`www.lightreading.com/service-provider-cloud/netflix-shows-why-telcos-should-fear-aws/a/d-id/772913`). The Netflix OSS Center software is available on GitHub (`https://netflix.github.io/`). Due to these many contributions to cloud services and technical innovations, Netflix received many awards, which include the JAX 2015 Industry Innovation Award.

The Walt Disney Company has also been using AWS, especially for the Disney+ video streaming services (`www.cloudcomputing-news.net/news/2021/apr/29/the-walt-disney-company-renews-vows-with-aws-for-disney-global-rollout/`).

More technical details on cloud services are provided in later sections of this chapter.

Cloud Service Models

There are four cloud service models based on the service domain of what and who the cloud is used for. Figure 8-1 presents the four cloud service models based on service domain, which are public cloud, private cloud, community cloud, and hybrid cloud. A public cloud enables public systems and service access. Public clouds commonly have an open architecture (e.g., email and web services) and could be less secure due to its openness. A private cloud enables service access within an organization, where due to its private nature, it is more secure. A community cloud is a cloud that is accessible by a group of organizations. A hybrid cloud is a combination of a public cloud and private cloud, where the private cloud supports critical activities and the public cloud supports noncritical activities (`www.tutorialspoint.com/cloud_computing/cloud_computing_tutorial.pdf`).

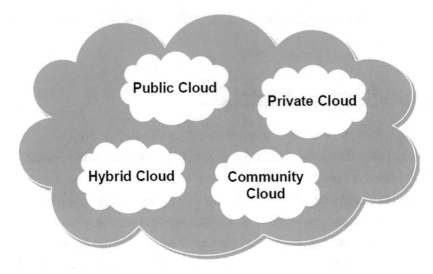

Figure 8-1. *Cloud Service Models Based on Service Domain*

There are three cloud service models based on functionality as presented in Figure 8-2. The function groups of Software as a Service (SaaS), Platform as a Service (PaaS), and Infrastructure as a Service (IaaS) are distinguished based on what the cloud can provide as a service. SaaS provides a variety of software applications as a service to end users. PasS provides a program executable platform for applications, development tools, etc. IaaS provides the fundamental computing and security resources for the entire cloud, which include backup storage, computing power, virtual machine (VM), etc. (`https://en.wikipedia.org/wiki/Cloud_computing`).

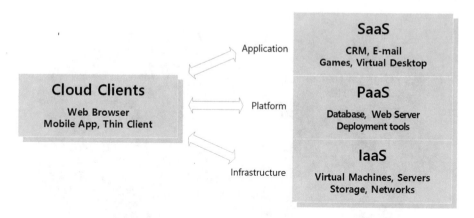

Figure 8-2. *Cloud Service Models Based on Service Functionality*

IaaS, PaaS, and SaaS are the basic three that cover the entire cloud service domain. However, there are many other cloud service models that can be claimed, where the form of XaaS in which X is where the initial of the service type is claimed. For example, NaaS can be used as "Network as a Service," DaaS can be used for "Database as a Service," BaaS can be used for "Business as a Service," CaaS can be used for "Cloud as a Service," etc.

Figure 8-3 summarizes the major benefits of cloud services. The main benefits of cloud services include high efficiency, reliability, and flexibility. Cloud services are especially attractive because cost-effective applications (apps) are provided as on-demand utilities received from the cloud over the Internet. User devices will access a cloud that matches the operating system (OS) and device's capability, so the user can easily manipulate and configure apps online where various development and deployment software tools are available online on the cloud, so nearly no additional software is needed on the user's device.

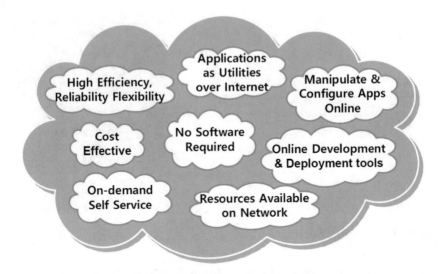

Figure 8-3. *Benefits of Cloud Services*

Figure 8-4 presents the cloud service characteristics. An essential characteristic of cloud computing is the on-demand self-service aspect, which means that the service applications that are needed can be found automatically or found by the user searching and can be downloaded and used immediately (assuming that the user is logged in and download authorization is obtained in advance). Some of the common characteristics of cloud services include broad network access, rapid elasticity, resource pooling, measured services, massive scale, resilient computing, homogeneity, geographic distribution, virtualization, service orientation, low-cost software, and advanced security.

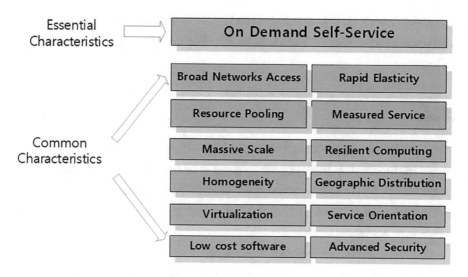

Figure 8-4. *Cloud Service Characteristics*

In cloud service support, IaaS is the lowest among the service models (when compared to PaaS and SaaS as presented in Figure 8-2) as it is based on using computer/server hardware components like storage memory, CPUs and GPUs for data processing, wired and wireless networks, virtual local area networks (VLANs), software packages/bundles, VMs, as well as security functions. PaaS is a level higher than IaaS and provides services like databases, web servers, and app deployment tools. SaaS is the highest cloud service model and is a software application (app) that can be downloaded from the cloud app store any time needed by the user. For example, smartphone apps are SaaS.

The lower service models need the support of the upper service models. What this means is that if a user accesses IaaS services, then the user needs to use the corresponding PaaS services to support the IaaS and download the SaaS on the user's device, so the matching IaaS and PaaS functions can be accessed and controlled by the installed SaaS app. Likewise, if a PaaS service is requested to be used by the user, then the corresponding SaaS app needs to be downloaded to the user's device.

However, if only SaaS is needed, then the SaaS app can be downloaded and used. More details on IaaS, PaaS, and SaaS are provided in the following.

IaaS

IaaS is focused on providing infrastructure support over the Internet, which include computing power, storage services, networking, and VM deployment. VMs are one of the main features of IaaS. IaaS enables control of computing resources by allowing administrative access to VMs through server virtualization features.

VM administrative command examples include saving data on a cloud server or creating a new web server. IaaS VM creation and service procedures are illustrated in Figure 8-5. The software owner or programmer creates a VM by combining the app with its OS in a software package. The VM is placed on the Storage Area Network (SAN) which is distributed to Virtual Switches (VSwitches). When a user needs the VM, a local VSwitch is searched and the VM is downloaded to the user's device. VMs are self-contained packages, as the app and the OS are both included, so the hypervisor on the user's device will execute the app using the OS functions. Due to the OS being included in the VM, the user's device can assess any type of app regardless of the OS requirements. On the other hand, since VMs have to include the OS, the file size of a VM is relatively large (www.tutorialspoint.com/cloud_computing/cloud_computing_tutorial.pdf).

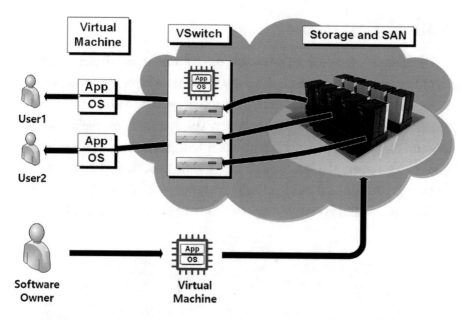

Figure 8-5. *IaaS VM Creation and Service Procedures*

IaaS provides flexible and efficient renting of computer and server hardware. A representative example of an IaaS service is a virtual desktop, which includes a package of various types of rentable computing resources that include VMs, storage, bandwidth, firewalls, IP addresses, monitoring services, etc. IaaS services are commonly rent payment based, which means that the resource type, usage time, and service package types determine the cost. The portability and interoperability with legacy applications are taken care of by the cloud, which has all types of older software to support full interoperability. IaaS also provides portable infrastructure resources that are used through Internet connections. IaaS also enables a method to maintain interoperability with other IaaS clouds.

PaaS

PaaS services are focused on providing development and deployment tools for app development. Figure 8-6 presents the PaaS service types. The application delivery-only environment of PaaS provides on-demand scaling and application security. The standalone development environment of PaaS provides an independent platform for a specific function. The open platform as a service model provides open source software to run applications for PaaS providers. In addition, the add-on development facilities enable customization to existing SaaS platforms.

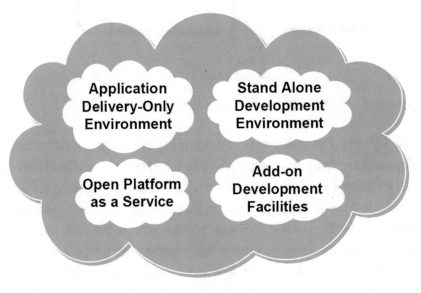

Figure 8-6. *PaaS Service Types*

The PaaS app runtime environment is presented in Figure 8-7. PaaS services are accessible by the integrated development environment (IDE) platform provided by the cloud servers. Users select the PaaS service type (e.g., data security, backup, recovery, application hosting, scalable infrastructure) in which the IDE will control the cloud server to provide that service to the user.

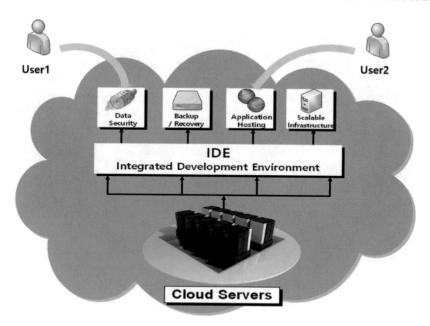

Figure 8-7. *PaaS App Runtime Environment*

A summary of PaaS benefits is presented in Figure 8-8 and is explained in the following. PaaS is focused on minimizing the administrative overhead of SaaS apps and frees the user from needing to be involved in any administration of the platform. PaaS is very effective in lowering the total cost of ownership, as the user does not need to purchase any hardware, memory, or server since PaaS provides all of this. PaaS also provides many scalable solutions by applying application resource demands based on automatic resource scale control. In addition, the newest version of system software (as well as older software versions) is provided to the users, as it is the cloud service provider's role to maintain software upgrades and install patches. In addition, keeping older versions of OSs and software packages helps to run and edit old programs, which is also very useful (www.tutorialspoint.com/cloud_computing/cloud_computing_tutorial.pdf).

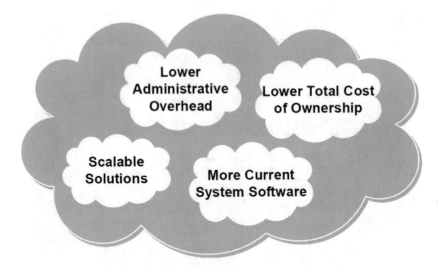

Figure 8-8. *Summary of PaaS Benefits*

SaaS

SaaS provides software applications as a service to the users. All software that is deployed on a cloud server is accessible through the Internet. Some of the main SaaS characteristics are summarized in the following. The on-demand availability is an essential feature of SaaS, as cloud software is available anywhere that the cloud is reachable over the Internet. Easy maintenance is important as no user software upgrade or maintenance is needed because the PaaS maintains all upgrades and manages the cloud's software and hardware platform making it suitable for user access any time. SaaS enables flexible scale-up and scale-down since the cloud system is under centralized management of all computing processes and access of data. SaaS enables shared data models, where multiple users can share a single data model and database. Because SaaS provides multiple tenant programming solutions (in which multiple programmers are ensured to use the same software version), there are no version mismatch problems among developed programs. This makes SaaS the optimal environment for large-scale software development by project groups with multiple programmers. Due to these features, SaaS is very cost-effective considering the pay based on usage models commonly applied and especially considering that there is no risk in buying the wrong software.

The open SaaS applications architecture is presented in Figure 8-9, where the users connect to the cloud through the client user interface (UI) in which the SaaS Orchestration system detects the requested app and provides app download to the user's device. Representative SaaS apps include directory, messaging, collaboration, and content web services (`www.tutorialspoint.com/cloud_computing/cloud_computing_tutorial.pdf`).

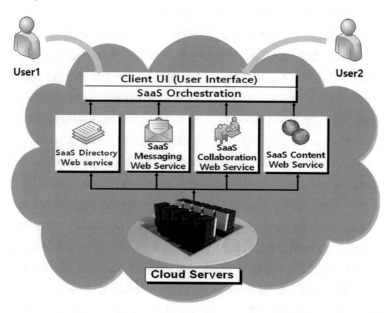

Figure 8-9. *Open SaaS Applications Architecture*

Containers, Dockers, and Kubernetes

In this section, details on containers, Dockers, and Kubernetes are introduced, which are cloud technology enhancements.

Containers are small program packages that are made to ensure an application can work in almost any computing environment, in an efficient and independent way. Containers have all the functions needed to process the application included in its package, which is why containers are platform independent and have great portability. Containers enable easy and efficient deployment of applications on any computing system in a scalable way. Many programs will not work because small mismatches and interface problems exist in the hardware, software, operating system, kernel, etc. A container is designed as an independent lightweight package of application programs and functions such that it can work on almost any computing platform. Containers are designed to be immutable, which means that once a container is deployed, it cannot be changed. Computers and servers process application instructions and data on their kernel using the operating system (OS) to control and manage the overall process. Container applications are isolated and use only a small part of the processing resources and memory to operate independently such that other processes on the same computer/server are (almost) not interfered with. Because containers share the OS's kernel processing resources, there is no need to run a separate OS instance for each container application, which results in smaller container files and higher resource (CPU, GPU, RAM) utilization. This is why containers are very good for cloud and edge computing applications (`www.aquasec.com/cloud-native-academy/container-platforms/what-is-a-container-complete-guide-2022/`).

For better understanding, VMs and containers need to be compared. VMs were explained in the preceding IaaS section. Figure 8-10 presents a comparison of VMs and containers and their operation environments.

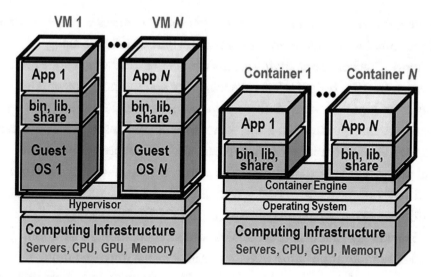

Figure 8-10. *Comparison of VMs and Containers and Their Operation Environments*

VMs are made by including the application program and including the necessary subdirectories that the application program needs, which also include "lib" for shared library files, "bin" for executable files, and "share" for data files. In addition, VMs include the OS that their application program needs. This makes VMs relatively large.

The server that executes the VM on its hardware needs to be equipped with a hypervisor, which enables VMs to be executed on a computing system by supporting the VM's OS while monitoring the application program's operation process. This is why the hypervisor is also called a virtual machine monitor (VMM). The VM is assigned a division of the computer/server's hardware and memory resources for processing. The computer/server's hardware and memory are virtually divided so that multiple VMs can be executed, in which each VM uses its own OS instance.

Containers are smaller than VMs because they include the application program and necessary subdirectory files (e.g., lib, bin, and share files) but do not include the OS files. The computer/server that executes the container needs to have a container engine and OS to assist the execution of the container program on the computing hardware while using memory. The container engine assists the OS to execute the application program, so the computer/server's hardware and memory are working with its original OS which makes all operations faster. The containers share a virtual division of the OS resources (with the help of the container engine), so each container program can efficiently share the hardware and memory resources of the computer/server (`www.netapp.com/blog/ containers-vs-vms/#:~:text=Conclusion%20Virtual%20machines%20 and%20containers,to%20run%20multiple%20OS%20instances`).

Docker is a platform that enables container creation. In addition, Dockers enable application development, delivery, and execution. A Docker image is a read-only file that provides instructions on how to create a container. Containers that are created from the Docker image can be executed on the Docker platform.

However, managing multiple containers distributed across multiple clusters through a cloud platform is very complex, time-consuming, and difficult. This is why **Kubernetes** was created. Kubernetes is an open source orchestration tool that enables control and management of multiple containers (and microservices) processed on computers/ servers that are distributed over multiple clusters on a cloud. Kubernetes is very resilient with an objective of zero downtime, which is enabled by its automated rollback, self-healing, and scalability features. Kubernetes automated self-healing features come from a combination of functions which include auto-restart, auto-placement, and auto-replication. Google was the original developer of Kubernetes, which is now supported by the Cloud Native Computing Foundation (CNCF). Kubernetes can be used on any public or private cloud platform due to its highly portable architecture. The top cloud platforms like AWS, Azure, Google Cloud, OpenStack, and bare metal machines all use Kubernetes.

Edge Computing and MEC

Cloud computing has become a necessity in all information, communication, and technology (ICT) services. Especially, as smartphones, smart devices, and Internet of Things (IoT) systems abundantly use cloud computing, there is a need to place the cloud computing resources closer to the users, near the edge of the network, which is where the name "edge" originated from (https://ieeexplore. ieee.org/document/8869772). Edge clouds help to reduce the time delay in providing cloud services to the users and help to reduce the network traffic. Edge computing can be seen as a similar function of CDNs using local content servers (LCSs) in video streaming services, but edge computing provides cloud services instead (https://en.wikipedia.org/ wiki/Edge_computing).

Figure 8-11 presents a multiple-access edge computing (MEC) edge cloud connected to a 4G LTE mobile communication network that is connected to the main cloud through the Internet. The term "multiple-access" in MEC refers to the fact that the MEC can be accessed from various wired, wireless, and mobile connections, which include 5G and 4G LTE mobile networks as well as Wi-Fi and Bluetooth wireless networks. The MEC provides SaaS, PaaS, and IaaS services to various user equipment (UE). Because the MEC cannot contain all apps, software, platforms, and hardware that the main cloud possesses, the MEC needs to make intelligent decisions on what to download from the main cloud server in advance. The MEC contains multiple hosts that contain multiple apps. MECs are located on or very near the base station (i.e., eNodeB (eNB) in 4G LTE or gNB in 5G) within the Radio Access Network (RAN) of the mobile communication network or near the Wi-Fi Access Points (APs) or gateways/routers of the local area network (LAN) (https:// en.wikipedia.org/wiki/Multi-access_edge_computing).

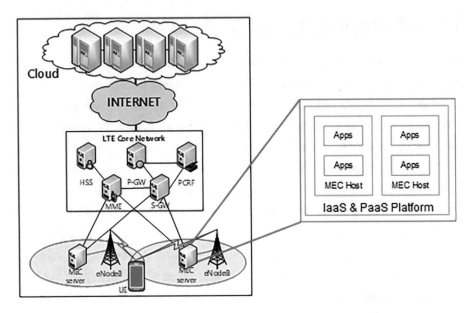

Figure 8-11. *MEC-Based Edge Computing Example*

Compared to conventional cloud computing, edge computing has many advantages. Without edge computing, cloud services directly supporting mobile devices through Internet connections commonly result in long time delays resulting in poor QoS performances, over usage of the network resources, excessive battery usage of IoT and smart devices, significant packet interarrival time jitter, and high probability of delay bound violation (DBV) for real-time multimedia services.

MEC servers offer real-time network information (e.g., network load and capacity) and information on the end devices connected to the servers (e.g., location information, etc.). MEC nodes (or servers) are usually colocated with the mobile communication network Radio Network Controller (RNC), macro base stations (i.e., eNB in 4G LTE or gNB in 5G), or APs in Wi-Fi networks. Edge servers may run multiple MEC hosts, where the MEC hosts can perform computation and storage through virtualized interfaces.

A Mobile Edge Orchestrator (MEO) is used to manage multiple MEC hosts and controls information flow for services. MEO services are offered to each MEC host to control the edge cloud resources and network topology while managing mobile edge applications.

Amazon AWS and Microsoft Azure Edge Cloud Services

For multimedia streaming, MMOGs, and XR metaverse services, cloud computing services are essential for on-demand application support, customer services, data storage, connectivity support, etc. This is why every company supporting multimedia streaming, MMOGs, and XR metaverse applications uses cloud computing services. However, because cloud centers are commonly located far away from the user, a large time delay occurs when the main cloud center is accessed. For multimedia streaming, MMOGs, and XR metaverses, most services need to be completed within a time delay bound, or the service may become unusable/useless. This is why local edge clouds are needed.

Two of the most popular edge cloud services are introduced in this section. The first one is the AWS edge cloud, and the other one is the Microsoft edge cloud Azure. AWS is one of the original cloud computing companies which now occupies over 40% of the world's cloud computing services and is used by almost all major companies, which include Netflix and Disney+ as described in the following. The second edge company introduced is Microsoft Azure, which is important because a large majority of personal computers and laptops use Microsoft Windows OSs and Office applications, which make interaction with Azure edge computing services very popular. More details of the AWS edge clouds and Microsoft Azure clouds are described in the following.

Amazon AWS Edge Computing Services

Amazon Elastic Container Service (ECS) is a container management service that is designed to operate optimally on the AWS cloud platform while being highly efficient and massively scalable. Amazon ECS clusters are formed based on the service characteristics of the company or group leasing AWS services. The global AWS cloud is divided into AWS Regions, and each AWS Region supports multiple edge computing domains, which are divided into Local Zones, Wavelength Zones, and AWS Outposts based on service size and network characteristics, as presented in Figure 8-12 (https://docs.aws.amazon.com/AmazonECS/latest/developerguide/cluster-regions-zones.html).

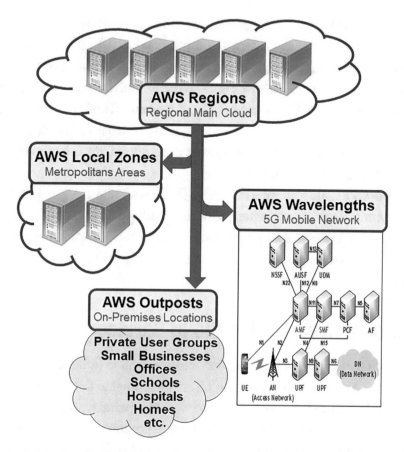

Figure 8-12. *AWS Region Connected to a Local Zone, Wavelength Zone, and Outpost Example*

AWS Region cloud services are extended through a Local Zone to provide a specific location that is sufficiently populated (but far from the AWS Region cloud center) with full AWS cloud services. So a Local Zone cloud is a direct extension of the AWS Region cloud brought closer to the users.

A Wavelength Zone cloud is an AWS edge cloud embedded into the 5G mobile communication network, so mobile devices (e.g., smartphones, smart devices, laptops, tablets, IoT, etc.) can easily use Amazon ECS as well as various cloud application services over the wireless network. Especially, the 5G Ultra Reliable Low Latency Communication (URLLC) mode provides networking services with extremely low latency and very high reliability, which can be used for control of remote/autonomous driving of cars and drones, MMOFPS and MMORTS games, XR and AR services, etc.

AWS Outpost is the smallest Amazon ECS service unit, which is used to provide AWS cloud services to private user groups, small businesses, offices, schools, homes, etc.

Amazon Elastic Kubernetes Service (EKS) is a Kubernetes container cluster control and management service supported by AWS. EKS is used to run and scale Kubernetes applications in the AWS cloud and edge systems or on private server platforms (on-premises) (`https://aws.amazon.com/eks/`).

Microsoft Azure Edge Cloud Services

Microsoft Azure edge computing services are divided into Azure public MECs and Azure private MECs, which are described in the following.

In order to provide Azure cloud services over wireless networks, Azure public MECs are embedded in the 5G mobile communication network or very near in the mobile operator data centers in highly populated areas (which are commonly metropolitan business districts). The Azure public MEC compute service types and architecture are presented in Figure 8-13. Azure public MECs are installed with 5G mobile network operators or ISPs. Especially, 5G URLLC services used with Azure public MECs can provide very fast and highly reliable wireless mobile Azure cloud service control that can be used for XR and AR services, metaverses, multimedia streaming, smart factories, MMOG real-time games, and autonomous/remote control of vehicles (e.g., cars, trucks, and drones).

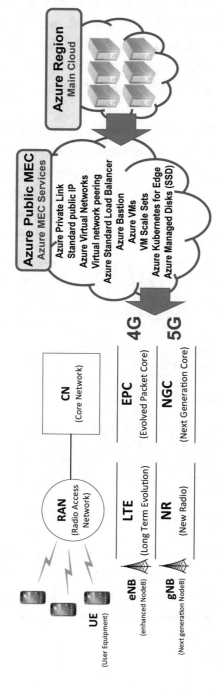

Figure 8-13. Azure Public MEC Services Example

Azure public MEC core services include Azure VMs, VM Scale Sets, Azure Private Link, Standard Public IP, Azure Virtual Networks, Virtual network peering, Azure Standard Load Balancer, Azure Kubernetes for Edge, Azure Bastion, and Azure managed disks (https://docs. microsoft.com/en-us/azure/public-multi-access-edge-compute-mec/ overview).

The Azure private MEC compute service types are presented in Figure 8-14. Azure private MEC compute services are for enterprise customers, telcos and system integrating companies, and application independent software vendors (ISV). The main services provided include the Application services and Azure Management services, which are delivered through the Azure Network Functions to the users.

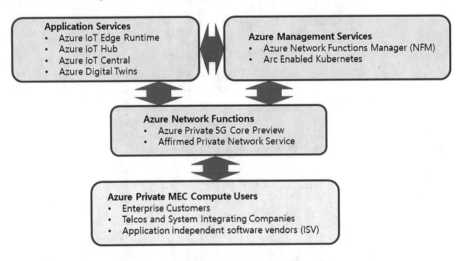

Figure 8-14. *Azure Private MEC Compute Services*

The Application services provided by the Azure private MEC include the Azure IoT Edge Runtime, Azure IoT Hub, Azure IoT Central, and Azure Digital Twins. Azure IoT Edge Runtime helps control cloud deployment and workload management across edge compute appliances, and Azure

IoT Hub serves as a center to support this service. Azure IoT Central is an application platform that enables device management and data ingestion. The service provides a predictable pricing model and global scale management. Azure Digital Twins enables sensors to form a business context-based mode of spatial relations, usage patterns, and business context that replicates physical assets and the work environment.

Azure Stack hardware and services include the Azure Stack Edge and the Azure Stack Hyper-Converged Infrastructure (HCI). Azure Stack Edge provides Windows and Linux VMs, Azure Backup, Azure Monitor, and Microsoft Defender for Cloud to Azure MEC user devices. Azure Stack HCI is a new HCI OS that provides advanced security, performance, and features of the Azure cloud to MEC users.

Azure Management services include the Azure Network Functions Manager (NFM) and Arc-enabled Kubernetes services. Azure NFM enables Virtual Network Functions (VNFs) deployment in support of private MEC services, such as deploying packet core and SD-WAN VNFs. Azure Arc-enabled Kubernetes supports attachment and configuration of Kubernetes clusters within the Azure cloud platform domain and outside with any Cloud Native Computing Foundation (CNCF) certified Kubernetes cluster.

Azure Network Functions serve the main role of connecting the users with the Azure private MEC features, where there are two types of functions which include the Private 5G Core Preview and the Affirmed Private Network Services. The Azure Private 5G Core Preview provides management and deployment of Azure cloud services for enterprise private mobile networks. The Affirmed Private Network Service provides managed private network services to 4G and 5G mobile network operators (MNOs) and service enterprises.

Summary

This chapter introduced cloud computing technologies including details of the service models SaaS, PaaS, IaaS as well as details on containers, Dockers, and Kubernetes. Just by seeing how AWS cloud services are used by Netflix and Disney+, the importance of cloud technology can be easily realized. In addition, edge computing and MEC technologies are introduced along with descriptions of AWS and Azure edge cloud services. In the following Chapter 9, which is the last chapter of this book, possible directions of future technical evolution as well as predictions on emerging technologies are provided.

CHAPTER 9

Emerging Technologies

In this chapter, some possible directions of future technical evolution are described, corresponding to each of the previous chapters of this book. Based on my experience, some personal predictions will be made in this chapter, which I hope most will come true. However, please forgive me if these predictions do not come true, as these predictions are only to help the reader see where technical evolutions could go toward. For the areas of XR as well as metaverse and multimedia streaming services, if these futuristic fields interest you, then pursuing a career in these areas could be beneficial. This is because these technologies are the foundation of the entire online entertainment, sports, game, education, and training business domain, which has extremely large financial support and investments made and will continue to need significant contributions in new technologies and creative content.

© Jong-Moon Chung 2023
J.-M. Chung, *Emerging Metaverse XR and Video Multimedia Technologies*,
https://doi.org/10.1007/978-1-4842-8928-0_9

Chapter 1. Introduction to Metaverse and Video Streaming Technology and Services

Chapter 1 introduces metaverse, XR, and multimedia streaming technologies and services. As presented, many of the core technologies used in metaverses and video streaming are the same, just used in slightly different ways to support distinguished service characteristics. Future evolution directions may progress to make metaverse and video streaming services crossover in many ways, which is why this book covers these two massive service domains together. As mentioned in Chapter 1, metaverse XR services need new creative socializing themes to be built into multiverses, and multimedia streaming services are driving to create unique content for only their platform. I predict that this will create a merge of metaverse XR services and multimedia streaming services as well as massively multiplayer online game (MMOG) services. The companies that successfully establish content sharing and collaborative creativity and have an excellent user platform with a good business model will become the leaders of these service domains.

However, there are several problems that metaverse services need to solve (`https://bernardmarr.com/7-important-problems-disadvantages-of-the-metaverse/`). Among many issues, user protection is most important, especially for children. Children need to be protected from any type of abuse or assaults in metaverses. Designing avatars that have filtered audio and video input (which can exclude inappropriate language and images) with protection bubbles (i.e., minimum distance requirements that regulate encounters with other avatars or objects that can prevent all types of abuse and assaults) needs to be basic features and requirements. These child protection features need to be monitored and governed to prevent crimes and offenses in metaverses. Some of these policies can be lightened or removed as the user passes certain ages or qualifies to join certain metaverses. Such protection features can be programmed into metaverse avatars and multiverses. This is important especially because there are too many video games and MMOGs that require players to be extremely aggressive (and violent) in order to continue to win and progress to the next stage. From a user perspective, metaverses, video games, and MMOGs provide nearly the same level of perceptive presence; therefore, when using them, the user may feel very little difference in these virtual environments. Desensitization of frequent gamers is a difficult issue, because after being indulged in an aggressive massively multiplayer online first-person shooter game (MMOFPS), massively multiplayer online real-time strategy game (MMORTS), massively multiplayer online role-playing game (MMORPG), or similar video games for a while, and afterward, if the user enters a metaverse, the user can get confused if they are interacting with game characters controlled by the game engine or avatars controlled by actual human users. This is why video games and MMOG developers and metaverse developers need to have agreements on distinguishing features to help avoid confusion. In addition, crime policing within metaverses is needed, in which policies need to be set by international organizations with the participation of local governments. Policing enforcement needs to be provided by the metaverse service company. This may create a slight delay in the development due to adding the programs needed to control and police the metaverse. But once established, more secure, stable, and accredited metaverses will be able to serve as safe places to conduct socializing, education, training, research, development, entertainment, and business. As mentioned in Chapter 1, to form a sustainable expanding metaverse, the social values of that metaverse need to be maintained as the number of users grows, which will become more and more difficult without these types of management and policing features.

Chapter 2. Metaverse XR Components

As mentioned in Chapter 2, a high-quality XR experience requires the user to feel immersive presence effects provided by the XR device. The feel of immersive presence can be created through a combination of providing the feeling of immersion and presence. The immersion effect is created by enabling the user to feel surrounded in the XR environment, and the presence effect is created by enabling the user to feel physically and spatially located within the XR environment. Cognitive presence and perceptive presence are the two types of presence that a high-quality XR service needs to provide. Cognitive presence is felt in one's mind and is triggered by imagination, while perceptive presence is felt through the human five senses (i.e., eyesight, hearing, touch, taste, and smell) or a few of them. Current XR devices can interact with two or three human senses (e.g., eyesight, hearing, and touch), but with only low precision, and have a long way to go before four or five human senses can be properly simulated by XR systems.

A futuristic system could be one that can read the user's brain waves to form selective images/information related to the application running and project this information to other users or use it to control the XR interface and avatar(s).

Among the five basic human senses, the sensation of touch, smell, and taste could be triggered using advanced neural stimulation technology in the future. For example, a user could be made to smell without infusing an order or fragrance, and taste/flavor can be experienced without actually eating, drinking, or chewing on anything. Considering that visual and acoustic effects have already been implemented in XR systems (and are expected to improve significantly more), this would be one way to accomplish a XR full five basic human senses (5HS) perceptive presence experience.

This is also an area I have a lot of interest in. In addition to serving as a professor in the School of Electrical and Electronic Engineering in the College of Engineering, I also serve as a professor (joint appointment) in the College of Medicine at Yonsei University (located in Seoul, South Korea). One of my medical specialties is in epilepsy treatment and optimizing brain surgery, which requires electroencephalogram (EEG) brain signal analysis using advanced medical signal and image processing AI techniques. One of my papers on epilepsy treatment using EEG brain signals and AI technologies can be found at `https://ieeexplore.ieee.org/document/9262846`, which was conducted with Yonsei University's Severance Children's Hospital (located in Seoul, South Korea). In this paper, my research team introduces a new AI technology to help distinguish EEG brain signals for accurate epilepsy medical diagnosis. This paper was mentioned to show that brain signals are being used in precision medical treatment and could be used in futuristic mind reading and control systems (like the research ongoing at Neuralink).

Based on this fact, I predict that "cognition" will soon be recognized as the sixth human sense and be used to enhance XR technology to enable "cognitive reality (CR)" systems to be made. Cognition is the basis of knowledge and understanding which involves memory and experience through human senses. The five human senses (i.e., eyesight, hearing, touch, taste, and smell) are the inputs to cognition which are the basis for responsive human behavior. However, cognition cannot be fully expressed with responsive human behavior, as images and details of human thought go beyond what can be expressed through human activity. CR device form factors will be XR devices where the headset supporter/frame (i.e., temples and nose pads of the glasses) can serve as the brainwave reader. At first, the brainwave reader may need to take a hat or helmet form (to connect the set of multiple sensor taps like in EEG 10-20 brainwave readers), but eventually it will turn into a headband form, and later the form of temples on XR glasses will be sufficient, and later wireless inner ear pieces (i.e., wireless earbuds) will be sufficient to read brainwaves for CR control and information access. Futuristic CR modules could be added to cochlear implants (with almost no size or weight increasement) to provide CR functionality as well as multiple medical support functions.

Therefore, XR services could be enhanced with selective cognitive functions added to enhance immersive presence effects and be used to transfer selected visual images and information. Two or more users using CR could establish "telepathic reality (TR)" interaction, which includes telepathy of images and information between XR users supported through wirelessly interconnected CR devices. Such CR and TR systems could be used in communications as well as art, design, construction, education, entertainment, games, sports, industry, factories, transportation, business, and the military. But especially CR and TR could be used for patients with medical disadvantages, such as behavioral disorder or paralysis, as CR and TR could be used to provide medical support to assist communication and control of motion and utilities. In addition, CR and TR could also be used for patients with Alzheimer's disease and dementia as gap fillers to assist activities and communication when loss of memory occurs and help prevent accidents and make automated requests for emergent medical assistance.

Chapter 3. XR HMDs and Detection Technology

Chapter 3 focused on XR devices, covering the XR operation process as well as feature extraction and detection technologies. The details of XR technologies applied in state-of-the-art devices are also introduced. From Chapter 3, it is evident that the difficulty in AR implementations is where the major challenge of XR technology evolution lies in. AR technology is necessary as it is the user's interface to the real-world environment as well as actual objects, pets, and people. AR requires a very short time delay, high display quality, and fast (massive) content access. This results in high energy consumption due to the significant amount of data processing and communication required. These tough requirements make the AR evolution slow and expensive. Due to these reasons, many AR projects have failed or have been significantly delayed. Unless AR technology improves, MR and XR devices will have to focus on VR applications with limited or no AR access.

As mentioned in Chapter 1, my personal desire is to drive technology evolution toward a XR smart device in eye glasses form that has a weight within the 10 to 40 grams range (the lighter the better), which is basically standalone but can switch to wireless tethered mode to connect to the 5G edge cloud or the user's smartphone only when needed (through Bluetooth, Wi-Fi, 5G, or 6G device-to-device (D2D) networking technologies). This XR smart glasses device will need 5G or 6G mobile communication support to assist the control channel as well as the two 8K videos (or higher) supporting the left-eye-view and right-eye-view displays. Using 5G technology, the control channel could be networked using an Ultra Reliable Low Latency Communications (URLLC) channel, and the two 8K videos could be delivered through two enhanced mobile broadband (eMBB) channels. Even though 5G URLLC and eMBB modes are extremely advanced, they are not sufficient to provide reliable real-time high-quality XR services. URLLC channels can satisfy the time delay and reliability performance of real-time XR services but cannot support the two 8K video streams sufficiently due to limitations in bitrates. On the other hand, two 5G eMBB channels can be used to support the two 8K video streaming channels as it can support sufficiently high bitrates, but eMBB cannot satisfy the time delay and reliability requirements of high-quality real-time XR services (especially in mobile environments). This is why 6G technology will be needed for futuristic high-quality real-time XR services. With this objective, I have been conducting research and development to enhance the performance of 5G and 6G systems where my papers https://ieeexplore.ieee.org/document/8959359, https://ieeexplore.ieee.org/document/9780598, and https://ieeexplore.ieee.org/document/9488321 could help to provide a view of the state-of-the-art level in this technical field. These papers also use deep learning technology, where related AI emerging technologies will be described in the following.

Chapter 4. Deep Learning for Metaverse XR and Multimedia Systems

As described in Chapter 4, deep learning is an advanced form of machine learning, and machine learning is an advanced form of AI. Deep learning enables a system to conduct highly complex tasks with high levels of accuracy, which can exceed human performance levels in many cases. Deep learning will be used in every technology area that has been described in this book, where a few examples are provided in the following.

Confirming valid user login and private data access in metaverses and video streaming services needs high levels of accuracy, which is where deep learning can help. Proper user access checking, user authentication, and access authorization as well as user behavior monitoring can be conducted with the help of deep learning technology. In addition, deep learning algorithms like Deep Reinforcement Learning can be used to learn user patterns and provide an optimized recommendation list of content and control options customized to the user's needs. In addition, the user data can be encrypted and stored in blockchains such that user records and transactions are immutable and cannot be tampered with. A representative Deep Reinforcement Learning algorithm called Deep Q-Network (DQN) has been used on blockchains to enhance the data protection, security level, and transaction speed (which is measured in transactions per second (tps) units). Applying AI technologies to blockchain networks is an area that I have worked on where my papers `https://ieeexplore.ieee.org/document/8840847` and `https://ieeexplore.ieee.org/document/9133069` could help to provide a view of the state-of-the-art level in this technical field.

Chapter 5. XR and Multimedia Video Technologies

Chapter 5 focuses on the video encoding and decoding technologies used in XR services, metaverses, and video streaming services, which include the H.264 Advanced Video Coding (AVC), H.265 High Efficiency Video Coding (HEVC), H.266 Versatile Video Coding (VVC), and holography technologies. The H.264 AVC standards were first published on August 17, 2004, and the latest upgrade version 14.0 was published on August 22, 2021. The H.265 HEVC standards were first published on June 7, 2013, and the latest upgrade version 8.0 was published on August 22, 2021. H.265 was designed to be 50% more efficient than H.264 in compression efficiency while being able to support higher video resolutions reaching up to 8K (i.e., 8192×4320) video and 360° videos. The latest version of H.266 VVC is version 1.0 which was released on August 29, 2020. H.266 was designed to be 50% more efficient than H.265 HEVC in compression efficiency while being able to support higher video resolutions reaching up to 16K video.

The next video standard H.267 has yet to take any clear form and may be published sometime between 2026 and 2028. Until then upgrade versions of H.265 and H.266 will be released. Although it is too early to define the modes of H.267, I can make some bold predictions on what features may be considered. H.267 could include goals to enhance the compression efficiency by more than 50% compared to H.266 while supporting higher-resolution videos reaching up to 32K or 64K and possibly even up to 128K. As AI technology becomes more advanced (like in deep learning), AI based video compression technologies can become very effective, where I predict that AI will be used in the H.267 video compression standards, which will significantly help to reduce the encoding and decoding complexity and time. It would be very beneficial to display devices if the H.267 decoding time and complexity could be kept similar to the H.265 or H.264 decoding levels, in which

AI could help. As XR devices and metaverses become extremely more popular in the future, XR based video modes could be included into the H.267 standards. If XR modes (or maybe even CR and TR modes) are included in H.267, then it would be necessary to also include encoding (compression) of the other senses signals like audio, touch, taste, smell, and maybe even cognition information. This is because the video data would not be separable to the other senses data; thus, a coordinated encoding would be a preferred method. I also expect for H.267 to include more diverse Multiview (MV) modes like Mobile MV (MoMV), Multiverse MV (MvMV), and Holography MV (HoMV), but maybe under different mode names.

Chapter 6. Multimedia Streaming with MPEG-DASH

Chapter 6 focuses on multimedia streaming using Moving Picture Experts Group (MPEG) – Dynamic Adaptive Streaming over HTTP (DASH). MPEG-DASH is used in all OTT services, which is why understanding how it works is important in metaverse and multimedia streaming services. Because DASH is a pull-based protocol that is controlled by the Client device that plays the multimedia, as player devices evolve, DASH technology also has to evolve. For example, as mentioned above regarding the evolution of H.276 future multimedia codec technology, the network adaptation techniques used in DASH will have to change correspondingly. For example, for metaverse XR devices to be supported, new display advertisement techniques need to be designed based on the XR device's display characteristics. This will require new changes in the Multimedia Presentation Description (MPD). In addition, if new modes like the proposed MoMV, MvMV, and HoMV were to be added, then the video frames (e.g., I, P, B frames) may change, and correspondingly the Group of Pictures (GOP) format will need to change. In addition, as new networks are made, MPEG-DASH technology will have to change to fit the network characteristics. For example, in Beyond 5G (B5G) and 6G mobile communication networks, Non-Terrestrial Networks (NTN) technology that uses Low Earth Orbit (LEO) satellites (like in Starlink) and drones as mobile base stations of the mobile network are under standardization. These types of networks have different time delay and error rate characteristics which need to be considered when designing new MPEG-DASH technology.

Chapter 7. Content Delivery Network (CDN) Technology

Chapter 7 focuses on content delivery network (CDN) technologies. CDNs are used by all global OTT services, and obviously all global metaverse and video streaming companies use CDNs. A common trend is for a company to lease CDN services until the company becomes large enough where a positive return on investment (ROI) of having the company's own CDN becomes definite. Around this time, or before, the company will start investing into their own CDN. It is expected for this trend to continue, but economic recessions may make companies more conservative in making large CDN investments. One future trend I expect is that CDNs and cloud companies will merge, or CDN companies will add on more cloud features, and/or cloud companies will add on more CDN features. I expect for this trend to continue to a point where several combined CDN and cloud companies will exist. Through this process, many new support technologies making the CDN more efficient in usage of network bandwidth while being able to support higher-quality multimedia streaming services will be achieved. AI technologies like deep learning will be used to predict future changes in real time such that CDN hierarchical content delivery as well as CDN caching services and content updating operations will improve in performance significantly. In addition, big data technology can be used on the CDNs with cloud support to analyze regional unstructured data in addition to the structured data to provide better predictions of content popularity and changes in network traffic distribution. Fast and reliable control of big data systems would be needed for this purposes in which my papers https://ieeexplore.ieee.org/document/9623558 and https://ieeexplore.ieee.org/document/8605312 could help to provide a view of the state-of-the-art level in this technical field.

Chapter 8. Cloud Computing and Edge Cloud Technologies

Chapter 8 focuses on cloud computing and edge cloud technologies, where descriptions on how Amazon Web Service (AWS) cloud services are used to support Netflix and Disney+ are introduced. Two trends are expected in the future. First, I predict that the usage of cloud computing will significantly grow and become even more important for metaverse services, XR devices, and various multimedia streaming services. Second, I predict that in the future, edge computing will also become very commonly used, and edge computing cloud technologies will become available in more diverse forms (adding on to the multiple-access edge computing (MEC), fog computing, and cloudlet technologies). Therefore, AWS edge cloud services, Microsoft Azure edge cloud services, Google Cloud, as well as other edge cloud services will grow in business revenue as the number of users and service utilization will rapidly grow. In addition, the influence of AI will assist cloud computing and edge cloud technologies to grow more rapidly, and the Software as a Service (SaaS), Platform as a Service (PaaS), and Infrastructure as a Service (IaaS) will expand to include a wider variety of cloud service models. Optimizing the performance of cloud and edge computing systems is an area that

I have worked on where my papers `https://ieeexplore.ieee.org/document/9693102`, `https://ieeexplore.ieee.org/document/8674579`, and `https://ieeexplore.ieee.org/document/8692395` could help to provide a view of the state-of-the-art level in this technical field.

Future Plans

As I have explained above, there is a great amount of planning, designing, research, development, manufacturing, integration, marketing, accounting, investing, financing, and advertising that needs to be done in each of these areas. I hope that you find interest in these areas as each has great importance and significant influence for the users and especially for the companies and the related global markets.

I deeply thank you for reading my book and sincerely hope it helped you in some way. In the future, I plan to upgrade the content of this book in the following edition as new technologies continuously evolve. I appreciate your time and interest and wish you a joyful and successful career.

Index

A

Accelerated segment test (AGAST), 137
Accelerometer, 88, 101
Access points (APs), 276, 295
Accurate predictions, 78
Acer AH101, 107
Acer OJO, 107
Acornsoft, 7
Activation function, 145
Adaptation Set, 241
Adaptive cloud offloading, 121
Adaptive loop filter (ALF), 215, 223
Adaptive MV resolution (AMVR), 219
Adobe Flash Player, 189
Adobe HTTP Dynamic Streaming, 234
Adobe Lightroom, 81
Adorable Representative M.C. for Youth (ARMY), 26
Advanced Research Projects Agency (ARPA), 4
Advanced speech, 178
Advanced Video Coding (AVC), 193
Advertisements, 247
Aerospike, 81

Akamai, 252
Alexa, 175–177
Alexa Service Platform (ASP), 176, 177
Alexa Skills Kit (ASK), 176
AlexNet, 174
AlphaGo Master system, 171
Alpha House, 54
Amazon, 24
Amazon Alexa, 154
Amazon AWS, 297–303
Amazon Fire tablets, 55
Amazon Fire TV, 55
Amazon Prime, 46
Amazon Prime Video, 54
Amazon's Echo, 175–177
Amazon Unbox, 45
Amazon Web Service (AWS), 279, 316
  cloud support, 280, 281
  Microsoft Azure, 297–303
AMD Radeon RX 5700 GPU, 108
Analog color TV, 34
Android, 186
Android 10 source code, 101
Angry Birds Space, 81
Annedroids, 54
Apple, 24

© Jong-Moon Chung 2023
J.-M. Chung, *Emerging Metaverse XR and Video Multimedia Technologies*,
https://doi.org/10.1007/978-1-4842-8928-0

B

C

F

G

Printed in the United States
by Baker & Taylor Publisher Services